T0339700

THE IVORY TOWER OF BABEL

THE IVORY TOWER OF BABEL

WHY THE SOCIAL SCIENCES ARE FAILING TO LIVE UP TO THEIR PROMISES

David Demers

Algora Publishing
New York

Library of Congress Cataloging-in-Publication Data —

Demers, David, 1953-
  The ivory tower of Babel: why the social sciences are failing to live up to
their promises / David Demers.
      p. cm.
  Includes bibliographical references and index.
  ISBN 978-0-87586-879-0 (soft cover: alk. paper) — ISBN
978-0-87586-880-6 (hard cover: alk. paper) — ISBN 978-0-87586-881-3
(ebook) 1. Social sciences — Philosophy — History. I. Title.
  H61.D3379 2011
  300.1 — dc22
                                2011015347

Printed in the United States

All pictures in this book are
public domain except where noted.

Dedicated to the memory of
Professor Simon Dinitz

A portion of the royalty from the sale of this
book is donated to the Walter Reckless/Simon Dinitz
Scholarship Fund at The Ohio State University

TABLE OF CONTENTS

BABYLONIANS, SCHOLARS AND TOWER BUILDING

According to Biblical legend, several millennia ago — sometime after the Great Flood — the Babylonians, who were descendants of Noah, settled in Shinar, a fertile plain between the Tigris and the Euphrates rivers that is now part of Iraq. Using bricks instead of stone, they began building a mighty city and a ziggurat, which was a stepped pyramid that could reach heights of 30 stories.

The Babylonians, who spoke one language, believed the ziggurat could channel the power of heaven to the earth. The Book of Genesis quotes them as saying: "Come, let us build ourselves a city and a tower with its top in the sky, and so make a name for ourselves; otherwise we shall be scattered all over the earth."[1]

But Yahweh, the God of Israel, was angered by this insolent attempt to circumvent "his" authority. "Then the Lord said: 'If now, while they are one people, all speaking the same language, they have started to do this, nothing will later stop them from doing whatever they presume to do. Let us then go down and there confuse their language, so that one will not understand what another says.' Thus the Lord scattered them from there all over the earth, and they stopped building the city. That is why it was called Babel, because there the Lord confused the speech of all the world."[2]

---

[1]Genesis 11: 4, *Saint Joseph Edition of the New American Bible* (New York: Catholic Book Publishing Co., 1992).
[2]Genesis 11: 6-9.

The writer of this tale, Christian theologians say, had two major motives. One was to illustrate the increasing wickedness of the human race — a wickedness reflected in the presumptuous attempt to create an urban culture apart from God. The second motive was to explain the existence of diverse languages around the world. The name "Babel" was apparently analogous to the Hebrew word *balal*, which means "muddled" or "to confuse."

Like the Babylonians, social scientists for the past two centuries or so have been building a tower of sorts, only this time the attempt is to build one composed of knowledge rather than bricks. The primary goal of these scholars — anthropologists, communication scholars, economists, political scientists, sociologists and social psychologists[3] — has been to solve problems of social integration. The Babylonian tower was designed in part to unite people to one geographical area. Similarly, social scientists see their tower of knowledge as a means for solving social problems — such as poverty, crime, drug abuse, inequality, discrimination, unemployment, abuse of power — that alienate people and groups from modern society.

According to the Bible, the Babylonians failed because of divine intervention. Social scientists aren't finished building their tower. But, according to many critics, the results so far look less like a tower of knowledge for solving social problems than an "Ivory Tower[4] of Babel" — one in which social scientists routinely dispute each other's theories and data, and even uncontested or well-supported findings rarely influence public policy. Disputes over the nature of truth and knowledge are so commonplace in the social sciences that many scholars believe a social

---

[3]Psychologists are excluded from the list because their focus is mainly on the individual, not the social structure, culture or values. Geography and archeology also are omitted, because of lack of space. Business and education are seen here as applied fields, because they borrow methods and theories from the social sciences.

[4]The term "ivory tower" was first used in Song of Solomon 7:4, but its meaning today stems from an 1837 poem by French writer Charles Augustin Sainte-Beuve, who used it to describe the poetical (ivory tower) attitude of Alfred de Vigny compared with the more socially engaged Victor Hugo, author of the novels *Les Misérables* and *The Hunchback of Notre Dame*. Merriam-Webster's defines *ivory tower* as "a place of mental withdrawal from reality and action"; Wiktionary.com defines it as "a sheltered, overly-academic existence or perspective, implying a ... lack of awareness of reality or practical considerations."

In Judeo/Christian history, the ivory tower was associated with purity. In modern usage, however, the term has come to mean a sheltered academic perspective that is disconnected from or unaware of reality or practical matters. *(Photograph of stained glass window in St. Ignatius Church, Chestnut Hill, Massachusetts, by John Workman; used with permission).*

science which uses methods from the natural sciences — such as experiments, survey research, quantitative statistics — is incapable of generating knowledge that can solve social problems. As Bent Flyvbjerg, a Danish professor of planning, put it:

> If we want to re-enchant and empower social science ... then we need to ... drop the fruitless efforts to emulate natural science's success in producing cumulative and predictive theory ... we must focus on issues

of values and power ... we must ... communicate the results of our research to ... citizens. If we do this, we may successfully transform social science from what is fast becoming a sterile academic activity, which is undertaken mostly for its own sake and in increasing isolation from a society on which it has little effect and from which it gets little appreciation.[5]

Many mainstream social scientists — those who believe that knowledge is constructed through a rigorous, quantitative scientific process similar to that in the natural sciences — disagree. But even when they produce what appears to be meaningful data or theory, they and their research rarely have a significant influence on public policy, many critics point out. According to public administration professor Cheol H. Oh,[6]

despite the tremendous increase in attention to the importance of information in the [policy] decision-making process, "recent research indicates that governmental policymakers make little use of information;[7] at best, social science research findings alter policymakers' understandings and/or definitions of policy problems over a long period of time."[8]

This precarious state of affairs has even led some scholars to conclude that the whole idea of a social science guiding public policy is a complete

---

[5]Bent Flyvbjerg, *Making Social Science Matter: Why Social Inquiry Fails and How It Can Succeed Again* (Cambridge, United Kingdom: University Press, 2001), p. 166.

[6]Cheol H. Oh, *Linking Social Science Information to Policy-Making* (Greeenwich, CT: JAI Press, 1996), pp. 9-10.

[7]Oh cites these scholars to back up his statement: C. E. Nelson, J. Roberts, C. Maederer, B. Wertheimer, and B. Johnson, "The Utilization of Social Science Information by Policymakers," *American Behavioral Scientist, 30*: 569-577 (1987); W. E. Pollard, "Decision Making and the Use of Evaluation Research," *American Behavioral Scientist, 30*: 661-676 (1987); and A. L. Schneider, "The Evaluation of a Policy Orientation for Evaluation Research," *Public Administration Review, 46*: 356-363 (July/August 1986).

[8]Robert F. Rich and N. Caplan, "What Do We Know about Knowledge Utilization as a Field/Discipline — The State of the Art," paper presented at the Research Utilization Conference, University of Pittsburgh (September 1978); Carol Weiss, "Introduction," pp. 1-20 in *Utilizing Social Research in Public Policy Making*, edited by Carol Weiss (Lexington, MA: D.C. Heath, 1977); and Carol Weiss, "Knowledge Creep and Decision Accretion," *Knowledge, 1*: 384-404 (1980).

myth — a ritual that serves no purpose other than to feed professors' egos and to deflect criticism that elites and their institutions are failing to correct society's ills. Public policy researcher Robert Formaini writes:

> [S]cientifically-based (i.e., justified) public policy, a dream that has grown every larger since the Enlightenment and that, perhaps, has reached its apogee toward the close of our own [20th]century, is a myth, a theoretical illusion. It exists in our minds, our analyses and our methods only because we seek to find it and, typically, we tend to find that which we seek.[9]

In their defense, some mainstream social scientists acknowledge that their research has had little direct impact on public policy. But they insist this isn't their fault.

First, they point out that policymakers often ignore the research they produce, relying instead on their own or their political party's ideology or the influence of constituents or special interest groups.

Second, social science defenders say their universities rarely reward them for solving social problems or for influencing public policy. In some cases, they are even punished in annual reviews. Universities reward scholars for publishing scientific books and journal articles. The clarion call in academe is "publish or perish," not "solve social problems or perish."

Third, some defenders of social science also argue that it is unreasonable to expect social science research to have strong, direct impacts on public policymaking. A more realistic view is that the impact of research is more subtle and more long-term. It takes time, they argue, for social scientific knowledge to filter into the "public sphere" and into public policy.

---

[9]Robert Formaini, *The Myth of Scientific Public Policy* (New York: Transaction Publishers, 1990), p. 1.

And fourth, some defenders blame the lack of impact partly on the 21st century trend toward the "corporatization" of higher education,[10] which they say places greater emphasis on generating revenues for universities than on solving social problems or impacting public policy. As state allocations have declined, many administrators have increased pressure on academic units to generate more federal or private grants, public donations and profit-making programs. If they fail to do this, administrators may downsize or eliminate the programs.

Are the critics right? Are the social sciences capable of generating knowledge that can solve social problems? Is that why they have little impact on public policy? Or is it because universities are not rewarding the faculty who seeks to influence public policy and because politicians ignore the results of social scientific research? Are the social sciences failing to live up to their promises? Have they outlived their usefulness? Have they become, or are they becoming, an Ivory Tower of Babel?

These are the questions this book seeks to answer.

David Demers
Summer 2011

---

[10]Cary Nelson, "From the President: Ethics and Corporatization," American Association of University Professors website, retrieved November 2, 2010, from <www.aaup.org/ AAUP/pubsres/academe/2010/JF/col/ftp.htm>.

CHAPTER 1

JESSE JACKSON VS. THE PROFESSORS

August 8, 1997
Marriott Hotel
Chicago

The Reverend Jesse Jackson enters the hotel banquet room, embraces the lectern and preaches about the struggles and successes of the civil rights movement. At one point, he tells his audience of more than one thousand journalism and mass communication professors that people often ask him how he can remain optimistic when so many of the movement's goals are unfulfilled. "Because," he says, "the civil rights movement has achieved many of its goals and has had a significant impact on public policy." The audience of mostly liberal professors, who are members of the Association for Education in Journalism and Mass Communication (AEJMC), give him a standing ovation.[1]

Jesse Jackson in 1983 *(Public domain photograph donated to Library of Congress by U.S. News & World Report)*

After Jackson leaves the room, former Illinois Senator Paul Simon, who is a professor of political science at Southern Illinois University in

---

[1]AEJMC is the nation's largest national association representing scholars (about 5,000) who teach in journalism and mass communication programs.

Carbondale, and five leading scholars
in the field of mass communication
take the stage, including Stanford
University's Steven Chaffee.[2] The
purpose of the panel is to comment on
the impact that mass communication
research has had on public policy or
in solving social problems.[3] But in
striking contrast to the upbeat
presentation of Jackson, the panelists
are unable to identify specific
examples. In fact, the discussion
focuses more on the lack of impact.

"Chaffee tried really hard," Alex
Tan, who was president of AEJMC at

The late Sen. Paul M. Simon of Illinois
(U.S. government public domain photograph)

the time and organizer of the panel, said many years later.[4] Unfortunately
— or perhaps fortunately for the panelists — the session ended early,
because Jackson had used more than his allotted time.

THE IMPACT PROBLEM

Social scientists from different disciplines periodically create panels like
the one above to assess how well their discipline is doing in terms of
impact in the real world. The results are not always this dismal.[5] They vary
by discipline and other factors, such as whether scholars obtain grants for

---

[2]The other panelists are Sharon Dunwoody of the University Wisconsin-Madison,
Oscar Gandy and George Gerbner of the University of Pennsylvania, and Ellen Wartella of
the University of Texas at Austin

[3]Everette Dennis, who was at the time executive director of the Freedom Forum,
moderated the panel. I contacted him (he's now a professor at Fordham University) and
several members of the panel, but they were not able to recall much detail from the session.
Chaffee and Simon have died since then panel was conducted, but I did contact Chaffee soon
after the session and he provided more comments about the issue, which are offered later.

[4]Personal conversation in October 2008.

[5]In Chapter 6, I'll present some examples of mass communication research having an
impact on public policy.

their research. Those who get grants generally have a greater chance of influencing public policy, because the funding agency, usually a state or federal agency or a private foundation, is specifically asking for information or research data. This doesn't guarantee impact, because policymakers often ignore even government-funded research. But, other things being equal, getting a grant increases the chances of impact. The inability of the AEJMC panelists to identify specific impacts of mass communication research may stem in part from the fact that their field of study typically receives fewer grants than other social science disciplines.[6]

In contrast, the field of economics, when compared with other social sciences, probably has the most significant direct impact on policymaking in government and private industry. In fact, the 26,000 economists who are employed in government, private industry and university jobs probably have more influence than all of the other social sciences combined.[7] Of course, this involvement doesn't guarantee impact or success in solving economic problems. In fact, many critics are quick to point out that, despite more than two centuries of research in economics, Western capitalist nations are still unable to solve basic economic problems, such as unemployment, poverty, and cycles of growth and recession. A good example, of course, is the recession of 2008.

From 1990 to 2007, the U.S. Gross Domestic Product — a measure of economic productivity — had grown every year. But the upward trend collapsed in fall 2008. In one month (September 26 to October 27), the Dow Jones Industrial average lost 27 percent of its value, going from 11,143 to 8,174. By March 9, 2009, the index had fallen to 6,547, which was 50 percent less than its high mark of 13,056 in 2008. Economists were not necessarily responsible for the crash, but the most disturbing aspect of the crash is that economists didn't even see it coming. "[L]ast fall's crash took the economics establishment by surprise," *The New York Times*

---

[6]Most of the research money for mass communication is spent on health-related issues, such as the effects of alcohol and smoking advertising.

[7]See Chapter 7 for details.

reported in March 2009.[8] "Since then, former Federal Reserve chairman Alan Greenspan has admitted that he was shocked to discover a flaw in the free market model and has even begun talking about temporarily nationalizing some banks."[9]

Many, if not most, economists willingly concede their field of study lacks precision. "The dismal record of forecasting crashes and recessions [that] we economists have is not new," Hernán Cortés Douglas, a professor of economics at Catholic University of Chile, wrote in 1992, well before the 2008 crash.

> The crash of 1929 and the Great Depression came as an unexpected avalanche to economists, particularly those in the hall of fame. Fourteen days before Wall Street crashed on Black Tuesday, October 29, 1929, Irving Fisher, America's most famous economist, Professor of Economics at Yale University, said: "In a few months I expect to see the stock market much higher than today." ... [W]hy do they [economists] utterly fail over and over again at forecasting economic downturns? Why do they have to adjust their projections over and over in times of trend change?[10]

In 1997, business consultant William A. Sherden empirically confirmed Douglas' intuition: economic and market forecasts have no more predictive validity than basing a prediction on the previous day's performance (i.e., the best predictors of events today will be those of yesterday). Sherden found that the only discipline that could provide a

---

[8]Patricia Cohen, "Ivory Tower Unswayed by Crashing Economy," *The New York Times* (March 5, 2009), pp. C1, C6.

[9]Yet, even though economists had failed to predict the crash, the *Times* reported that most economics departments were refusing to change their basic theories about capitalism. "The financial crash happened very quickly while 'things in academia change very, very slowly,'" David Card, a labor economist at the University of California, Berkeley, told the newspaper. Card pointed out that during the 1960s economists believed unemployment and inflation were tied together: as one went up, the other went down. However, they were proved wrong in the 1970s, which experienced both high unemployment and inflation.

[10]Hernán Cortés Douglas, "What Macroeconomists Don't Know," Gold-Eagle.com (January 24, 2002), retrieved May 12, 2009, from <www.gold-eagle.com/editorials_02/cortes012402pv.html>.

reasonable amount of prediction was meteorology, but that was only for one-day forecasts.[11] John Horgan, a science journalist and director of the Center for Science Writings at Stevens Institution of Technology, summed up the problems facing economists in 2011:

> The recent recession provides a powerful demonstration of social science's limits. The world's smartest economists, equipped with the most sophisticated mathematical models and powerful computers that money can buy, did not foresee — or at any rate could not prevent — the financial calamities that struck the United States and the rest of the world in 2008.[12]

Quoting philosopher Paul Feyerabend, Horgan adds: "Prayer may not be very efficient when compared to celestial mechanics, but it surely holds its own vis-à-vis some parts of economics."

Even more damning to the legitimacy of a discipline than a failure to predict, though, is the failure of its members to agree on fundamental problems and issues or identify quality research. "Economists were divided over whether the $787 billion economic-stimulus package passed last month is enough," *The Wall Street Journal* reported in March 2009 after surveying 49 economists. "Some 43% said the U.S. will need another stimulus package on the order of nearly $500 billion. Others were skeptical of the need for stimulus at all."[13]

THE KNOWLEDGE PROBLEM

Economics isn't the only field of study in the social sciences that has had difficulty finding agreement — or what scientists call *intersubjectivity* — among its practitioners. Postmodernism, a field of study that has admirers

---

[11]William A. Sherden, *The Fortune Sellers: The Big Business of Buying and Selling Predictions* (New York: John Wiley & Sons, 1997).

[12]John Horgan, "A Prescription for the Malaise of Social 'Science,'" *The Chronicle of Higher Education* (Feb. 13, 2011), retrieved Feb. 14, 2011, from <http://chronicle.com/article/A-Prescription-for-the-Malaise/126311>.

[13]Phil Izzo, "Obama, Geithner Get Low Grades From Economists," *The Wall Street Journal* (March 11, 2009), p. A4.

in both the humanities and the social sciences, was licking its wounds after a hoax was played on one of its scholarly journals. And mainstream, quantitative mass communication scholarship was put to the test when the editor of a scholarly journal decided to examine the levels of agreement among paper reviewers.

The Sokal Hoax

In May 1996, a New York University mathematical physicist decided to test the rigor and validity of postmodernism by sending a "bogus" paper to one of its scholarly journals. Postmodernism is a theory or perspective (depending upon the observer) which asserts that modernism — with its emphasis on scientific rationality, empiricism, realism, objective truth, progress — is failing to solve problems and is in decline. Scientific objectivity, postmodernists argued, is being replaced by a relativistic conception of the world, one in which truth and knowledge are subjective and relative, and reality is constructed rather than given by mass media and symbols.[14]

Physicist Alan D. Sokal sent the bogus article to the editors of *Social Text*, a postmodern cultural studies journal published by Duke University Press.[15] The article asserted that quantum gravity has progressive political implications and that the "New Age" concept of "morphogenetic field"

---

[14]For more on postmodernism, see Dominic Strinati, *An Introduction to Theories of Popular Culture* (New York: Routledge, 1995); David Harvey, *The Condition of Postmodernity: An Enquiry into the Origins of Cultural Change* (Cambridge, MA: Blackwell, 1989); Herbert W. Simons and Michael Billig (eds.), *After Postmodernism: Reconstructing Ideology Critique* (Thousand Oaks, CA: Sage, 1994); and Jürgen Habermas, *The Philosophical Discourse of Modernity: 12 Lectures*, trans. by Frederick Lawrence (Cambridge, MA: MIT Press, 1987).

[15]Sokal got the idea for his "experiment" after reading Paul R. Gross and Norman Levitt's *Higher Superstition: The Academic Left and Its Quarrels With Science* (Baltimore: Johns Hopkins University Press, 1994). Gross and Levitt argued that the success of getting published in postmodern journals was based not on the quality of the work but rather on its "academic leanings — papers displaying the proper leftist thought, especially if written by or quoting well known authors, were being published in spite of their low quality."

could be a leading theory of quantum gravity.[16] Sokal wrote in the conclusion that because "physical 'reality' ... is at bottom a social and linguistic construct," a "liberatory science" and "emancipatory mathematics" must be developed to replace "the elite caste canon of 'high science'" with a "postmodern science" that supports a "progressive political project."

Pure poppycock, and the journal's editors initially did raise concerns about its quality. They asked Sokal to revise it. He refused. But the editors, who didn't recognize the subterfuge, accepted the article for publication. Sokal revealed the hoax the day the article was published.[17]

> My goal isn't to defend science from the barbarian hordes of lit crit (sic) (we'll survive just fine, thank you), but to defend the Left from a trendy segment of itself ... There are hundreds of important political and economic issues surrounding science and technology. Sociology of science, at its best, has done much to clarify these issues. But sloppy sociology, like sloppy science, is useless or even counterproductive.

The incident created a firestorm of controversy about the validity of postmodernism and cultural studies. Sokal was interviewed on public radio, and a number of books and articles were written about the topic, both pro and con.[18] The editors of the journal accused Sokal of unethical conduct. Critics also suggested that Sokal's phoney paper never would have been published had it undergone a formal outside peer-review process. At the time, *Social Text* did not subject its submissions to the more rigorous

---

[16]Alan D. Sokal, "Transgressing the Boundaries: Toward a Transformative Hermeneutics of Quantum Gravity," *Social Text 14* (Spring/Summer 1996), pp. 1-2.

[17]Alan D. Sokal, "A Physicist Experiments with Cultural Studies," *Lingua Franca,* 6(4) (May/June 1996). Retrieved October 25, 2010, from <http://www.physics.nyu.edu/faculty/sokal/lingua_franca_v4/lingua_franca_v4.html>.

[18]See, e.g., Steven Weinberg, "Sokal's Hoax," *The New York Review of Books* (August 8, 1996), p. 12; Babette E. Babich, "Physics vs. Social Text: Anatomy of a Hoax," *Telos, 107* (1996); Michael Holquist and Robert Shulman, "Sokal's Hoax: An Exchange," *The New York Review of Books* (October 3, 1996), p. 54; Michel Callon, "Whose Impostures? Physicists at War with the Third Person," *Social Studies of Science, 29*(2): 261-86 (1999); and Alan D. Sokal and Jean Bricmont, *Fashionable Nonsense: Postmodern Intellectuals' Abuse of Science* (New York: Picador, 1998).

double-blind peer-review process, in which neither the authors nor the reviewers know the identity of each other. However, the editors did incriminate themselves when they conceded they accepted the paper for publication partly because it was the only paper submitted by a "real scientist" (the rest were scholars from the humanities). In other words, the editors published it possibly because they felt a paper written by a natural scientist helped legitimize postmodernism as a concept, and they, in turn, felt an obligation to validate Sokal.

The Sokal incident draws attention to the fact that nonscholarly considerations sometimes enter into the decision to publish journal articles. Of course, it also raises questions about the validity of postmodern scholarship. Nevertheless, most scholars recognize that one case study is hardly sufficient to indict an entire field of study. Mistakes happen. More cases would be needed to draw more definitive generalizations, and, ideally, those cases would be drawn from a formal double-blind peer-review process.

Reviewer Agreement Study

Those two problems — the need for more cases and a formal outside review process — were overcome when the editor of *Mass Communication & Society*,[19] a mainstream social science research journal, decided in 2001 to test the validity of agreement among his reviewers. Another advantage of this study is that it examined mostly mainstream, quantitative social scientific papers. Mainstream researchers often claim quantitative research, which quantifies concepts and measures, produces higher levels of agreement than qualitative research, which is more impressionistic.

The research question was simple: If two scholars review the same research paper, how often will they agree with each other in terms of its quality? A high level of agreement doesn't guarantee that scholars are able to objectively identify "knowledge." After all, the history of natural and

---

[19]The journal is published by the Mass Communication & Society Division of the Association for Education in Journalism and Mass Communication. At the time, I had just completed four years as editor of the journal.

social science is filled with examples of widely accepted theories that later were found to be flawed.[20] However, a low level of agreement would certainly cast a shadow on assertions that mainstream quantitative social science is capable of generating objective truth-based observations. All sciences ultimately are built on intersubjective agreement, or the idea that scholars agree with each other on what constitutes knowledge. Lack of intersubjectivity in terms of assessing manuscripts doesn't necessarily mean science cannot produce knowledge, because many factors influence the evaluation process. But examining the degree of agreement among reviewers is a starting point.

Scholarly journals usually operate on what is called a "double-blind review process." That means the authors of papers submitted and the people who review those papers will never know each other's identities before the paper is published.[21] The purpose of double-blind review is to make the review process as objective as possible. When a scholar submits a paper for review at a scientific journal, the editor removes identifying information about the author and then usually sends the paper to two to four reviewers. Ideally, the editor sends the paper to scholars who are knowledgeable in the subject matter or theory discussed in the paper. In many cases, those reviewers are members of the editorial board of the journal. Most scholarly journals give editors the authority to choose their board members.

The editorial board for MC&S at that time contained 71 members, and all members had provided information about their areas of knowledge or research specialities. When a paper was submitted, the editor would identify the topic or theoretical area, and then, using a simple computer program, would link that paper to the speciality areas of the board members. In most cases, manuscripts were sent to four reviewers in the hopes that at least two reviewers would respond. Professors are busy people

---

[20]Thomas S. Kuhn, *The Structure of Scientific Revolutions* (Chicago: University of Chicago Press, 1962).

[21]Scholars who review the articles will be able to identify the author after the paper is published, but the reverse normally is difficult because the reviewers' names are never released..

and often do not respond in a timely manner.

The job of assessing the results was not difficult. An undergraduate assistant who worked part time for the journal put together a spreadsheet that included all of the articles submitted and their outcomes. On the forms provided, reviewers had three choices: They could "accept" or "reject" the manuscript, or request the author to "revise and resubmit." Over the four-year period, 119 manuscripts were sent out for review. By chance alone, one would expect one-third level of agreement (about 33%) between pairs of reviewers. But if social scientists are able to distinguish good research when they see it, the level of agreement should be much higher.

The editor asked many of his colleagues to estimate the level of agreement. Interestingly, most gave low figures. They intuitively expected the result to be low, perhaps because most of them have sent papers out for review and got back highly inconsistent results. No seasoned scholar in the social sciences could ever escape such an experience.

The colleagues were right. The level of agreement was 44 percent, just slightly better than by chance alone.[22]

This reviewer-agreement study raises serious questions about the ability of social scientists to recognize quality research. It certainly would warrant additional research. However, it is important to point out that the study does not mean that the social sciences are incapable of generating knowledge meaningful for solving social problems.[23] Many individual and structural factors influence the ability of scholars to judge the quality of research, some of which are beyond the control of scholars themselves. For

---

[22]If one takes into account the fact that not all categories have an equal probability of being selected (the reject category was much higher than the other categories), the difference was even more negligible.

[23]It is also important to point out that scholarly journals serve other purposes. One of the most important is to identify the founder of an idea, theory or process. In the 17th century, scholars and inventors often squabbled over who was the first to discover a new new idea or process. Sociologist Robert K. Merton found that 92 percent of cases of "simultaneous discovery" ended in dispute during that century. However, as the number of scholarly journals increased, the number of disputes dropped: 72 percent in the 18th century, 59 percent in the latter half of the 19th century, and 33 percent in the first half of the 20th century. Robert K. Merton, *The Sociology of Science: Theoretical and Empirical Investigations* (Chicago: University of Chicago Press, 1973).

example, the definitions of "accept," "reject" or "revise" can vary widely among scholars. In addition, most scholars are busy and some spend far less time judging a paper than they should. The level of agreement among reviewers would likely increase if reviewers had an unlimited time to review an article.

But even more disconcerting than the low level of agreement was the fact that even though social scientists widely agree the review process is flawed, there is no sustained debate about that process or the implications it has for delegitimizing the social sciences as social institutions. This is the case even though questions about the review process often arise at conferences or in personal conversations.

A good example occurred in 2006, when the Association for Education in Journalism and Mass Communication sponsored a panel session whose purpose was to provide advice to graduate students and assistant professors about how to publish in academic journals. At one point, one of the audience members pointed out that sometimes the process isn't very "scientific" — that reviewers often vary widely in their reviews. The former editor of MC&S then presented the results of his reviewer-agreement study, adding that "chance may very well play a big role in whether you get your research published." The editor expected this data would generate some follow-up discussion. But it did not. No one was interested in debating the merits of the double-blind review process. Flawed or not, they just wanted tips on how to get published so that they could get tenure. In the hackneyed sports metaphor, winning the game was far more important than fixing bad rules. The double-blind review process is an institutional activity so deeply embedded into academic culture that challenging it is akin to opening Pandora's box and unleashing forces that very well could delegitimize the social sciences themselves.

Of course, the fact that social scientists can't agree on everything doesn't mean an academic discipline is incapable of generating knowledge or solving social problems. Few scholars would dispute the notion that economists have produced a great deal of useful knowledge about economic processes. But the inability to detect basic economic problems and agree on how to fix them constantly fuels criticism of the social sciences. Can economics and other social sciences really generate enough useful knowledge to solve problems or influence public policymaking? The relevance of this question is heightened even more by the fact that economics is often said to be the "hardest" science of the social sciences. Compared with other social sciences, economics shares far more common ground with the natural sciences, which, of course, have been very successful in understanding and explaining various aspects of the physical world. But if economics is the "hardest" social science and it has difficulty solving economic problems, then what can be expected from the other social sciences?

ASSUMPTIONS UNDERLYING SOCIAL SCIENCE

To proclaim that a social science has a meaningful impact on public policy or on solving social problems, two assumptions must be made. The first, simply enough, is that the role of social science is to fix problems. After all, if fixing the world isn't or shouldn't be one of the primary goals of the social sciences, then there is no need to evaluate the performance of the social scientific research. The second assumption is to show that the social sciences are capable of generating knowledge that can fix problems. This is a more complicated matter.

Assumption #1: Role of Social Science

Historians and social scientists widely agree that modern social sciences emerged mainly in response to social problems created by industrialization and urbanization in the 18th and 19th centuries. As societies become more complex (or structurally differentiated, as the sociologists say), so do their problems, such as crime, economic and political inequality, bigotry and prejudice, overpopulation, urban decay, divorce, unequal access to education, economic instability and war.

Most early social scientists, including Auguste Comte, Adam Smith and Émile Durkheim, were concerned with developing methods and approaches for reformatory action. On the other hand, some, like Karl

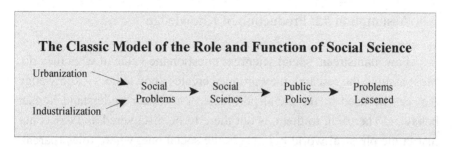

The Classic Model of the Role and Function of Social Science

Urbanization ⟶
Industrialization ⟶ Social Problems ⟶ Social Science ⟶ Public Policy ⟶ Problems Lessened

Marx, believed revolutionary, not evolutionary, change was the best solution. But not every social scientist, then or now, assumes that fixing social problems is a main goal of social science. English sociologist Herbert Spencer argued that science should not interfere with the workings of nature; rather, its goal should be limited to understanding how nature works. American sociologist William Graham Sumner agreed.

Although most contemporary social scientists disagree with Spencer and Sumner, some agree that fixing social problems should not be the most important goal of research. Instead, they contend that the search for truth, or curiosity, alone, justifies the existence of the social sciences. Some scholars maintain the humanities can justify themselves solely on the inspiration and curiosity. But can social science do the same?

Most social scientists, today as well as in the 19th and 20th centuries, don't think so. Instead, they subscribe to what might be called the "classic model of the role and function of social science," which is summarized and simplified in Figure 1.1. At the far left, industrialization and urbanization — two key trends of modernization — are held to be the primary causes (or structural conditions underlying) of social problems. The social sciences are expected to study and generate knowledge about how to fix these problems. In turn, politicians and government bureaucrats are expected to use that scientific knowledge to generate public policies — laws, rules, procedures, etc. — for resolving or ameliorating those social problems. Businesses and citizens may also use the knowledge to help them make decisions.

Assumption #2: Production of Knowledge

Few mainstream social scientists question the value of what they do. Most assume the research they produce creates knowledge — knowledge that can be used to fix social problems or to better understand human behavior. The truth, to them, is out there to be discovered and exists not just in the physical world but also in the social one, where roles (parent, employee, student, voter) connect individuals to institutions and provide a set of expectations that guides individual behavior. In fact, social scientists tend to assume that roles and other social phenomena (values, beliefs, rules, laws) are so powerful in influencing human behavior that they trump individual action, or free will. When people assume a new role, such as a promotion at the office, they often even exhibit new behaviors and values that contradict previous ones. The role makes the individual; it "determines" behavior and thoughts.

The concept of determinism (see sidebar on next page) strongly influenced the social sciences during much of the 19th and 20th centuries. As late as 1979, one of the most popular textbooks in sociology, written by methodologist Earl Babbie, argued that the deterministic posture of the social sciences represents its most significant departure from more other ways of thinking about the world.

> Science is based on the assumption that all events have antecedent causes that can be identified and logically understood. For the scientist, nothing just happens; it happens for a reason.[24]

By studying roles and other social phenomena, mainstream social scientists believe they can explain and predict a lot of human behavior without even taking personality, motivations, reasons or psychology into account. And the best way to generate this knowledge, they point out, is through experimental studies, survey research and quantitative statistics. These methods produce objective knowledge for use in the policymaking

---

[24]Earl Babbie, *The Practice of Social Research*, 2nd ed. (Belmont, CA: Wadsworth, 1979), p. 41.

DETERMINISM VS. FREE WILL

In the humanities and social sciences, there is no shortage of writings on the concepts of determinism and free will. Virtually every introductory philosophy book has a discussion, and there seems to be widespread agreement on a conceptual definition. Runes' definition is representative: Determinism is the "doctrine that every fact in the universe is guided entirely by law ... all facts in the physical universe, and hence also in human history, are absolutely dependent upon and conditioned by their causes. In psychology: the doctrine that the will is not free but determined by psychical or physical conditions." Thus, to say that a human act or decision is determined is to argue that, given the antecedent conditions of the actions, people could act or think in no other way. The doctrine of determinism usually implies that people are not responsible for their actions, because they are causally determined by biological or social forces out of their control.

The concept of determinism can be refined further in the distinction between supernatural and natural determinism. Supernatural determinism is the belief that human action, as well as all natural phenomenon (such as earthquakes, floods), is caused or determined by gods, devils or some other supernatural deity. Natural determinism is the belief that actions are determined by the impersonal workings of nature. Economic laws of supply and demand fit into this category. The emergence of natural determinism was tied closely to the growth of the physical sciences during the 17th and 18th centuries. Some scientists who subscribe to natural determinism reduce action or mental processes to materialistic forms (i.e., chemical or physiological forces).

This view asserts that people are like puppets or robots, controlled by nature.

In contrast to determinism, the doctrine of free will, or voluntarism, "ascribes to the human will ... freedom of indeterminacy," which is "the will's alleged independence of antecedent conditions, psychological and physiological," Runes writes. "A free-will in this sense is at least partially uncaused or is not related in a uniform way with the agent's character, motives and circumstances," according to Runes. Free will also is often defined as the ability to detach oneself from any inner motivation or to choose between alternative courses of action. Although free will is the basis of responsibility, this does not mean that behavior is arbitrary. A decision to act has to be an expression of the person who makes it. This decision may take motivational factors into account, but the decision is not causally determined by them.

In the social sciences, the debate between determinism and free will is often framed in slightly different terms. For sociologists, the question is usually one of agency versus structure, or whether social actors (individuals or groups) can engage in volitional, purposive action as opposed to the determined or constrained aspects of the social structure (e.g., roles). For uses and gratifications communication researchers, it is a question of active versus passive usage of the mass media. Although the terminology differs in sociology and U&G research, the basic question is the same: Is human action the product of deterministic forces or a free will?

Dagobert D. Runes (Ed.), *Dictionary of Philosophy* (Ames, IA: Littlefield, Adams & Co., 1959).

arena. The role of the social scientist is to generate knowledge, not to implement policy. Policymaking is for bureaucrats and politicians. The social scientist should not become actively involved in the political process, because that can compromise the objectivity of the research and knowledge. As political scientist Robert Dahl wrote in the 1950s:

> The empirical political scientist is concerned with what is ... not with what ought to be. He finds it difficult and uncongenial to assume the historic burden of the political philosopher who attempted to determine, prescribe, elaborate, and employ ethical standards — values, to use the fashionable term — in appraising political acts and political systems. The behaviorally minded student of politics is prepared to describe values as empirical data; but, *qua* "scientist" he seeks to avoid prescription or inquiry into the grounds.[25]

The view that social scientists should produce knowledge but not get involved in public policy still dominates, as sociologist James A. Crone's recent introductory text book shows.

> Many sociologists contend that our role is to state only what is ... not saying what should occur ... [T]hey worry that they or other sociologists may go beyond their role in being objective. They fear that if the general public no longer sees sociology as objective, sociology will lose its credibility ... Consequently, a number of sociologists conclude that ... maybe it is better to stay away from recommending solutions. Instead, we need to leave this area to the policymakers.[26]

But over the last couple of decades the detached role has come increasing attack. A smaller, but powerful, group of scholars who work in the social sciences, often called "humanists," believe social scientists should play an active role in policymaking. They work under the

---

[25]Robert A. Dahl, "The Behavioral Approach in Political Science: Epitaph for a Monument to a Successful Protest," *American Political Science Review, 55*(4): 763-772 (December 1961), pp. 770–771.

[26]James A. Crone, *How Can We Solve Our Social Problems?* 2nd ed. (Thousand Oaks, CA: Pine Forge Press, 2011), pp. 5-6.

assumption that people have free will and are not simply robots in a universe of causes and effects. Humanists use the methods of the humanities rather than the natural sciences (mostly qualitative rather than quantitative) to study human behavior. Humanists dismiss the idea of nature as a primary determinant of human behavior. To them, knowledge about the social world is not "out there" to be discovered. Knowledge is not absolute. It is relative, bounded by time, place and context. Truth in one culture or society may be a myth in another. Humanists contend that humans, as objects of study, are completely different from the inanimate objects or forces that natural scientists study. Humans have the ability to make decisions; they have free will. Inanimate objects or forces, like gravity, cannot think and thus have no free will. According to media studies scholars James Carey and Clifford Christians:

> Humans live by interpretations. They do not merely react or respond but rather live by interpreting experience through the agency of culture ... It is, then, to this attempt at recovering the fact of human agency — the ways persons live by intentions, purposes, and value — that qualitative studies are dedicated. Thus we do not ask "how do the media affect us" (could we figure that out if we wanted to?), but "what are the interpretations of meaning and value created in the media and what is their relation to the rest of life?"[27]

Cary also writes that cultural studies

> does not seek to explain human behavior, but to understand it. It does not seek to reduce human action to underlying causes or structures but to interpret its significance. It does not attempt to predict human behavior, but to diagnose human meanings. It is ... an attempt to bypass

---

[27]Clifford Christians and James W. Carey, "The Logic and Aims of Qualitative Research" pp. 342-362 in G. H. Stempel & B. H. Westley (Eds.), *Research Methods in Mass Communication* (Englewood Cliffs, NJ: Prentice-Hall, 1981), pp. 346-347.

the ... empiricism of behavioral studies and the esoteric apparatus of formal theories and to descend deeper into the empirical world.[28]

In short, humanists working in the social sciences tend to focus on the reasons people themselves give to understand their behavior. The goal is not to explain or predict human behavior or motivation as a product of external forces or factors but to understand how people construct the world in their own minds and how they interpret it. To humanists, reality is a social construction, which means that people, not nature or supernatural forces, are mostly or completely responsible for creating social phenomena such as organizations, institutions, rules, customs and values, and social problems, too. Thus, humanists reject quantitative methods and instead marshal their evidence through historical research, qualitative interviews and ethnography. And, unlike mainstream social scientists, most humanists begin with the assumption that all research is value-laden and, consequently, they encourage scholars to get involved in the political process, often through social movements. In fact, if research suggests that a public policy is more harmful than good, then scholars are morally obligated to do all they can to quash the policy.

Not all humanists are critics of mainstream social scientific research. Most humanists actually work in the humanities (philosophy, music, fine arts, English or literature, and history) and produce scholarship or works of art (novels, plays, paintings, music) that are often indifferent to the debate whether social science is capable of generating meaningful knowledge. But for many, if not most, of the humanists who work in social science programs, opposition to mainstream social science (which they sometimes call "scientism") defines a major part of their own research program. The humanist approach routinely criticizes mainstream social scientific methods. In fact, humanists have produced thousands of books and tens of thousands of scholarly articles lambasting mainstream social science research. Much of the criticism draws its intellectual strength from early

---

[28]James W. Carey, "Mass communication Research and Cultural Studies: An American View," pp. 407-425 in J. Curran, M. Gurevitch and J. Woollacott (eds.), *Mass Communication and Society* (Beverly Hills, CA: Sage, 1979), p. 418.

Marxist (humanist) theory, hegemonic theory, Critical Theory (capitalized because it refers to a specific theory), cultural theory and postmodernism.

All of these intellectual movements, in turn, draw some inspiration from French philosopher Jean-Jacques Rousseau, who won an essay contest in 1750 after asserting that science, technology and urbanization were leading to the moral degradation of society. All of the other contestants argued just the opposite: that science and reason would bring progress and prosperity. Rousseau maintained, however, that civilization made people cruel and selfish and robbed them of their freedom and individuality.

> [O]ur minds have been corrupted in proportion as the arts and sciences have improved. Will it be said, that this is a misfortune peculiar to the present age? No, gentlemen, the evils resulting from our vain curiosity are as old as the world. The daily ebb and flow of the tides are no more regularly influenced by the moon, than the morals of a people by the progress of the arts and sciences. As their light has risen above our horizon, virtue has taken flight, and the same phenomenon has been constantly observed in all times and places.[29]

Although many contemporary critical scholars believe, like Rousseau, that a social science based on the natural sciences cannot adequately address and solve social problems, some do concede that mainstream social scientific research is capable of generating knowledge. Their complaint, though, is that the knowledge is being used not for the benefit of society but as a tool or weapon for controlling people and organizations. The critics point out that elites in government and private industry sometimes use the knowledge generated from mainstream research to create advertising or public relations campaigns for the purpose of manipulating people into buying goods and services or voting for a political candidate.[30] A good

---

[29]Jean-Jacques Rousseau, "A Discourse on the Moral Effects of the Arts and Sciences," in Jean Jacques Rousseau, *The Social Contract and Discourses*, translated with an Introduction by G. D. H. Cole (London: J. M. Dent and Sons, 1923, originally published in 1750), retrieved from <http://oll.libertyfund.org/title/638/71081 on 2010-03-20.

[30]Bill Israel, *A Nation Seized: How Karl Rove and the Political Right Stole Reality, Beginning with the News* (Spokane, WA: Marquette Books, 2011).

example is the story of a PR practitioner who, in the 1930s, was able to persuade the fashion industry to introduce forest green as the main color for fall fashions to encourage women to purchase Lucky Strike cigarettes, which were packaged in forest green, a color that would match the women's clothes.[31]

Critical scholars also have argued that mainstream "scientific knowledge" is often used to mask or explain away differentials of power and wealth in society. Society often views unemployment, crime and poverty as individual problems (e.g., laziness, immoral character), not as problems stemming from the political, economic or social structure (e.g., lack of access to education and jobs, discrimination). Although some critical scholars acknowledge the ability of social science research to generate some knowledge, most assert that such research is not very valuable in terms of solving social problems. Quantitative research, they claim, is too artificial, too superficial. It has done little to eliminate major social problems, especially crime and poverty.

In response, mainstream researchers point out that scholars who work in glass ivory towers shouldn't throw qualitative stones. Qualitative research, the quantitative researchers point out, is even "softer" and "mushier" than quantitative research. Two different qualitative scholars can study the same phenomena and reach totally different conclusions. That's no way to build knowledge and solve problems, the mainstreamers contend. Moreover, mainstreamers assert that humanist research in the social sciences — much of which is highly critical of government, industry, business and capitalism — appears to have even less impact on public policy or on public opinion than mainstream research. One reason is that critical scholars are often marginalized by the mainstream institutions and elites. Another is that critical scholars have not been able to generate a following among ordinary citizens. Although critical scholars often speak about justice or emancipation for everyone, the scholars themselves rarely try to educate the public or get them involved in social movements. Mainstreamers point out that critical scholars have no incentive for doing

---

[31]Stuart Ewen, *PR! A Social History of Spin* (New York: Basic Books, 1996).

that. After all, most of them draw comfortable salaries ($50,000 to $150,000) from their university jobs. They prefer not the praise of the public but the admiration of other scholars in their field.

But even if critical scholars had the incentive to rouse the masses, they would have a difficult time recruiting followers because, as the mainstreamers point out, critical writings are difficult for ordinary people to understand. Critical humanist scholars have developed a highly complex lexicon that is accessible only after years of study. This has led some journalists and scholars to poke fun at critical scholarship. In 1996, New Zealand professor Denis Dutton, a philosopher, created an annual Bad Writing Contest. The 1998 first-place winner wrote the following paragraph in a scholarly journal:

> The move from a structuralist account in which capital is understood to structure social relations in relatively homologous ways to a view of hegemony in which power relations are subject to repetition, convergence, and rearticulation brought the question of temporality into the thinking of structure, and marked a shift from a form of Althusserian theory that takes structural totalities as theoretical objects to one in which the insights into the contingent possibility of structure inaugurate a renewed conception of hegemony as bound up with the contingent sites and strategies of the rearticulation of power.[32]

---

[32]Denis Dutton, "The Bad Writing Contest: Press Releases 1996 to 1998," retrieved October 21, 2010, from <http://denisdutton.com/bad_writing.htm>. The passage was taken from Judith Butler, "Further Reflections on the Conversations of Our Time," *Diacritics*, 27(1): 13-15 (Spring 1997), p. 13. Also see Denis Dutton, "Language Crimes: A Lesson in How Not to Write, Courtesy of the Professoriate," *The Wall Street Journal* (February 5, 1999), retrieved October 21, 2010, from <http://denisdutton.com/language_crimes.htm>. Setting aside for the moment various grammatical and sentence structure problems, Butler's paragraph can be roughly translated as follows: Power and oppression in free-market countries cannot be explained solely through an ahistorical theory that blames just the social structure (e.g., capitalism). The theory must also take into account (a) the role of mass media and other cultural institutions in generating ideological content that falsely justifies or legitimates inequities of power and wealth and (b) that false ideology and the social structure can change as social conditions and powerful elites and institutions change.

To be fair, most humanists or critical scholars are not fans of foggy prose. But emeritus professor and poet John Carey of England argues that scholars should write to express rather than to impress. He says: "To write exclusively for a learned or academic readership seems to me hostile to the spread of knowledge ... "[33] Carey also told a newspaper columnist that most of his colleagues in English departments "found the idea of addressing the ordinary, intelligent reader repugnant. They wrote for each other and did not take pains to make their writing attractive. On the contrary: They tend to use obscure theoretical terms as if to signal their membership of an enclosed order, unconnected with the ordinary world. So the ordinary world wisely ignores them."[34]

Perhaps the most interesting element of the conflict between mainstream social scientists and critical humanist scholars is that both groups can be faulted for failing to have a greater influence on the public policy process. Scholars from both camps are often good at identifying and clarifying social problems. But most of the credit for ameliorating some social problems, such as race and sex discrimination, goes not to the social scientists who study them, but to social activists like Jesse Jackson, who actively work for change in the political arena.[35] Indeed, finding examples of professors who play an active role in policymaking is not easy. When a panel of four journalism historians studying the civil rights movement between 1930 and 1950 recently was asked if any U.S. college professor had played a significant, active role in the civil rights movement during that time period, none of the panelists could identify a single individual.[36] On

---

[33]Quote obtained from John Carey's website at <www.johncarey.org/ about.html>.

[34]Nick Cohen, "Academia Plays into the Hands of the Right: The Cuts in Arts, Humanities and Social Science Courses Can Be Seen as a Self-inflicted Wound," *The Guardian* (January 30, 2011), retrieved February 6, 2011, from <http://www.guardian.co.uk/ commentisfree/2011/jan/30/nick-cohen-higher-education-cuts>.

[35]Of course, social scientific research can indirectly affect public policy through social movement organizations, which sometimes draw upon research to bolster their campaigns. But the assumption of this book is that there is no reason why scholars should have less direct effect than social movements.

[36]Some social scientists believe sociologist W. E. B. Du Bois, a champion of civil rights during the early 20th century, had a major impact. However, Du Bois himself apparently didn't seem to agree. Late in life he became disillusioned with the slow pace of change in the United States and moved to Africa. See Chapter 8 for details.

the policymaking stage, social science is almost always a supporting actor, rarely a star. This generalization even applies (especially) to presidential commissions and task forces, which, as will be discussed later, rarely influence policy decisions.

In summation, critical scholars contend that most mainstream social science research at most times and in most places has little effect on public policy or on ameliorating social problems. That's because, they believe, mainstream social science research is unable to generate meaningful knowledge. Some critics even argue that mainstream research more ritualistic than strategic. Its main function is not to solve social problems, but to build egos and regulate young scholars' entry into the exclusive Ivory Tower Club.

WHAT'S AT STAKE?

The issue of whether social scientific research is living up to its promises may seem like small potatoes when compared with other social problems, such as unemployment, poverty, crime, drug abuse and child abuse. Closer inspection reveals, however, that hopes for assuaging those problems depend, at least in part, on some institution or organization generating meaningful knowledge about them. If universities are unable to create a discipline or institution that can generate such knowledge, then maybe an even more fundamental question needs to be asked: Should society continue to financially support the social sciences?

This is not a rhetorical question. Although the social sciences have been around for nearly two centuries and many government agencies here and abroad depend upon social science research to achieve their goals, there is no guarantee that government funding for research and teaching will continue. Ask any United Kingdom social scientist or humanist. In 2010, the UK government announced that it will cut £600 million (about $1 billion U.S.) from the budgets two dozen public universities. All state funding to humanities and social science programs will be cut. Courses in science, engineering, technology and math will be exempted from the cuts. According to new stories, the hard sciences were exempted because these disciplines generate lots of research money for the universities and it's easy to see their impact on public policy or on improving industrial processes and everyday life. In contrast, politicians —both liberal and conservative — had a more difficult time seeing the impact or value of the humanities and social sciences.

Critics charged that the government had utilitarian agenda: to produce more graduates for work in industry and business. "Universities across the country that do not meet the government's arbitrary definition of usefulness — but nonetheless transform and enrich our economy and society — are to be brutalised," said National Union of Students President Aaron Porter.[37]

"If they [humanities and social sciences] are to survive," London *Observer* commentator Nick Cohen wrote, "they must persuade students to pay £7,000 to £8,000 a year, a task that may be beyond many of them. It tells you all you need to know about the political class's commitment to culture that the Department for Business rather than the Department for Education is in charge of universities."[38] But Cohen assigned some of the blame for the cuts to liberal academics.

> [A]cademics ... have been naive to the point of stupidity about the [political] right. They assumed that Conservatives did not mean what they said and would not take money from institutions which have gone out of their way to alienate the intellectually curious. People write well when they have something say. The willingness of too many academics to write badly has told their fellow citizens that they are not worth listening to or fighting for.[39]

---

[37]Quote is taken from journalist Andy Worthington's website, dated November 22, 2010, and retrieved April 28, 2011, from <http://www.andyworthington.co.uk/2010/11/22/did-you-miss-this-100-percent-funding-cuts-to-arts-humanities-and-social-sciences-courses-at-uk-universities>. Porter, by the way, did not run for re-election after he was heavily criticized for failing to do more to stop the tuition increases.

[38]Cohen, "Academia Plays into the Hands of the Right."

[39]*Ibid.* One British academic who wrote a letter to the editor in response to Cohen's article is worth quoting here: "The piece of gobbledegook by Judith Butler could be simply translated as 'the Marxist revolution hasn't arrived yet and we have to explain why.' But that wouldn't get you a lectureship. Sociology is jam-packed with similar rubbish. With the demise of social mobility has come the shifting of the personnel and perspective in the subject to the right. Thus the concentration on non-controversial approaches such as identity,

In response to the expected cuts, The Academy of Social Sciences in January 20, 2011, launched a public relations campaign to convince the public that social scientists had learned their lesson.[40] "Muddled messages and aloof attitudes [among scholars] must be a thing of the past. Some social scientists at least must communicate their worth in intelligible, everyday words if they are to demonstrate the value of their work to those of us outside of academe."[41] The Campaign and its participants will lobby members of Parliament; create a popular vision of what social science can do; clearly identify for the public what social science is and what might happen without it; encourage social scientists to publicize their work more widely; place social science stories in the media, on Internet, radio and television; find, encourage and support social scientists who are talented popular communicators; engage with the blogosphere to stimulate discussion and suggestions for further activity; and clarify the benefits of a social science education. To pay for the cost of delivering these messages, the Academy is raising £250,000 from the social science community.

Although public relations campaigns are certainly useful, especially in the long run, it would be naive to expect that this campaign will turn things around anytime soon. Even a massive protest in London had little affect on the politicians. On March 29, 2011, shortly after some universities announced they were tripling the cost of tuition (from $4,500 to about $14,000 U.S.), more than 250,000 students and citizens demonstrated in the

---

symbolism and cultural relativism and a convoluted prose style reminiscent of the Bloomsbury lot. They, of course, were all well-heeled and writing just before the beginning of the Great Depression. How ironic that they might be hoisted on their own structuralist hegemony." James Andrade, letter to the editor, *The Observer* (February 6, 2011), retrieved February 21, 2011, from <http://www.guardian.co.uk/commentisfree/2011/jan/30/nick-cohen-higher-education-cuts>.

[40]The campaign's website address is <www.campaignforsocialscience.org.uk>.

[41]Kate Roach, "Social Scientists Explain Many Things – But Can They Explain Themselves? David Willetts Understands Why Social Sciences Matter, But We Need to Do a Better Job of Convincing the Wider Population," *The Guardian* (February 3, 2011), retrieved February 21, 2011, from <www.guardian.co.uk/commentisfree/2011/feb/03/social-sciences-david-willetts?INTCMP=SRCH>.

streets.[42] Violence broke out. Some students and police were injured and some protesters were arrested. But as of this writing, UK universities were still preparing to absorb the cuts and raise tuition.

The humanities and social sciences in the United States have not yet faced such a crisis. Part of that may stem from the fact that public higher education is more decentralized in the United States. Universities report mostly to state governments, not the federal government. However, some critics believe both state and federal governments could cut a substantial amount of research grant funding to the humanities and social sciences.[43] The federal government currently spends about $1.1 billion to fund research in the social sciences.[44] Although social science scholarship cannot be expected to work miracles, taxpayers in a democracy do have the right to expect a return on their investment. If the knowledge derived from social scientific research (as well as humanistically oriented research on social problems) is not being used in the policymaking process or is not in other ways making society better, then it behooves social scientists to justify why their research is "politically impotent" and to fix the problem. And if the problem cannot be fixed, then why spend money on an institution that isn't providing something of value in return?

Given that the stakes are so high, one might expect that American social scientists would be actively working to improve the influence their work has in the real world. But there is no significant national debate underway about the role of social science research in public policymaking (at least outside the field of public policy research, whose job is to investigate that role). That was also the case in the UK, by the way, before the government cut funding to the humanities and social sciences.

---

[42]Katherine Price, "Students March for an Alternative," *The Boar* (March 29, 2011), retrieved April 8, 2011, from <http://theboar.org/news/2011/mar/29/students-march-alternative>.

[43]The social science industry in the United States is composed of 178,000 professors and Ph.D. researchers who collectively earn more than $13.6 billion in wages (excluding benefits), with most of that coming from taxpayers. Bureau of Labor Statistics, United States Department of Labor, retrieved from http://www.bls.gov/oes/ current/oes_nat.htm. Data are for the year 2009.

[44]U.S. National Science Foundation, NSF 09-300, *Federal Funds for Research and Development* (November 2008, annual).

CHAPTER 2

SHOULD SOCIAL SCIENCE FIX THE WORLD?

$\mathbf{N}$inetecnth century French philosopher Auguste Comte (1798-1857) was a genius whom biographers have called arrogant, egotistical and ungrateful. But he also had a soft spot for the welfare of humanity and argued that the social sciences could emulate the natural sciences (especially biology) and fix social problems.[1]

> Far from being of theoretical interest alone, the social sciences, *like the natural sciences, must ultimately be of concrete benefit to man and play a major part in the amelioration of the human condition.* In order for man to transform his nonhuman environment to his advantage, he must know the laws that govern the natural world, "For it is only by knowing the laws of phenomena, and thus being able to foresee them, that we can ... set them to modify one another for our advantage ... Whenever we effect anything great it is through a knowledge of natural laws ... *From Science comes Prevision; from Prevision comes Action*"[2] [italics added].

Comte coined the term "positivism" to refer to his new philosophy. This basically was the idea that the methods and general theoretical

---

[1]Lewis Coser, *Masters of Sociological Thought: Ideas in Historical and Social Context* (New York: Harcourt Brace Jovanovich, Inc., 1971).

[2]*Ibid.,* p. 4. The quoted material is from Auguste Comte, *The Positive Philosophy of Auguste Comte,* vol. 1, translated and condensed by Harriet Martineau (London: Bell, 1896; reissued by Cambridge University Press, 2009), pp. 20-21.

approaches in the natural sciences could be
used to study and understand human
behavior. He believed knowledge came from
studying or experiencing phenomena in the
real world, or through empirical observation.
Armed with this knowledge, scholars could
generate "laws" of human behavior similar
to those in the natural sciences. Those laws,
in turn, could be used to create a "religion of
humanity," one that could cure society's ills.
Comte coined the term "sociology" to refer
to the social science that would lead this
effort.

Auguste Comte

Comte developed positivism partly in response to the "negativism" of
traditional ways of thinking, which held that the world was what it was and
could not be changed. People should just accept it. At the heart of this way
of thinking was scholasticism, a doctrine that the Bible and some of the
writings of Aristotle essentially comprised all the knowledge that people
ever needed to know. Proponents of scholasticism objected to Comte's idea
of a science that actively sought to study the natural world and to use the
knowledge gained to make the world a better place. They feared, rightly so,
that a positivist social science would chip away at the power of traditional
authorities in the church and state.[3]

When Comte was in his mid-twenties, he devised a theory called the
Law of Three States, which contended that humankind went through three
stages of intellectual development: theological, metaphysical and scientific.
In the theological stage, humans attribute the states of the natural and social
world to supernatural beings who created it. In the metaphysical stage,
humans attribute the world to abstract forces. The scientific stage was
conceived as the "positive" state.

---

[3]Comte built his ideas of the writings of previous thinkers associated with the Age of
Reason, including Francis Bacon, Rene Descartes, Adam Smith, Jean Baptiste Say, and
Immanuel Kant.

WHAT IS POSITIVISM?

Many definitions of positivism can be found in the social science literature. In fact, despite the alleged emphasis on precision in scholarship, scholars in the social sciences find that they often misunderstand each other.

A good example of this occurred in 1961 at a symposium in Tübingen, Germany. Attendees expected British scholar Karl Popper to defend positivism and neo-Marxist German-born theorist Theodore Adorno to attack it. "However, because Popper unequivocally denounced positivism, the anticipated confrontation did not materialize," much to the amusement of the audience, according to one scholar.* Popper basically defined positivism as a highly inductive approach, one that focused almost exclusively on empirical (real-world) observations when building a more general theory. His perspective is derived from the Vienna School's concept of "logical positivism," which argued that knowledge could only be obtained through empirical obser-vation or sensory experience. Adorno, on the other hand, criticized a positivism that was highly deductive and assumed that knowledge could be generated from the testing of hypotheses derived from a more general theory. His view of positivism came from Comte.

Despite these misunderstandings, most definitions of positivism today usually emphasize the following:

(1) *radical empiricism,* or the idea that knowledge is derived only through empirical (inductive) observation (i.e., sensory experience); (2) *determinism,* or the idea that forces in nature (biological, psychological, social or cultural) are the true cause of human behavior, thereby rejecting free will as a basis for understanding behavior; (3) *universal laws of human behavior,* or the idea that behavior can be explained by invariant laws similar to physiological laws of the universe; (4) *a rejection of theology, ethics, and metaphysics,* which contain ideas that cannot be empirically verified; (5) *a methodology based on the natural sciences,* including mathematical explanations for human behavior; (6) *a belief in the strict separation of fact and value,* along with the idea that social scientists can objectively observe and measure human activity, and (7) *a belief in the idea that social science knowledge should be used to ameliorate social problems.*

For a readable introduction to positivism, see Loic Wacquant, "Positivism," in Thomas B. Bottomore and William Outhwaite (eds.), *The Blackwell Dictionary of Twentieth-Century Social Thought* (New York: John Wiley & Sons, 1992).

*Thomas D. Cook, "Postpositivist Critical Multiplism," pp. 21-62 in R. Lance Shotland and Melvin M. Mark (eds.), *Social Science and Social Policy* (Beverly Hills, CA: Sage, 1985), pp. 22-23.

Comte introduced positivism in a series of books he wrote from 1830 to 1842.[4] In 1848, English philosopher John Stuart Mill endorsed positivism, saying that if empirical laws were deduced from the principles of human nature, they could serve as a foundation for a scientific sociology.[5] Comte and English sociologist Herbert Spencer called traditional historical research, which was allied with humanist approaches, "a hopeless superficial facticity."[6] Other advocates of positivism would later criticize humanistic modes of inquiry, such as qualitative research methods and historical research, for being "unscientific" and "soft and fuzzy." A common complaint was that two qualitative researchers could study the same phenomena and reach two different conclusions. That, the positivists argued, was no way to generate a body of knowledge.

The most extreme form of positivism was known as logical positivism and was associated with a group of scholars known as the Vienna Circle. During the 1920s and 1930s, they met in Vienna and championed a "scientific world-conception" — one proclaiming that the only valid knowledge was knowledge derived "from experience, which rests of what is immediately given. Empiricism as the sole basis of knowledge set limits for the content of legitimate science."[7] If phenomena couldn't be measured or directly observed, they didn't exist. This radical empiricist approach basically rejected the idea that knowledge could be derived from reason (or rationalism), which played a major role in the humanities.

Although Comte believed that the social sciences should use the knowledge to generate solutions to social problems, do all social scientists feel that way?

---

[4]Auguste Comte, *The Course in Positive Philosophy.* The books were compiled into two volumes in 1853. *The Positive Philosophy of Auguste Comte*, trans. Harriet Martineau, (reissued by Cambridge University Press, 2009).

[5]Dorothy Ross, *The Origins of American Social Science* (Cambridge, UK: Cambridge University Press, 1991), p. 18.

[6]*Ibid.*, p. 20.

[7]"The Scientific Conception of the World: The Vienna Circle," in Marie Neurath and Robert S. Cohen (eds.), *Otto Neurath: Empiricism and Sociology* (Dordrecht: D. Reidel Publishing Company, 1973), p. 309.

A BRIEF HISTORY OF THE ROLE OF SOCIAL SCIENCE

Plato

Comte was not the first scholar to argue that knowledge should be used to help humanity. That distinction might go to the ancient Greek philosophers, especially Plato, who created an ideal system of government in which knowledge played a key role. Plato began with the assumption that people are easily corrupted by power. He argued that people should not rule for personal enjoyment but for the good of the state. He believed educated people (or a "philosopher king") were best suited to rule.[8] He advocated a universal educational system for men and women.

Plato also argued that restrictions must be placed upon rulers and the military to prevent them from being corrupted. These restrictions include abolishment of wealth and the institution of family. Children would be reared in a group setting so none of them would have an advantage over the other, and the smartest and wisest would be groomed as guardians (rulers). Plato criticized timocracy — a form of government in which ambition for honor, power and military glory motivates rulers — as well as totalitarianism, oligarchy and democracy. He said democracy is flawed because of its susceptibility to rule by unfit sectarian demagogues.

Plato's concept of government, especially its collectivist elements, has drawn many critics and some admirers over the centuries.[9] But his idea that knowledge and wisdom should guide policymaking has been widely admired and two thousand years later influenced Comte and a diverse group of philosophers during what has been called the "Age of Enlightenment."

---

[8]Plato, *The Republic*, translated with introduction and notes by Francis MacDonald Cornford (New York: Oxford University Press, 1945).

[9]One of the more disliked aspects of Plato's ideal government was the notion that babies with physical defects should be killed.

The Age of Enlightenment

The Enlightenment — sometimes called the "Age of Reason," "Enlightenment project" or "modernity" — is a term scholars have given to a time period in which new and controversial ideas about political rule, the role of the individual in society and science were introduced.[10]

During the 17th and 18th centuries, scholars and philosophers in Europe, England and America argued that human reason (especially scientific reasoning) — rather than superstition, tradition or religious dogma—should guide human affairs. German philosopher Immanuel Kant (1724-1804) defined Enlightenment (*die Aufklärung*) as emancipation from "man's" self-incurred immaturity.[11]

The Enlightenment movement is reflected in the writings of Francis Bacon, Jeremy Bentham, Thomas Hobbes, John Stuart Mill and John Locke in England; Jean-Jacques Rousseau, Voltaire, Montesquieu, and Denis Diderot in France; Adam Smith and David Hume in Scotland; and Thomas Jefferson, James Madison, Benjamin Franklin and Thomas Paine in America. Their books and articles embraced reason and scientific knowledge and eschewed ideas based upon traditional authority, dogma and religious speculation. They opposed tyranny and oppression and believed ordinary people should have a greater role in governing their communities. Many, such as Locke, advocated democracy. Most also supported free speech for ordinary people and believed humans could, through scientific research, solve social problems and make the world a better place.[12]

---

[10]The term "modernity" is often used to refer to the social and cultural outcomes stemming from the ideals of the Enlightenment itself.

[11]Immanuel Kant, "Beantwortung der Frage: Was ist Aufklärung?" ("Answering the Question: What Is Enlightenment?"), *Berlinische Monatsschrift* (*Berlin Monthly*) (December 1784).

[12]For a sampling of the writings of these individuals and others associated with The Enlightenment, see Isaac Kramnick (ed.), *The Portable Enlightenment Reader* (New York: Penguin, 1995).

Voltaire

Voltaire (real name François Marie Arouet) is perhaps the single best representative of the Enlightenment. His *Lettres Philosophiques*, published in 1734, defined the essence of the Enlightenment. In it, he advocates religious tolerance and extolls the virtues of science, reason and empiricism over religion, armchair theorizing and religious dogma. Voltaire also argues that the purpose of life is not to reach heaven through penitence but to assure happiness to all humans through progress in the sciences and arts. Voltaire criticizes powerful religious and political elites and praises people who study law and science.

> Whilst that the barons, the bishops, and the popes, all laid waste [to] England, where all were for ruling; *the most numerous, the most useful, even the most virtuous, and consequently the most venerable part of mankind, consisting of those who study the laws and the sciences,* of traders, of artificers, in a word, of all who were not tyrants — that is, those who are called the people [brackets and italics added].

Voltaire also declares that books, as a repository of knowledge, are a positive force in society, because they help integrate people in a community.

> What we find in books is like the fire in our hearths. We fetch it from our neighbors, we kindle it at home, we communicate it to others, and it becomes the property of all.[13]

The ideals of the Enlightenment were also reflected in Voltaire's personality. He was irreverent, extremely witty and not afraid to criticize authorities. This made him a popular, entertaining guest at parties thrown by the nobility. Once, when the philosopher Montesquieu fell asleep while reading a speech, Voltaire commented: "Wake him up. He seems to

---

[13]Voltaire, "Lettre XII: sur M. Pope et quelques autres poètes fameux," *Lettres Philosophiques'* (1733).

imagine that he's in the audience." On another occasion a noblewoman who returned to court after an absence complained that "the things they say about me are incredible! They even say I retired to the country in order to give birth to twins." Voltaire responded: "Don't be disturbed ... I only believe half of what I hear in court." During a visit to England, he was surrounded by an English mob who wanted to hang him because he was a Frenchman. But, drawing on his wit again,

Voltaire

he responded: "Men of England — you wish to kill me because I am a Frenchman. Am I not punished enough in not being born an Englishman?" The mob cheered and escorted him safely to his lodgings.

But his wit also got him into trouble, especially among aristocrats who were opposed to the ideals of the Enlightenment. In 1717, Voltaire was imprisoned in the Bastille for mocking a nobleman. In 1726, he engaged in a dispute with a leading French family. The family had him beaten up. He was given a choice between exile and prison. He chose the former, spending about two years in London, where he learned English and studied the writings of Locke, Hobbes and the scientist Isaac Newton. What he most admired about the English was the greater level of tolerance they had for freedom of speech and the press. Although radicals were still punished for treason and seditious libel, England by this time was no longer licensing publishers or engaging in prior restraint. Voltaire's admiration for freedom of speech is often associated with the phrase: "I disapprove of what you say, but I will defend to the death your right to say it." Although he didn't really say that, the statement does accurately reflect his thinking.[14] When he returned to France in 1729, he sought to spread the ideas he learned.

---

[14]The quote first appears in Evelyn Beatrice Hall (writing under the pseudonym of Stephen G Tallentyre), *The Friends of Voltaire* (1906), which summarized Voltaire's beliefs on freedom of thought and expression.

In 1734, he wrote *Lettres Philosophiques*, much of which was about his experiences in England. But French authorities were not amused. A warrant was issued for his arrest, and he fled, traveling through a number of European nations. Voltaire wrote a number of other historical and theatrical works after 1749, but his Enlightenment masterpiece was *Candide*,[15] a novel written in 1758 that attacked religious fanaticism and the injustices of class status and war. The story is about Candide, a naive young disciple of Doctor Pangloss, who preaches that this is "the best of all possible worlds." The character of Pangloss represents established religion, which held that people should accept all forms of suffering and evil and always look for the silver lining. This perspective, of course, is at odds with the idea of making the world better. Candide suffers many indignities and becomes disillusioned with the world. He concludes that the best approach is "cultivating his own garden" — in other words, to reject utopian dreams and live within one's capabilities.

Impact of the Enlightenment on Social Science

Drawing upon the ideas of the Enlightenment thinkers and Comte, most scholars doing social science research during the late 19th and early 20th centuries believed knowledge generated from scientific research should be used to make the world a better place. Frank Lester Ward (1841-1913), the founder of American sociology, "was convinced that man could help direct the course of social change." Ward practiced what he preached, devoting "a great deal of energy to social reform."[16] He supported free public education and full social and political equality for women. He also wrote a book promoting the role of social scientists as change agents.[17]

---

[15]Voltaire, *Candide,* 2nd ed., trans. Robert M. Adams (New York: W. W. Norton, 1991; originally published in 1759).

[16]Elbert W. Stewart and James A Glynn, *Introduction to Sociology* (New York: McGraw-Hill Book Company, 1971), p.16.

[17]Lester F. Ward, *Applied Sociology: A Treatise on the Conscious Improvement of Society by Society* (Boston: Ginn, 1906).

Albion W. Small (1854-1926), who founded the first sociology department in the United States, embraced Ward's call for social reform. Small urged sociologists to do three things: organize "all the positive knowledge of man and society," formulate an "equilibrium of a perfect society," and find ways "for changing the actual into the ideal." The latter he called "Dynamic Sociology." The purpose of sociology, according to Small, was to equalize social relations. He maintained that sociology

Albion W. Small

emerged in part because of socialism, which has "mercilessly exposed social evils" but has not provided good "remedies." Borrowing philosopher Georg Wilhelm Friedrich Hegel's concept of dialectical idealism, Small posited that "conventionality is the thesis; Socialism is the antithesis; Sociology is the synthesis."[18]

But Small was not always consistent when it came to casting sociology in the social change role. In 1897, he would back off his call for an active sociology and embrace a sociology that was more scientific, more objective.

> The shortest way to ... solve social problems is not to try to solve them at all for a long time, but to learn how to state them.

> The men of scientific temper and the men of business methods ... that realistic study of social facts simply as facts, without any interposition of our opinions and feelings, is the only credible guarantee of the respectability of subsequent conclusions.[19]

Small never explained his change of heart, but social science historian Dorothy Ross convincingly speculates that the election of 1896 was at least partly responsible. Republican presidential candidate William McKinley

---

[18]Quoted material Ross, *The Origins of American Social Science*, pp. 125-126.
[19]*Ibid.*, p. 134.

trounced Democrat William Jennings Bryan (known as "The Great Commoner" because of his concern for working-class Americans), effectively ending a momentum leftist radicals had built up during the 1890s.[20] This was not a good time for sociology to be too radical. Nevertheless, Ross points out that Small did not completely abandon the call for a politically active sociology.

> Small's ultimate aim remained that sociological science be turned into action, but effective action now required acceding to what "living people think good for themselves."[21]

American sociologist Edward A. Ross (1866-1951) also advocated social reformism. He, too, tried to influence the public policymaking process. In the third edition of his *Principles of Sociology*, he wrote, "Must we be content with such betterments of society as come of themselves? Or may we put in a hand to bring about desired changes? Surely the latter!" He added:

> We suppress smallpox, typhus, diphtheria, the bubonic plague — why should we not endeavor to banish such social maladies as prostitution, juvenile delinquency, child exploitation, trampery, mob violence, family disintegration, religious rancor and race antagonism? Indeed, attack upon the maladjustments among us is the logical consequence of developing a social science; for *what is the use of working out causes and effects, of discovering how certain things condition other things, if we are to do nothing with this knowledge?*[22] [emphasis added]

Edward A. Ross

---

[20]*Ibid.*, pp.134-138.

[21]*Ibid.*, p. 136.

[22]Edward Alsworth Ross, *Principles of Sociology,* 3rd ed. (New York: Appleton Century Crofts, Inc., 1938), p. 642.

In 1900, Ross was dismissed from his post at Stanford University after the university's benefactor, Jane Eliza Lathrop Stanford, demanded he be fired for criticizing the use of Chinese immigrant labor to build the rail lines for Southern Pacific, which the Stanford family owned. The firing helped promote the concept of academic freedom and the development of tenure in the American university system.[23]

Many European scholars also believed social science should actively seek to make things better. French philosopher and sociologist Émile Durkheim (1858-1917) is representative.

> Because what we propose to study is above all reality, it does not follow that we should give up the idea of improving it. We would esteem our research not worth the labour of a single hour if its interest were merely speculative.[24]

Before the 20th century, the number of empirical studies, especially quantitative studies, was limited, partly because the field of statistics was still developing and partly because most scholars had limited access to resources. Durkheim's study of suicide was an exception.[25] Using statistics gathered from various European nations and communities, he concluded that suicide rates were higher in Protestant areas than in Catholic areas. He attributed the difference to social practices in the churches: Catholic churches exercised greater control over

Émile Durkheim

---

[23]Warren J. Samuels, "The Firing of E. A. Ross from Stanford University: Injustice Compounded by Deception?"*The Journal of Economic Education, 22*(2): 183-190 (Spring 1991).

[24]Émile Durkheim, *The Division of Labor in Society* (New York: Macmillan, 1933), p. xxvi (Trans. of *De la Division due Travail Social*, doctoral dissertation, completed in 1893).

[25]Émile Durkheim, *Suicide* (London, Routledge and Kegan Paul, 1952; originally published in 1897). The methodology of Durkheim's study has been criticized, but it nonetheless is admired because it was emulated by other social scientists.

their parishioners. Protestants had more freedom. In terms of solving social problems, the implication is that suicide can be reduced if communities can find other means for integrating Protestants into a community, such as encouraging them to volunteer for nonprofit organizations. Even though the methodology of Durkheim's study has been questioned, his study nonetheless served as a model for other scholars who wanted to conduct quantitative research.

Although most 19th-century social scientists believed social science should work to fix society's problems, there were some notable exceptions. English sociologist Herbert Spencer's (1820-1903) idea of evolution, which emphasized that social change (increasing complexity in society) occurred naturally rather than through direct intervention from humans, was strongly opposed to intervention. He agreed with Comte that human behavior was the product of universal laws, but Spencer maintained that the laws should be studied "in order not to act collectively."[26] As a hard-core individualist, Spencer argued that society must be free from governmental or reformist intervention. The only role Spencer was prepared to give the state was that of protecting individual rights and society against outside enemies. Everything else was to be left to the free market. Hence, Spencer — not biologists, as is commonly believed — coined the phrase, "survival of the fittest."[27]

> The intervention of government in social affairs, Spencer argued, must distort the necessary adaptation of society to its environment. Once government intervenes, the beneficent processes that would naturally lead to man's more efficient and more intelligent control over nature will be distorted and give rise to a reverse maleficent process that can only lead to the progressive deterioration of the human race.[28]

---

[26]Coser, *Master's of Sociological Thought*, pp. 99-100.

[27]Biologists today do not normally use the term "survival of the fittest." They prefer "natural selection," which does not require that only the fittest survive, but that all organisms capable of reproducing are fit enough to survive.

[28]*Ibid.*, p. 101.

There is a fair amount of
evidence to support Spencer's idea
that social engineering on occasion
may produce adverse consequences.
Public drunkenness and fist-fighting
declined after Prohibition was
enacted, but that, in turn, led to
bootlegging and organized crime
syndicates. Requiring children to
wear safety helmets while bike riding
has reduced head injuries
substantially, research has shown,
but it may also reduce bike riding,
because many kids don't like to wear
helmets. Ironically, some research
shows that lack of exercise from bike

Herbert Spencer

riding may pose an even greater threat to the health of children than head
injuries.[29] These examples draw attention to what social scientists have
called *the unanticipated consequences of change*. Quite simply, this is the
idea that solving one problem sometimes creates another.[30]

Another opponent of social engineering was William Graham Sumner
(1840-1910), who taught the first class in sociology in America and
"vigorously opposed Ward's idea of social planning."[31] Sumner adopted
Spencer's approach. Although Spencer's ideas were very popular in the late
1800s, history has not been kind to them (or to Spencer). In fact, he is the
most reviled sociologist in history, because his idea about the survival of

---

[29]D. L. Robinson, "Head Injuries and Bicycle Helmet Laws," *Accident Analysis and Prevention, 28*(4): 463-475 (1996).

[30]This is known in the social sciences as "the law of unintended consequences," which means that an intervention in a complex system can create unanticipated and often undesirable results. The idea goes back to Adam Smith but was popularized in the 20th century by sociologist Robert K. Merton, who also used the term "latent functions" to refer to the idea and its impact on social organizations. See Robert K. Merton, "The Unanticipated Consequences of Purposive Social Action," *American Sociological Review, 1*(6): 894-904 (December 1936).

[31]Stewart and Glynn, *Introduction to Sociology*, p. 16.

the fittest often was used to justify mistreatment of factory workers and to explain why the poor were poor: They were biologically inferior.[32]

20th Century Views on Fixing Social Problems

The social-science-should-fix-problems philosophy began shifting directions in the early part of the 20th century. Social scientists were still committed to solving social problems, but they were becoming more "scientific," more mainstream, and thus less willing to level strong criticisms against mainstream social, political and economic institutions. Advancements in methods and statistics influenced this trend. Russian mathematician Aleksandr Lyapuno "rediscovered" probability and sampling theory,[33] which enabled social scientists to estimate errors in experimental and survey research with great precision. It even allowed them to make generalizations about extremely large populations (tens of millions of people) based upon small samples (fewer than 500 people). Social science was looking more and more like the natural sciences: more professional and more likely to embrace the idea that research should be objective rather than ideological. Social science historian Dorothy Ross writes:[34]

> The professionalization of American social science should be understood not only as an ally of science in the search for authority, but also as a product of the structure of American society ... American

---

[32]For more on the ideas of Comte, Ward, Sumner, Spencer and other early sociologists, see Craig Calhoun, "Sociology in America: An Introduction," pp. 1-38 (Chapter 1) in Craig Calhoun (ed.), *Sociology in America: A History* (Chicago: University of Chicago Press, 2007). Ironically, if one uses birth rates as a measure of a species to survive, the poor would top the list, because birth rates were much higher among that group than the wealthy. The wealthy deliberately had fewer children so their estates would be intact as they were passed on from generation to generation.

[33]French-born mathematician Abraham de Moivre introduced the central limit theorem in an article published in 1733, but it wasn't until 1901, when Lyapunov proved how it worked mathematically, that scientists saw its practical value. See Andreas Hald, *History of Mathematical Statistics from 1750 to 1930* (New York: Wiley & Sons, Inc., 1998), Chapter 17.

[34]Ross, *The Origins of American Social Science*, pp. 160-161.

capitalists, modernizers, and politicians quickly recognized the economic and social benefits of modern knowledge and supported a rapid expansion of higher education ... The decentralized American colleges, competing for students and prestige, allowed the new disciplines to multiply quickly and establish their independence.[35] It can be argued that this decentralized institutional structure was itself responsible for the scientistic orientation of American social science.

American philosopher John Dewey (1859-1952), who witnessed the emergence and growth of the natural and social sciences in the late 19th and early 20th centuries, also played a key role in legitimizing science and positivism. Like Comte, Ward and Ross, he believed that science should be used to solve social problems and to create a better world. Knowledge and education were also critical for a democracy. People need to be informed to make good decisions in and out of the voting booth. Unlike Plato, Dewey had faith in democracy as a political system.

That science is the chief means of perfecting control of means of action is witnessed by the great crop of inventions which followed intellectual command of the secrets of nature ... Railways, steamboats, electric motors, telephone and telegraph, automobiles, aeroplanes and dirigibles are conspicuous evidences of the application of science in life ... [Science] has brought with it an established conviction of the possibility of control of nature in the interests of mankind and thus has led men to look to the future, instead of the past ... To subjugate devastating disease is no longer a dream; the hope of abolishing poverty is not utopian. Science has familiarized men with the idea of development, taking effect practically in persistent gradual amelioration of the estate of our common humanity.[36]

---

[35]Ross gives credit for this sentence to Bernard Berelson, *Graduate Education in the United States* (New York: McGraw-Hill, 1960), chaps 1, 2 and to Joseph Ben-David and Awraham Zloczower, "Universities and Academic Systems in Modern Societies," *European Journal of Sociology, 3*: 45-84 (1962).

[36]John Dewey, *Democracy and Education: An Introduction to the Philosophy of Education* (New York, The Macmillan Company, 1916). Quote is taken from Chapter 17.

Walter Lippmann (1889-1974), Park's contemporary, disagreed. Participatory democracy could not work, Lippmann argued in *Public Opinion*, which was published in 1922,[37] because it was impractical for the average citizen to be well informed about many issues in a modern, complex bureaucracy. A successful democracy would have to rely heavily on trained experts in government and political science. The role of the press, Lippmann argued, was to inform the public about the conclusions reached by these experts. Dewey responded that Lippmann's vision of democracy was elitist and that the

John Dewey, circa 1885 *(Photo courtesy of The John Dewey Center at Southern Illinois University)*

basis of democracy is not information but conversation and debate. In other words, process was just as important as the decision itself.

Yet, despite these disagreements, both Dewey and Lippmann agreed that scientific knowledge was crucial for a well-run state. Dewey argued that knowledge was best obtained through reflective thought, a process that involved identifying problems, proposing hypotheses (informally or formally), and testing the ideas. This way of thinking — that knowledge was best gained not from armchair theorizing or speculation but from interacting with the real world — was often called pragmatism. Dewey, though, preferred to be known as an instrumentalist.[38] He believed that science could give humans control over nature for the purpose of improving human life.

By the 1930s, social scientists were using sophisticated quantitative experimental and survey research techniques, and the U.S. government employed many of them to analyze the social problems tied to the Great Depression. One consequence of increasing interdependence between the

---

[37]See Walter Lippman, *Public Opinion* (New York: Harcourt, Brace and Company, 1922).

[38]John Dewey, *Experience and Education* (New York, The Macmillan Company, 1938), p. 54.

government and social scientists was the near-elimination of radical attacks upon capitalism by positivistically oriented researchers. Many mainstream social scientists took for granted the existing political and economic order. Crime, for example, was defined as deviant behavior, not as a flaw in the structure of capitalism itself, such as high unemployment, lack of access to education or capitalists' desire to protect their wealth. Differentials in wealth were defined as natural workings of the market, not as a flaw in the structure of inheritance laws, which allowed generations of wealthy to remain wealthy. And differentials in intelligence were defined as stemming from genetics and proper breeding, not from structural differentiation (unequal access to education, jobs, resources, etc.).

By the 1940s, quantitative positivist researchers dominated the social sciences. They were attracting the lion's share of federal and state research grant dollars as well as prestige from the institution itself. One of those researchers was Carl Hovland, a Yale social psychologist who conducted a number of studies in an attempt to understand the effects of military films designed to inform soldiers and motivate them to fight.[39] The findings were used in recruitment and training of soldiers.

During the war, few scholars questioned the methods and goals of a positivist social science. Leonard A. Salter Jr., an associate professor of agricultural economics at the University of Wisconsin, expressed this sentiment in 1943.

> Always the purpose of social science is to assist in the resolution of social conflicts and confusions. This responsibility is most keenly felt in times like the present, for war is the extreme aftermath of unresolved social problems. Today every social science must ask whether the problems that preoccupy it are adjusted in terms of current relevance and on a scale commensurate with the real problems of humanity.[40]

---

[39]Carl I. Hovland, Arthur A. Lumsdaine and Fred D. Sheffield, *Experiments on Mass Communication* (Princeton: Princeton University Press, 1949).

[40]Leonard A. Salter Jr., "Global War and Peace, and Land Economics," *The Journal of Land & Public Utility Economics, 19*(4): 391-396 (November 1943), p. 391.

By the late 1940s, the number of social scientists at U.S. universities had swelled to more than 20,000. Optimism was high. Very few scholars were questioning the purpose of social science. Its goal was to correct social ills. As Bernard Barber, a sociologist of science, wrote in 1952:

> It seems not at all unlikely that in the future we may witness a reciprocal process of social change in which social science earns support for itself by its achievements and in which these achievements in turn create a solid conviction of the Order of Human Nature. It seems not unlikely that we may gradually learn that human nature is no more arbitrary, capricious, chance-y [sic], indeterminate, random, or inexplicable than physical nature or biological nature. Science in our society will not really achieve full maturity until social science comes of age with its sisters, the natural sciences.[41]

Indeed, social scientists had a good reason to celebrate just two years later. The U.S. Supreme Court relied upon social scientific research to justify in part its decision in *Brown v. The Board of Education* (1954),[42] which struck down legal segregation. Among the research cited was the book *An American Dilemma: The Negro Problem and Modern Democracy*,[43] which was based on a 1944 study of race relations in America. The Carnegie Foundation funded the study and hired Swedish economist Gunnar Myrdal to conduct it. The "moral dilemma," Myrdal pointed out, was the co-existence of American liberal ideas about human rights, freedom and equality and the miserable conditions that most blacks faced, including discrimination and lack of access to jobs and resources. He concluded that whites were largely responsible for the problems blacks faced.

---

[41]Bernard Barber, *Science and the Social Order* (Glencoe, IL: The Free Press, 1952), p. 262. See page 246 for the statistics on the number of social scientists, which were taken from the National Roster of Scientific Personnel.

[42]*Brown v. Board of Education of Topeka,* 347 U.S. 483 (1954).

[43]Gunnar Myrdal, *An American Dilemma: The Negro Problem and Modern Democracy* (New York: London, Harper & Brothers, 1944). The Supreme Court also cited research conducted by educational psychologists Kenneth B. Clark and Mamie Phipps Clark.

An American Dilemma offered hope that social scientific research could play a significant role in public policymaking and in solving social problems. But the celebration was cut short in the 1960s.

The Great Society Program

In the early 1960s, President John F. Kennedy and his liberal administration had devised an ambitious guided social change project, one that sought to eliminate poverty and racism in America. They called it the Great Society program, and it was built in large part upon the ideas and writings of two well-known social scientists: economist John Kenneth Galbraith and political scientist Michael Harrington.

John Kenneth Galbraith

In his book *Affluent Society* (1958), Galbraith pointed out that even though America had become the richest country in the world, nearly one-fourth of its people were still living in poverty.[44] In *The Other America* (1962), Harrington chronicled poverty in America. His book inspired a number of Great Society social welfare programs, including heath care and expanded social security benefits.[45] A theme common to both books was that poverty was a systemic problem — a problem stemming from flaws in the structure and function of a free-market economy — not an individual problem (i.e., poor people are poor because they are lazy).

Kennedy was assassinated Nov. 22, 1963, so he was never able to see the Great Society programs implemented. But six months to the day after the assassination, on May 22, 1964, Johnson formally launched the programs after a speech at the University of Michigan. He created 14

---

[44]John Kenneth Galbraith, *The Affluent Society* (Boston: Houghton Mifflin, 1958). In 2009, the poverty rate was about 15 percent, slightly lower than the rate in the late 1950s but higher than the rate after Great Society reforms.

[45]Michael Harrington, *The Other America: Poverty in the United States* (New York, Macmillan, 1962). Harrington called himself a socialist, but he was highly critical of communism.

separate task forces to address a wide range of mostly domestic issues. The typical task force had nine members, most of whom were government bureaucrats and academicians, including many social scientists. Johnson and his administration also relied heavily on the advice of economist Robert Lampman, whose chapter on poverty in the 1964 Economic Report to the President became the foundation for Johnson's antipoverty programs.[46] Yale University Nobel Prize economist Frank C. Genovese called Lampman "the intellectual architect of the war on poverty."[47] Decades later, Klaus P. Fischer would write:

> In waging "war on poverty," both Kennedy and Johnson relied on a new and committed group of social scientists turned social advocates. Armed with the tools and techniques of social science, these planners and policy specialists would provide the organizational strategies to implement Johnson's Great Society programs.[48]

More than 400 pieces of legislation were enacted as part of the Great Society program, including affirmative action. The goal of affirmative action was to eliminate discrimination that was embedded into the structure of American society. Affirmative action changed the rules on how employees were hired and how contracts for government jobs were awarded. Affirmative action and other Great Society programs did have some effect. The poverty rate declined, going from about 22 percent in 1960 to 12 percent in 1968, mostly because of increased government assistance through welfare programs. Medical benefits also were extended to the poor (Medicaid) and to older Americans (Medicare).

---

[46]Under the Kennedy Administration, sociologist Daniel Patrick Moynihan also played a key role as under secretary of labor. However, he was not favored in the Johnson Administration and left his post in 1965.

[47]Frank C. Genovese, "In Memoriam: Robert J. Lampman, 1920-1997," *The American Journal of Economics and Sociology* (January 1998), retrieved November 1, 2008, from <http://findarticles.com/p/articles/mi_m0254/is_n1_v57/ai_20538773/pg_2?tag= artBody;col1>.

[48]Klaus P. Fischer, *America n White, Black, and Gray: The Stormy 1960s* (London: Continuum International Publishing Group, 2006), p. 146.

However, President Richard Nixon began dismantling some of the programs after he was elected in 1968. By the late 1960s, many critics proclaimed that the Great Society program had failed to meet its objectives of ending poverty, racism and discrimination. Liberals were angry. According to American labor leader and political activist Sidney Lens,

> The Great Society, in retrospect, lapsed into a coma two years after its birth and died a year later ... [I]ts failure puts to rout the thesis that men are poor because society cannot afford to raise them out of their poverty, because there is a paucity of economic riches. They are made poor or kept poor either by the indifference or the deliberate intent of other people.[49]

Great Society supporters maintained that the program failed because of the costly war in Vietnam and the public's unwillingness to support massive federal welfare spending. Liberals also argued that social scientists never really got a chance to test their public policy programs. Two or three years is hardly enough time to change centuries of discrimination and poverty. Conservatives countered that some of the Great Society programs actually created more problems than they solved. A favorite target was social welfare, which, the critics conceded, might have lowered the poverty rate, but welfare also lessened the incentive for people to work, thus creating what conservatives called a new generation of people dependent upon government handouts (a new social problem, in their view).

After reviewing the Great Society programs, political scientist Henry J. Aaron concluded that the connection between actual policy and science was not strong.[50] The Head Start program, for example, received negative evaluations from some scholars, yet the program continues to be popular. The college work-study program was very popular but was never even evaluated. And the Job Corps program, which received mixed reviews, was cut back. But from the perspective of many social scientists, the most

---

[49]Sidney Lens, *Poverty: America's Enduring Paradox: A History of the Richest Nation's Unwon War* (New York: Thomas Y. Crowell Company, 1969), p. 320.

[50]Henry J. Aaron, *Politics and Professors: The Great Society in Perspective* (Washington, D.C.: Brookings Institution, 1978).

unsettling aspect of the debate wasn't failure of the Great Society program but the fact that Nixon and his administration were ignoring their advice. If the advice of social scientists is ignored, then what is the value of social scientific knowledge?

Policy Studies Research

The 1970s didn't do much to enhance the role of social science as an agent of change. Two new problems emerged.

The first was that quantitative research methods were having a difficult time explaining human behavior. For decades many mainstream social scientists believed that with better measurement and better theories, social science could reveal the causes of many social problems. However, most quantitative survey research studies — even those that employed lots of variables in sophisticated multivariate models — were unable to explain many human behaviors. In most cases, the data could account for only 10-30 percent of the variance. If social science was going to fix problems, it would need more explanatory power. Hence the catchphrase "more research is needed" became a popular way to end a scholarly research article. Translated, it meant: "If we social scientists could just improve our measurement techniques and add more key variables, we could fix this social problem."

But explaining more variance was never achieved, even with more and more advanced statistical techniques. Consequently, some mainstream researchers backed away from the presumed commitment to solve social problems. At that time, a popular introductory sociology textbook for college students advised:

> Although the modern sociologist *hopes his findings will help the human race,* he sees his task as primarily the intellectual quest for knowledge and explanation ... [T]he sociologist must study and learn; society, *hopefully* can put his knowledge to use.[51] [emphasis added]

---

[51]Stewart and Glynn, Introduction to Sociology, pp. 4, 8, 16 and 21, respectively.

The second major problem impinging upon the status of social science was the findings from public policy research. A growing number of empirical and anecdotal studies were being conducted on the question of whether social sciences were actually having an impact on public policy. The results strongly suggested that the social sciences had far less impact on public policy than many scientists had previously believed.

For example, Raymond W. Mack studied the impact of Presidential Commissions and found that their recommendations are not respected at top levels of government. Too frequently, he says, the fate of scholars who devote part of their professional lives to such efforts is to see their findings and recommendations ignored or rejected. Citing Princeton University's Charles F. Westoff, who served on the Commission on Population Growth and the American Future from 1970 to 1972, Mack wrote:

> The loss, in my judgment, was not the failure to adopt a particular set of recommendations, or even the harsh criticism of the research procedures and findings. *It was, rather, the failure ... to penetrate the policy realm with the principle that empirical research is relevant ...* The probability is high of a disappointing response or no response from the White House to social science findings and recommendations.[52] [emphasis added]

In 1979, Robert F. Rich, professor of law and political science at the University of Illinois, summed up the sentiment among policy researchers: "The adaptation of scientific knowledge to meet the needs of society is a recurring theme in western thought. Scientists, philosophers, and sociologists have argued that social change is directly related to changes in modes of knowing, changes in the way in which information is

---

[52]Raymond W. Mack, "Four for the Seesaw: Reflections on the Reports of Four Colleagues Concerning Their Experiences as Presidential Commissioners," in Mirra Komarovsky (ed.), *Sociology and Public Policy: The Case of Presidential Commissions* (New York: Elsevier, 1975), pp. 145, 147. A common practice in politics when a controversy erupts is to create a task force or commission to investigate the problem. This action makes it appear as though the elites in charge are genuinely interested in solving the problem, even if they are not.

generated."[53] However, Rich pointed out that the impact of social science research appears to be waning.[54] He added that "with the exception of studies carried out during World War II, the influence of the social sciences as a field and social scientists as experts was quite limited. "The field developed as an autonomous social system and it continued as such with minimum regard for its social utility."[55]

With autonomy comes less accountability, a condition that pleases scholars who dislike government oversight. But other scholars did not see this is as a strength. In 1971, a small group of concerned social scientists created the Policy Studies Organization.[56] Its goal was to enhance the impact of social science on public policy. One of the early members of the group said she was "astonished when I was doing my doctorate that ... the Park Service was unaware of watershed research and that professors were unaware how the Park Service felt about forestry practices."[57] The creation of PSO, according to its website, "was not a call for any sort of strict utilitarianism, but simply a feeling that much good could be done by bringing together people who felt that policies (and not just government policies, but policies of companies, of universities, and indeed of all kinds of institutions) should be informed policies."

Today, the main purpose of PSO is to disseminate information, according to its president, Paul J. Rich. PSO publishes 10 academic journals and has published more than 250 books related to the topic of policy studies. The organization also sponsors conferences, convention panels, and conducts workshops on policy evaluation methods around the

---

[53]Robert F. Rich, *Social Science Information and Public Policy Making* (New Brunswick: Transaction Publishers, 2001; originally published in 1981 by Jossey-Bass), p. 2.

[54]*Ibid.*

[55]For this sentence, Rich cites N. S. Caplan, "The State of the Art: What We Know About Utilization," in L. A. Braskamp and R. D. Brown (eds.), *New Directions for Program Evaluation: Utilization of Evaluative Information,* No. 5 (San Francisco: Jossey-Bass, 1980).

[56]The Policy Studies Organization home page is <http://www.ipsonet.org>.

[57]The 1972 founding issue of *Policy Studies Journal* also declared: "Who today dares to oppose relevance and who would disagree with the statement that scientists must contribute to the reduction of human suffering and the resolution of social problems?"

world, placing special emphasis on win-win policy analysis. More than 3,600 universities and institutions are members, and its individual members come from more than 93 countries. Oddly, though, the organization has never collected empirical data measuring the extent to which the information it produces influences public policy.[58] But that's the way it should be, some say.

Should Relevance Drive Social Science?

Although PSO obviously hopes that some of the information it disseminates affects public policy, President Rich would not speculate on whether social scientific research is having more impact today on public policy than it did before PSO was created. Nevertheless, he said some of the research in the social sciences has led to "progress."

He cited political scientist Seymour Martin Lipset's ("a lifelong friend") contributions to understanding the conditions under which democracy as a political institution can survive. Lipset argued that the "chances for democracy were higher if income were higher," Rich said. "I think that is a discovery most of us now accept — that economic progress and democratization have to go hand in hand. You cannot have economic growth without democracy and democracy without economic growth."

Rich also cited the research of Larry Diamond and others at the Hoover Institution, a "think-tank" at Stanford University created in 1919 by Herbert Hoover, who was president of the United States from 1929 to 1933. The Hoover Institution is influential among conservatives. Diamond is a senior fellow at Hoover, founding co-editor of the *Journal of Democracy*, and co-director of the International Forum for Democratic Studies of the National Endowment for Democracy. He wrote *The Spirit of Democracy: The Struggle to Build Free Societies Throughout the World*, which examines the sources of global democratic progress and the future prospects of democracy. Diamond theorizes that the fate of democracy is not driven by historical events or even structural forces but by the passion

---

[58]Telephone interview March 11, 2009, with PSO President Paul J. Rich..

and zeal of individual people. "It is a consequence of struggle, strategy, ingenuity, vision, courage."[59]

Rich, who was once himself a Hoover fellow, also said his own research, which focuses on how rituals help legitimize institutions, has had an impact. "I have tried to put forth over the years that ... there is an element of the theatrical to politics that you ignore at your peril." For example, intelligent leaders know the importance of flags and military bands. "Pageantry, drama, theater are all essential to democratic governments; that's the reason why Denmark, Sweden and Canada are successful ... because they have the ability to legitimize rule through ritual." He said he has advised college presidents and politicians on the use of rituals to legitimize the government. "I was adviser to the royal family in Qatar and the ruler at that time wanted to legitimize the armed forces and ... He asked me if I could develop ... regimental dresses and traditions."[60]

PSO president Rich dismisses the empirical research in policy studies which has shown that social science research in general has had relatively little impact on public policy. He said it was a "meaningless debate." Many social scientific studies have little impact, he said, because they are poorly devised and executed.

> A great deal of higher education is wasting the time of faculty who will never make an intellectual contribution — and students who will not amount to anything ... *Comme ci, comme ça*. They are not all going to be worthwhile contributors ... Think of the appalling fact that a million students are banging away at a piano. Only a few will become accomplished [play concert venues] ... Social science does not have a monopoly on trying to be relevant. A great deal of medical science also isn't relevant.

Rich's "theory" implies that only a handful of elite social scientists is capable of having a significant impact on public policy, and that's why the

---

[59]Larry Diamond, *The Spirit of Democracy: The Struggle to Build Free Societies Throughout the World* (New York: Times Books, 2008).

[60]From 1981 to 1990, Rich was adviser, principal lecturer, and head of supervisory programs for the Ministry of Education in Qatar.

policy research on the impact of social science research shows that most research doesn't have an impact. Even a critic would have to concede that competition among scholars is generally a good thing.

But a devil's advocate would point out that Rich's theory assumes a level playing field. Quality of research is not the only factor driving whether some research impacts public policy and some doesn't. Money, power and connections all come into play. And without a level playing field, the devil's advocate asks, how can one determine if those who are having a disproportionate impact on public policy are actually the ones who are producing the best research and theories? In other words, is the conservative research that comes out of the Hoover Institution influential because it is the best research or because the Institution has the financial and political resources to promote that kind of research to policymakers?

On the same day in 2009 the interview with President Rich was conducted, a news story about President Barack Obama's philosophy on science and its role in the public policymaking process appeared in newspapers across the country. The headline was "Obama Conveys Faith in Science." Here are the first two paragraphs:

> WASHINGTON — From tiny embryonic cells to the large-scale physics of global warming, President Barack Obama urged researchers Monday to follow science and not ideology as he abolished contentious Bush-era restraints on stem-cell research.
>
> "Our government has forced what I believe is a false choice between sound science and moral values," Obama said as he signed documents changing U.S. science policy and removing what some researchers have said were shackles on their work. "It is about ensuring that scientific data is never distorted or concealed to serve a political agenda — and that we make scientific decisions based on facts, not ideology."[61]

"I discussed all this at lunch today with a friend," Rich responded via e-mail the next day. "We agreed that curiosity and not relevance should

---

[61]Wire reports, "Obama Conveys Faith in Science: In lifting the Ban, He Rejects False Choice between the Two," *The* (Spokane) *Spokesman-Review* (March 10, 2009), retrieved from <http://www.spokesman.com/stories/2009/mar/10/obama-conveys-faith-in-science>.

guide folks. It has led to more in the end! The PSO leadership feels that trying to apply relevance as a test to dissemination is a slippery slope. Scholarship and excellence, yes."[62]

The Humanist Turn

During the 1980s and 1990s, the ratio of mainstream social scientists to critical humanists in the social sciences — after decades of growth — began declining. The number of professors in sociology, political science, mass communication and some of the other social science disciplines who identified with humanistic scholarship was increasing. One survey of the literature also showed that political scientists, who are overwhelming oriented to a behavior-positivist position, were becoming less hostile toward the humanities and historical research.[63]

The origins of this trend can be traced to the 1960s, when the war in Vietnam invigorated neo-Marxist professors who were highly critical of the so-called "military-industrial complex." These scholars complained that the military and government were using the mainstream research to develop ways to manipulate the news media, soldiers and the public. Indeed, the Department of Defense even had a name for it: *perception management.*

Actions to convey and/or deny selected information and indicators to foreign audiences to influence their emotions, motives, and objective reasoning as well as to intelligence systems and leaders at all to influence official estimates, ultimately resulting in foreign behaviors and official actions favorable to the originator's objectives. *In various ways,*

---

[62]E-mail from Paul Rich, March 10, 2009. Rich also has criticized the tenure system in higher education, arguing that it encourages a lack of accountability for professors. "Is it protecting human rights, or is it sometimes simply protecting laziness?" See Paul Rich, "Time to End Tenure: Job Protection Blocks Accountability in Academia," *Carolina Journal,* 4(3) (December 1994/January 1995), excerpted from Rich's book, *Sacred Cow: Tenure and the Demise of Academic Accountability* (John Locke Foundation, 1994). Also available online at <www.paulrich.net/ publications/carolina_journal_vol4_nr3.html>.

[63]Don Skemer, "Drifting Disciplines, Enduring Records: Political Science and the Use of Archives," *The American Archivist, 54*(3): 356-369 (Summer 1991).

perception management combines truth projection, operations security,
cover and deception, and psychological operations.[64] [emphasis added]

Ph.D. students of these antiwar professors were graduating in greater numbers and were assuming professorial positions at many universities across the country. They, in turn, were educating the next generation of critical, mostly humanist scholars. Some quantitative scholars also jumped ships, partly because of disillusionment over the failure of quantitative methods to explain more variance in human behavior and partly because mainstream social science failed to have more impact on public policy.[65] A visible indicator of the shift to the humanist side occurred in 1999, when a controversy erupted in the American Sociological Association over whether the next editor of *American Sociological Review* — its flagship, positivistically oriented scholarly journal — should be a quantitative researcher or a qualitative one. Up to that point in time, all of the recent editors had been quantitative. Joe R. Feagin, the new president of ASA and a humanist scholar, wanted a change. He asserted that qualitative research has more impact on public policy than quantitative research.

"From the beginning, sociology has included a rich variety of qualitative and quantitative research methods," Feagin, a sociology professor at the University of Florida, wrote in the *Chronicle of Higher Education.*

> However, since World War II, many leading sociologists have stressed the need for ... testing of rigidly framed, deductive propositions by quantitative data and methods. Many sociologists have taken the command for statistical rigor to heart. Indeed, *one reason why sociology does not currently have more social impact is its over-emphasis on advanced statistical methods and a neutrality toward society's marked inequalities.* Like other social scientists, too many sociologists have lost

---

[64]*Department of Defense Dictionary of Military and Associated Terms*, Joint Publication 1-02 (April 12, 2001).

[65]It was rare, though, to see a humanist turn into a positivist.

touch with the moral and practical concerns from which our field emanated.[66] [emphasis added]

Feagin blamed the "shift away from broader concerns" on sociology's increased dependence on government grants for research. To back up his humanist position, he cited what he called "tour-de-force articles" in the 1993 book *A Critique of Contemporary American Sociology.*[67]

[S]ince World War II, sociology has been reshaped into a discipline whose most prestigious members are often linked to government agencies, foundations, or other bureaucracies that supply much of the money for social research ... *In other words, the postwar accommodation of money sources that prefer to support only certain research topics and quantitative methods has often bred superficiality in sociology — as well as in some other social sciences, such as political science.* The social survey, a prevailing research technique, typically involves surface-level readings of human behavior. [emphasis added]

ASA ended up taking the diplomatic route. It appointed two co-editors, one with a qualitative background and one with a quantitative.

RECENT EVENTS

In the decade since those appointments, not much has changed. Most scholars in the social sciences, whether humanist or positivist, continue to believe the social sciences should fix social problems or empower ordinary people to push for change. "Sociologists have a crucial role to play in conducting scientifically rigorous research that yields useful information for policymakers and community leaders," University of Minnesota sociologist and department chair Ronald Aminzade wrote in a departmental

---

[66]Joe R. Feagin, "Soul-Searching in Sociology: Is the Discipline in Crisis?" *The Chronicle of Higher Education* (October 15, 1999), p. B4.

[67]Ted R. Vaughan, Gideon Sjoberg and Larry T. Reynolds (eds.), *A Critique of Contemporary American Sociology* (New York: Rowman & Littlefield, 1993).

newsletter in 2005. "Our faculty members have no desire to hide in an ivory tower. They undertake projects to address critical social needs, advise community groups and serve on their boards, serve as court consultants, and provide expert testimony at legislative hearings."[68]

A 2011 textbook for undergraduate students, written by sociologist Crone, advises students that

> [F]rom its beginning, the ... discipline of sociology focused on the study of social problems and how these problems could be solved. Contemporary sociologists have the same focus. We too are curious about how society works, why it works the way it does, and what may happen in the future. We too are interested in how social conditions create social problems. And we too are interested in how we can change social conditions to solve our social problems.[69]

In sum, the evidence shows that the social sciences emerged in the 19th century specifically to address the social problems created by industrialization and urbanization. They did not emerge solely to satisfy the curiosity of its adherents or to placate a human drive for inner meaning. Although traditional humanities can justify themselves on these criteria, relevance is crucial for legitimizing the role of social science.

The goal of solving social problems continues to be important in the social sciences, even though the movement toward quantitative research and objectivity in research increasingly isolated scholars from the political process. But a debate still rages in the social sciences about the nature of knowledge. Can positivism or its variants create knowledge that is meaningful for public policy decisions? Are humanistic methods better? Or is human behavior so complex and unpredictable that neither approach works? And if the social sciences are incapable of producing knowledge or solving social problems, should they be eliminated from the academy?

---

[68]Ronald Aminzade, "From the Chair," *Facets* (Minneapolis: College of Liberal Arts and Department of Sociology, 2005), p. 2.

[69]James A. Crone, *How Can We Solve Our Social Problems?* 2nd ed. (Thousand Oaks, CA: Pine Forge Press, 2011), p. 4.

CHAPTER 3

THE ATTACK ON POSITIVISM

"What I can't understand is why owners of Ford automobiles are more likely than nonowners to remember our advertising," said Frank Flustor, the director of marketing research for Ford Motor Company.[1] Flustor made the comment during a meeting in the mid-1980s with executives at a national market research company whose telephone calling facility was located in Phoenix, Arizona.

Flustor's question surprised some of those at the meeting. A well-documented finding in marketing research is that owners of various products generally have higher awareness of advertising for those products than do nonowners. The most

Edsel Bryant Ford, former president of Ford Motor Company, was viewed by many neo-Marxists as a capitalist who exploited American workers and consumers.

frequently cited explanation: advertising reinforces and legitimates the owner's previous behavior or decision to buy the product. Or, as one participant told the group, drawing on the terminology of social psychologists: "Cognitive dissonance. People who make a decision are much more likely to remember information that reinforces the decision than

---

[1]Not his real name. Information about this incident available upon request.

information that challenges that decision. They seek stability, not insecurity, in their cognitive structure."

Marketing research is big business in North America. Corporations spend nearly $9 billion to understand consumers and markets.[2] This figure is actually about three times larger than the U.S. government spends on research in health, space, energy, transportation, environment, agriculture commerce and justice.[3] And in contrast to much of the research in the social sciences, marketing research has immediate, practical applications. The results help businesses improve their products and services, advertising and public relations campaigns, and marketing plans. No one in that room that day questioned the idea that quantitative research could generate meaningful knowledge about consumer behavior. That was a given.

But many scholars in American universities, then as now, are skeptical. Some believe quantitative research and the positivist paradigm are virtually worthless in terms of generating genuine knowledge about human behavior. Others believe quantitative research can generate knowledge, but they say that knowledge is used for the wrong purpose — to enhance the pocketbooks of capitalists and the wealthy. Marketing research also is often criticized for creating false needs and wants that are not essential for living a fulfilling life. From the critics' perspective, market researchers and mainstream social scientists are unwitting agents of the capitalists. They do research that helps the rich get richer as opposed to helping create a more equal and just society.[4]

---

[2]The worldwide total is $25 billion. Data obtained from the CASRO (Council of American Survey Research Organizations) 2007 Data Trends Survey, retrieved Jan. 19, 2009, from <www.casro.org/pdfs/2007%20CASRO%20Data%20Trends%20Survey.pdf>.

[3]"Domestic Research Priorities," National Science Foundation (April 1988), cited in Joan Petersilia, "Policy Relevance and the Future of Criminology — The American Society of Criminology 1990 Presidential Address," *Criminology 29*(1): 1-15 (1991), pp. 3-4. The rank order of expenditures per capita is: health, $32.04; space, $19.32; energy, $11.19; transportation, $4.34; environment, $4.34; agriculture, $3.47; education, $1.21; commerce, 53 cents; and justice, 13 cents. For more info, see visit <www.clarkson.edu/dor/documents/summary%20FY09%20funding% 20priorities.pdf>.

[4]In response, some mainstream scholars say the critics are hypocritical, because many draw comfortable salaries at their universities.

A BRIEF HISTORY OF CRITICISM

Criticism of positivism and mainstream social science is nothing new. In 1785, about a decade after Enlightenment philosopher and economist Adam Smith (1723-1790) published his famous book, *Wealth of Nations*,[5] Whig leader Charles James Fox complained: "There is something in all these subjects which passes my comprehension; something so wide that I could never embrace them myself nor find anyone who did."[6] Smith believed the goal of economics was to solve economic problems. Ironically, though, his theory of the "invisible hand" suggested that the best course of action was to do nothing. A free market, one in which the government played a very limited role, was expected to create the best of all possible economic worlds.

Before the American Civil War, the social sciences were loosely connected fields of study, according to social science historian Dorothy Ross.[7] Economics, sociology and political science didn't exist as separate departments. Instead, they were subjects examined mostly in courses on moral philosophy. After the Civil War, the social sciences began emerging as separate disciplines. This increased the tension between professors of theology and social science. Some of the controversy was fueled by the debate over Charles Darwin's *Origin of the Species,* which had been published less a decade before.[8] Darwin (1809-1882) argued that all species of life are descended from common ancestry, and differentiation in life forms resulted from what he called "natural selection." Although many theologians reacted with horror, Darwin's evolutionary theory was widely admired among social, biological and natural scientists during his lifetime and, later, by the public.

---

[5]Adam Smith, *An Inquiry into the Nature and Causes of the Wealth of Nations,* Vol. X, The Harvard Classics (New York: P. F. Collier & Son, 1909–1914; originally published in 1776).

[6]John Rae, *Life of Adam Smith* (London: Macmillan & Co., 1895), p. 285.

[7]Dorothy Ross, *The Origins of American Social Science* (Cambridge, UK: Cambridge University Press, 1991), p. 53.

[8]Charles Robert Darwin, *The Origin of Species,* Vol. XI, The Harvard Classics (New York: P. F. Collier & Son, 1909–14; originally published in 1859).

Political science and economics were the first social sciences to gain a foothold in colleges, according to Ross. Sociology was established as a separate discipline in 1880s. Most of the early social scientists believed the universe contained laws that could be applied to human behavior. The goal of social science was to identify those laws and push for social reform. In sociology, a fair number of the early professors formerly were clergymen who believed that solving social problems meant changing the social structure. Most religions, in contrast, were focused on changing the individual. Some even discouraged changing the social structure. As *Candide* pointed out, the emphasis was on salvation, not on real-world problems.

The sociological focus on changing the social structure and culture (i.e., institutions, values, beliefs) meant that the status quo needed to be challenged. Consequently, most sociologists, then as now, were liberal and reform-oriented. Some even wanted revolutionary change. The bulk of these scholars drew their intellectual inspiration from the writings and philosophy of German intellectual Karl Marx (1818-1883). They later would become the strongest critics of positivism and mainstream (reform-oriented) social science.

Marx and the Contradictions of Capitalism

Marx himself was not an outspoken critic of positivism, nor was he opposed to a social science that used quantitative methods. In fact, many scholars believe that later in life he endorsed such methods. But his critical theories about the evils of capitalism fit in well with attacks on positivism and mainstream social scientific research, and his descendants took full advantage of this.

According to Marx, every economic system grows to a state of maximum efficiency while at the same time developing contra- Karl Marx dictions that contribute to its decay. Marx referred to this as the "materialist conception of history," or "dialectical materialism." The basic idea was that the economy (or labor) is the major source of social change in history. In turn, ideas, customs, values and norms are all dependent upon how a society was economically structured. For example, people in capitalist countries today believe that anyone has the opportunity to go from rags to riches. However, only a very small proportion of the population will actually get rich. The belief, nevertheless, has the effect of reinforcing the unequal distribution of wealth and power in society, a fundamental feature of modern capitalism.

In 1867, when the first volume of *Das Kapital* (*Capital*) was published,[9] Marx drew attention to the structural contradictions inherent in capitalism, including the paradox of competition. He pointed out that market competition forces capitalists to innovate (e.g., make better machines for production), which in turn reduces the cost of goods and services. Profit margins would then fall. To remain competitive, companies have to lay off workers, replace them with more machinery and/or lengthen the working day and cut wages. Over time, the entire economic system becomes increasingly oligopolized, because many companies go bankrupt or are purchased by competitors.[10] Society becomes bifurcated into the many poor and the few rich. As wages fall and ranks of the unemployed increase, people become frustrated. They develop "class consciousness," which means they can see how industrialists and business owners have exploited them. The role of class consciousness, according to Marx, was to motivate the working classes or "proletariate" to revolt and replace capitalism with a new communist order, one that eliminates political or economic inequalities.

In the late 1880s, events in America as well as in Great Britain and many other places in Europe seemed to offer proof of Marx's theory.

---

[9]Karl Marx, *Capital: A Critique of Political Economy,* Vols. 1-3, trans. by Samuel Moore and Edward Aveling (New York: International Publishers, 1987).

[10]It's remarkable that Marx was able to predict oligopolistic practices well before businesses became large corporations. Today, most of us buy our office supplies from three major companies, our automobiles from fewer than 10 companies, our gasoline from a dozen companies or less, and 10 percent of our retail goods from one company (Walmart).

Factory workers, including children, worked long hours for little pay. Most of the profits from business went to the owners and their financier bankers, as Marx predicted. Pamphlets distributed in the 1880s called the worst of these capitalists "Robber Barons." This included oil magnate John D. Rockefeller, bankers Jay Gould and J. P. Morgan, and steel tycoon Andrew Carnegie. They were accused of exploiting workers and consumers. Rockefeller's Standard Oil Company, for example, controlled 90 percent of the oil distributed in the United States and made illegal pacts with the railroad companies to ship oil for below-market prices, running competitors out of business.

Adam Smith's "invisible hand" was becoming a "visible fist," it seemed. The free market seemed powerless to prevent such abuses. In response, millions of Americans became sympathetic to the idea of socialism, including scholars like sociologist Albion Small (see Chapter 2). Class consciousness appeared to be growing in America, but the revolution never materialized. Instead, America began reforming itself. Standard Oil Company was forced to break up into a number of smaller companies that now competed with each other. The federal and state governments enacted a number of laws or regulations that broke up monopolies in other industries, placed greater sanitary regulations on the meat-packing industry, improved working conditions for factory workers, recognized the right of laborers to unionize, limited working hours for children, improved housing conditions and increased penalties for government abuse of power. These reforms helped shore up some of the weaknesses in capitalism. They took the spirit out of the socialist movement. America, it was now believed, could correct its problems without help from the extreme political left.

Many social scientists in the late 1800s were activists for change, but their impact on the system was very limited. The steam behind the reforms came from social movements, progressivism and the press. Newspapers and magazines crusaded for change (the so-called muckraking press). Social science, as an intellectual discipline, was very concerned about the debate, but it contributed relatively little to the movement partly because it was still trying to define itself as a discipline. By World War I, much of this work had been completed. And, as the social sciences gained more power and authority, so did the criticism of them — only this time, the criticism came not from theologians but from the academic community itself.

Why Isn't Capitalism Collapsing?

In the 1920s, about four decades after Marx's death, many of his followers conceded something had gone wrong. There had been no revolutions in capitalist countries. In fact, the only communist-inspired revolution in the world had taken place in a quasi-feudalist state, Russia, where the Bolsheviks overthrew the Czar.

Was Marx wrong?

Many free-market economists at the time certainly thought so. They asserted that capitalism had corrected many of its evil ways. Wages were rising and now creating a large, contented middle class.

But Marx's followers weren't ready to buy into that rhetoric. They resurrected his earlier (1840s) writings on ideology[11] and used them to explain the lack of revolutions in capitalist countries. Marx and his associate Friedrich Engels defined *ideology* as a set of ideas or beliefs that promote, explain or justify a system of unequal class relations.[12] Ideology, they argued, conceals the fact that masses of people are exploited in capitalism to serve the interests of a small number of capitalists. Ideology, in other words, was a collection of false ideas that created a "false consciousness" in the working classes. As they put it:

> The ideas of the ruling class are in every epoch the ruling ideas ... The class which has the means of material production at its disposal, has control at the same time over the means of mental production, so that thereby, generally speaking, the ideas of those who lack the means of mental production are subject to it ... Insofar, therefore, as they rule as a class and determine the extent and compass of an epoch, it is self-

---

[11]A Frenchman named Destutt de Tracy coined the term "idéologie" in 1801. For a more thorough history of the concept, see Joseph S. Roucek, "A History of the Concept of Ideology," *Journal of the History of Ideas*, 5(4): 479-488 (October 1944).

[12]The term *ideology* also is more broadly defined as a set of beliefs or ideas. This definition is used by mainstream social scientists.

evident that they ... regulate the production and distribution of the idea of their age: thus their ideas are the ruling ideas.[13]

Antonio Gramsci

Marx's intellectual legacy was picked up during the 1920s by Italian communist leader Antonio Gramsci and some German scholars, who sought to explain the persistence of capitalism in part through theories of ideology. They argued that revolutions failed to emerge in capitalist countries because the working classes were unable to develop a revolutionary class consciousness, or at least one strong enough to move people to revolt. The critics blamed the mass media and other cultural institutions (family, education, church) for this state of affairs. These institutions, according to the critics, disseminated a "dominant ideology" — a set of beliefs that legitimates or justifies the existing social system and downplays its social, political and economic inequalities.

Italian communist Antonio Gramsci introduced the concept of "hegemony."

Gramsci, who was imprisoned during the reign of Fascist leader Benito Mussolini, called it "hegemony," which basically meant social control through cultural institutions, although the military and police were always there as backup should a revolutionary movement gain a following.[14] Without class consciousness, workers could not see how the capitalists were exploiting them and why they should revolt. Gramsci held out hope that Italy's northern working classes and southern peasantry could create a revolutionary alliance, but this never happened. Gramsci died of tuberculosis in 1937, several years after being released from prison.

---

[13]Karl Marx and Friedrich Engels, *The German Ideology* (London: Lawrence & Wishart, 1938; original work published in 1845), p. 39.

[14]Antonio Gramsci, *Prison Notebooks* (New York: International Publishers, 1971).

Max Horkheimer (front left), Theodor Adorno (front right), and Jürgen Habermas (in the background, right), in 1965 at Heidelberg

Frankfurt School

Collectively, the German scholars who came to be some of the harshest critics of positivism and mainstream social science research were later known as the "Frankfurt School." Like Gramsci, they, too, championed theories of ideology that became embedded in the curriculum of American colleges in the 1930s.[15] Most were Marxist scholars associated with the Institute for Social Research (*Institut für Sozialforschung*) at the University of Frankfurt am Main in Germany. Their theoretical perspective became known as Critical Theory (capitalized to distinguish it from theories that in general are critical). Max Horkheimer, who became the Institute's director in 1930, was the first scholar to define the term, which

---

[15]Scholars associated with the school did not go by that name, but the literature on their writings widely uses the designation.

he said involved critiquing and changing society. He criticized traditional science for seeking only to understand or explain society. Critical Theory's central tenet was that mass media news and entertainment content is embedded with false ideas (or ideology) that legitimize economic inequality in capitalist countries. But Horkheimer also criticized orthodox Marxism and communism, which he said had authoritarian tendencies.

Most of the Frankfurt School theorists believed that competitive capitalism and fascism eventually would be transformed into socialism, even though hopes for emancipation varied. Walter Benjamin was relatively optimistic, believing that "an intelligentsia interested in liberating the means of production" had the power to raise consciousness and promote critical ideas through mass media.[16] Theodor Adorno and Horkheimer were more pessimistic, claiming that the culture of neocapitalism is imposed from above, not by any indigenous culture. Neocapitalism promotes obedience, impedes critical judgment, and displaces dissent. Adorno believed mass media (movies, radio, newspapers, magazines) exerted social control through commercialization of popular culture. In other words, to earn a living, artists had to create works that could be sold for a profit in the marketplace. This came to be known as "commodification," the act or process of turning not-for-profit goods or services into commodities for sale. And the works that "sold" tended to be those that promoted traditional values and institutions, including capitalism as an economic institution.

In 1939, sociologist Robert S. Lynd, who helped some of the Frankfurt scholars get settled in the United States, published an influential book titled *Knowledge for What?*[17] Lynd maintained that the social sciences should model themselves more on the humanities, providing, among other things, a stronger critique of capitalism and its faults as an economic institution.[18]

---

[16]David Held, *Introduction to Critical Theory* (Berkeley: University of California Press, 1980), p. 108.

[17]Robert S. Lynd, *Knowledge for What? The Place of Social Science in American Culture* (Princeton, NJ: Princeton University Press, 1939). For a review of the book, see Cameron Fincher, "Recalling Robert S. Lynd's: Knowledge for What?" *IHE Perspectives* (Athens: Institute of Higher Education, University of Georgia, October 2001), pp. 1-6.

[18]Lynd was criticized for pushing a liberal agenda. He was, at the time, helping neo-Marxist scholar Max Horkheimer make the connections that enabled him to move the Frankfurt Institute from Germany to Columbia University. See Craig Calhoun, *Sociology in*

Private capitalism ... is proving a crude, recklessly wasteful, and destructive instrument for creating and diffusing welfare among a settled, highly interdependent population ... Private capitalism does not now operate, and probably cannot be made to operate, to assure the amount of general welfare to which the present stage of our technological skills and intelligence entitle us; and other ways of managing our economy need therefore to be explored.[19]

Herbert Marcuse, another member of the Frankfurt School, believed that, despite many obstacles, radical intellectuals, exploited minorities and the unemployed could join forces and lead a revolution. Marcuse wanted a social movement that would refuse to participate in the capitalist production of goods and services. He wanted "a non-instrumental relation between people and between people and nature."[20] Marcuse also argued

Herbert Marcuse in 1955 *(Photo courtesy of the Marcuse family, which owns the copyright)*

that mass media content (news, entertainment programming and advertising) in "advanced industrial society" creates false needs that integrated individuals into the existing system of production and consumption.[21] This produces a "one-dimensional" universe of thought and behavior that limits individual, critical thought and oppositional behavior. Marcuse, too, was critical not only of Western capitalist countries but the Soviet Union as well.[22]

America: A History (Chicago: University of Chicago Press, 2007), pp. 326-327.

[19]Lynd, *Knowledge for What?* p. 220.

[20]*Ibid.*, p. 76.

[21]Herbert Marcuse, *One Dimensional Man* (Boston: Beacon, 1964).

[22]Marcuse's book was required reading in a neo-Marxist course I took as an undergraduate student.

During the 1960s and 1970s, German scholar Jürgen Habermas became the most prominent contemporary member of the school of Critical Theory. His theories of communication have pushed for greater democratic participation. In his book, *Legitimation Crisis*, Habermas also argues that capitalism is failing as an economic institution.[23] Although he is not fully confident that a more "rational" society will emerge, he nonetheless looks forward to the end of capitalism and a time when the "pursuit of happiness" means something other than accumulating material objects.

Jürgen Habermas *(Photograph by Wolfram Huke, http://wolframhuke.de; licensed and used with permission through http://creativecommons.org/ licenses/ by-sa/3.0)*

In his book *Theory of Communicative Action*,[24] Habermas criticizes capitalism's economic and administrative institutions, including corporate capitalism, consumerism and the mass media, which, he says, generate cultural content that fails to stimulate an open and free discussion of social issues and problems. He argues that political parties and interest groups are subverting participatory democracy because they operate without much input from ordinary citizens. Positivistic social science research is of no help because it narrowly defines knowledge through empirical observation and "falsely" assumes that science can be objective. Democracy can thrive only when institutions give all citizens the right to debate matters of public importance. Habermas' "ideal speech situation" is based on an open, free and uninterrupted dialogue involving everyone, not just a small band of experts working in the government or the private sector.[25]

---

[23] Jürgen Habermas, *Legitimation Crisis*, trans. by T. McCarthy (Boston: Beacon Press, 1975).

[24] Jürgen Habermas, *The Theory of Communicative Action*, Volumes 1 and 2, translated by T. McCarthy (Boston: Beacon Press, 1984 and 1987, respectively).

[25] Jürgen Habermas, "On Systematically Distorted Communication," *Inquiry, 13*: 205-218 (1970) and Jürgen Habermas, "Towards a Theory of Communicative Competence," *Inquiry, 13*: 360-375 (1970).

But Habermas, unlike many of his critical colleagues, is not a pessimist. He does not reject the ideals of the Enlightenment, which include the pursuit of knowledge and truth. Modern society can still transform the world into a more humane and egalitarian place through what he calls "discourse ethics." This essentially means that truths about the world and about what is right or wrong can emerge when everyone is given a chance to speak their minds (i.e., engage in public discourse).[26] Habermas believes the Enlightenment is a noble, unfinished project; therefore, it should not be discarded. Instead it should be corrected. In this respect, he distances himself from more radical critics of positivism, including postmodernists and other members of the Frankfurt School, who believe most of the ideals of the Enlightenment project are misguided.

Other Critiques of Positivism

During the 1930s, less radical philosophers of social science also were taking potshots at positivism. The best known was Karl Popper, who grew up in Austria and lived mostly in Britain. Popper criticized the logical positivists for putting too much faith in the criterion of verifiability, or the idea that science could prove something true. Popper disagreed, saying that scientists could never control all of the variables that might affect some phenomena. A better approach is to falsify. Scientists can't prove, but they can disprove. They do this by testing the null hypothesis, not the research hypothesis.[27]

For example, a scholar might hypothesize that education reduces the chances of criminal behavior. *The more education people have, the less likely they are to be arrested for criminal behavior (street crime).* This is the research hypothesis. The null would simply say there is no relationship

---

[26]For an application of discourse ethics to the mass media, see Theodore L. Glasser and Peggy J. Bowers, "Justifying Change and Control: An Application of Discourse Ethics to the Role of Mass Media, pp. 399-424 in David Demers and K. Viswanath (eds.), *Mass Media, Social Control, and Social Change: A Macrosocial Perspective* (Ames: Iowa State University Press, 1999).

[27]Karl Popper, *The Logic of Scientific Discovery* (London: Routledge, 2002; originally published *Logik der Forschung* in 1934; translated by Popper himself into English in 1959).

between education and criminal behavior. If the data demonstrate a statistical relationship (or the variables are correlated), then the researcher rejects the null hypothesis and concludes that the data provide support the research hypothesis. However, the researcher cannot say the data proves a relationship, because other factors could be discovered that may account for the statistical relationship. It's possible, for example, to argue that the causal direction of the relationship is reverse. More criminal behavior leads people to devalue education.

During the 1940s and onward, humanists who criticized positivism were sometimes called antipositivists or postpositivists. The antipositivist movement received a boost in 1966 with the publication of a book titled, *The Social Construction of Reality.* Sociologists Peter L. Berger and Thomas Luckmann, building on the work of humanistically oriented philosophers and sociologists, promoted a philosophical perspective that they called "social constructionism." This was the idea that human beings, as opposed to invisible forces of nature, create society — its rules, values, institutions, etc. — as well as the everyday reality they experience.

> It should be clear ... that our approach is non-positivistic ... The sociology of knowledge understands human reality as socially constructed reality ... [Our conception of the sociology of knowledge ... does not imply that sociology is not a science, that its methods should be other than empirical, or that it cannot be "value-free." It *does* imply that sociology takes its place in the company of the sciences that deal with man *as* man; that it is, in that specific sense, a humanistic discipline. An important consequence of this conception is that sociology must be carried on in a continuous conversation with both history and philosophy or lose its proper object of inquiry. This object is society as part of a human world, made by men, inhabited by men, and, in turn, making men, in an ongoing historical process.[28] [italics in original]

---

[28]Peter L. Berger and Thomas Luckmann, *The Social Construction of Reality: A Treatise in the Sociology of Knowledge* (Garden City, NY: Doubleday & Company, 1966; Anchor Books edition, 1967), pp. 188-189.

Social constructionism challenged essentialism, which was the idea that laws, values and social institutions and social reality were created by supernatural beings or by nature — that what existed was the "natural order of things," the objective world.[29] Historically, essentialism was widely used to justify injustices and inequalities. This is one of the themes expressed in Voltaire's *Candide*, in which one character (Dr. Pangloss) constantly points out that "this is the best of all possible worlds." In other words, the world is the way it is and cannot or should not be changed. Early positivists were essentialists. They saw themselves as searching for the fixed, innate, immutable social facts with properties that transcended time and place. To them, however, the creator was nature (social physics), not gods.

The idea that reality is socially constructed, or subjective, rather than given in nature and objective, drew into question the positivist assumption that the development of laws, values, norms and institutions emerged from structural or natural forces beyond the control of individuals. Instead, to find the origins of these social phenomena, social constructivists urged scholars to study the specific historical conditions under which humans created them. For example, in the area of crime, social constructivists held that people in power (e.g., capitalists) constructed crime laws in ways to benefit themselves, their wealth and their way of life. Positivist sociology viewed theft as a violation of moral and legal codes, whereas social constructivists viewed theft as a law created by powerful people to uphold the human-created institution of private property.

Attacks on positivism grew rapidly in the late 1960s and 1970s, within and outside the social sciences. In sociology, Abraham Kaplan wrote an article about positivism for the 1968 edition of the *International Encyclopedia of the Social Sciences*, which concluded:

> In sum, the influence of positivism has been on form rather than substance — on methodology rather than on content. It has given new

---

[29]Plato often is cited as the originator of essentialism. He sought to define and essence of ideas and things that transcended the changes in the physical world. J. M. Irvine, *Disorders of Desire: Sex and Gender in Modern American Sexology* (Philadelphia: Temple University Press, 1990).

vigor to the ideals of clarity and precision of thinking, in a perspective in which the emphasis on theory is conjoined with an equal emphasis on the ineluctability of empirical data. *But too much self-consciousness as to methodology may have a repressive effect on the conduct of scientific inquiry. Unintentionally, and even contrary to its own purposes, modern positivism may have contributed to a "myth of methodology": that it does not much matter what we do if only we do it right.*[30] [emphasis added]

In the field of industrial and organizational psychology, the problem was that quantitative studies were producing inconsistent, conflicting results. Organizational psychologists Frank L. Schmidt and John E. Hunter noted:

> By the middle 1970s the behavioral and social sciences were in serious trouble. Large numbers of studies had accumulated on many questions that were important to theory development and/or social policy decisions. Results of different studies on the same question were typically conflicting ... As a consequence, the public and government officials were becoming increasingly disillusioned ... and it was becoming more and more difficult to obtain funding for research.[31]

In 1976, sociology of science professor Martin Rein criticized positivism for claiming it was value free.

> Briefly stated, my principal concern is to identify what alternative can be presented if we wish to reject what I call the decisionist assumptions held by the positivists. They take the view that values must be accepted as an arbitrary decision, posited by the will or by passion, while "factual" premises are grounded in reality ... In the value-critical

---

[30]Abraham Kaplan, "Positivism," *International Encyclopedia of the Social Sciences* (Detroit, MI: Gale, 1968). Available online at Encyclopedia.com. <www.encyclopedia.com/doc/1G2-3045000974.html>.

[31]Frank L. Schmidt and John E. Hunter, "Meta-Analysis," pp. 51-70 in Neil Anderson, Deniz S.. Ones, Handan Kepir Sinangil, Chockalingam Viswesvaran (eds.), *Handbook of Industrial, Work and Organizational Psychology: Volume 1, Personnel Psychology* (Thousand Oaks, CA: Sage, 2001), p. 52.

approach, not only are values treated as the subject of analysis, but it is assumed that analysis can never be independent of the value we hold.[32]

Also in 1976, Don Martindale, a humanist sociology professor at the University of Minnesota, wrote a book criticizing many of his colleagues and the department for embracing empirical (quantitative, positivist) research and specialization and for allegedly devaluing teaching and humanist research.

The 1970s opened with a style of hard-nosed scientism and sophistication which was soon followed by urgent togetherness and big brotherism ... [T]he writings of Minnesota sociologists in the 1920s tended to be broad ... global, imaginative ... in the 1960s they turned increasingly toward a narrow empiricism once more.[33]

In 1981, David Stockman, director of the Federal Office of Management and Budget in the United States, proposed reducing by 80 percent federal funding for research in the behavioral and social sciences. Normally, such a cut would generate outcries and protests. "But it did not," Schmidt and Hunter point out. "The behavioral and social sciences, it turned out, had no constituency among the public; the public did not care."[34]

---

[32]Martin Rein, *Social Science and Public Policy* (New York: Penguin Books, 1976), pp. 13-14.

[33]Don Martindale, *The Romance of a Profession: A Case History in the Sociology of Sociology*, 2nd ed. (New Delhi, India: Intercontinental Press, 1986), pp. 242-243. The first edition of the Martindale's book contained many personal attacks on faculty and administrators, and Martindale himself noted in a second edition that he had been ostracized from the department as well as the university as whole. He had hoped to rally humanist faculty into a powerful political force, but instead found himself alone on the issue. He retired in 1983 and died in 1985. Interestingly, the official history posted on the department's website contains no reference to Martindale's book (see <http://www.soc.umn.edu/about/history.html>. Social scientists are fond of criticizing traditional historians and elites for sanitizing history, but they, too, find it hard to rise above the politics of institutional life. One more ironic "footnote": The UM sociology department, with the assistance of Martindale's widow, created an endowed chair in the name of Martindale. "Money trumps politics every time," one UM insider confided.

[34]Schmidt and Hunter, "Meta-Analysis," p. 52.

In 1985, philosophy professor Roger Trigg criticized the social sciences for trying to follow the methods of the natural sciences. His view was widely shared by colleagues in his field.

> There has already been considerable disagreement over whether the social sciences should follow the methods of the natural sciences and share their assumptions. Are they to uncover the laws governing human behavior and explain its causes? This is to assume that the social world is indistinguishable from the natural world in important respects and may even be reducible to it. Many philosophers ... point out that the social world is constituted by the meanings and purposes of rational agents. The function of a social science is then to interpret and render intelligible rather than to invoke causes. People are different from physical objects and must be understood differently. This approach has been dubbed "humanist," as opposed to the "naturalist" approach of those taking natural science as a model.[35]

By the mid-1980s, positivism and mainstream social science were facing a major crisis. Even many mainstream social scientists were becoming disenchanted. The problem of explaining more variance is still around today, even though quantitative mainstream researchers often insert more and more variables into their sophisticated statistical models. If mainstream research can only explain a small part of human behavior, the critics were quick to point out, then how can it be expected to solve big social problems?

The Attack on Administrative Research

By the late 1970s, Critical Theory was exerting a major influence in the social sciences, especially in the disciplines of communication, sociology, political science, philosophy and English literature. Although scholars in the Critical Theory tradition emphasized different things and have had their share of disagreements, they did share the belief that

---

[35]Roger Trigg, *Understanding Social Science: A Philosophical Introduction to the Social Sciences* (Oxford, UK: Basil Blackwell, 1985), p. 2.

corporate mass media, among other institutions, were producing cultural content that kept ordinary citizens from recognizing the evils of capitalism.[36] For many of these scholars, the goal was to convince ordinary people that the rich and powerful were exploiting them and were using social science research as one of their tools of social control. In other words, social science research was really "administrative research," in the sense that it helped the government or those in power administrate over the masses. If this was true, then social scientists could be viewed as lackeys who failed to see how the knowledge they created was being used to maintain the status quo.

In the 1980s, Todd Gitlin was one of the best-known sociologists in the country promoting this view. During the Vietnam War, he was president of the Students for a Democratic Society. He later achieved national fame in the world of the academy with publication of his book, *The Whole World Is Watching*, which chronicles the student activist movement and media coverage of that movement during the Vietnam War.[37] In that book, he wrote that

> I work from the assumption that the mass media are, to say the least, a significant social force in the forming and delimiting of public assumptions, attitudes, and moods — of ideology, in short ... Such ideological force is central to the continuation of the established order ... economic and political powers of twentieth-century capitalist society, while formidable, do not by themselves account for the society's persistence, do not secure the dominant institutions against the radical consequences of the system's deep and enduring conflicts.[38]

---

[36]See, e.g., J. Herbert Altschull, *Agents of Power* (New York: Longman, 1984); W. Lance Bennett, *News: The Politics of Illusion*, 2nd ed. (New York: Longman, 1988); Stuart Ewin, *Captains of Consciousness: Advertising and the Social Roots of the Consumer Culture* (New York: McGraw Hill, 1976); Todd Gitlin, *The Whole World Is Watching: Mass Media in the Making and Unmaking of the Left* (Berkeley: University of California Press, 1980); Fred Powledge, *The Engineering of Restraint* (Washington, DC: Public Affairs Press, 1971); and Leon Sigal, *Reporters and Officials* (Lexington, MA: Heath, 1973).

[37]Gitlin, *The Whole World Is Watching*.

[38]*Ibid.*, p. 9.

In an article titled "Media Sociology: The Dominant Paradigm,"[39] Gitlin directed much of his criticism at Austrian-born sociologist and mass communication researcher Paul Lazarsfeld, who, during the 1940s and 1950s, was doing research that presumably helped support the "economic and political powers of twentieth-century capitalist society." As a young man during the 1920s, Lazarsfeld became associated with the Vienna Circle (that scholarly organization which denied the idea of all knowledge except that generated through experience). In the mid-1930s, Lazarsfeld emigrated from Germany to the United States, partly to escape the Nazis. Lazarsfeld founded Columbia University's Bureau for Applied Social Research and began conducting research for the U.S. government and private business, including mass media organizations. He is believed to have conducted the first quantitative research study of radio. He and his colleagues eventually wrote an influential book about the impact of radio and newspapers on voters.[40]

Lazarsfeld recognized the distinction between "administrative research" and "critical research."[41] He defined the former as research "carried through in the service of some kind of administrative agency of public or private character" and the latter as "posed against the practice of administrative research." But Lazarsfeld, according to Gitlin, failed to see the social control implications of administrative research.

> When I say that the Lazarsfeld point of view is administrative, I mean that in general *it poses questions from the vantage of the command-posts of institutions that seek to improve or rationalize their control over social sectors in social functions* ... From the administrator's point of view, the mass media system in its structural organization is of course

---

[39]Todd Gitlin, "Media Sociology: The Dominant Paradigm," pp. 73-121 in G. Cleveland Wilhoit and Harold de Bock (eds.), *Mass Communication Review Yearbook*, Vol. 2 (Beverly Hills, CA: Sage, 1981). Originally published in *Theory and Society*, 6(2): 205-253 (1978).

[40]Paul F. Lazarsfeld, Bernard R. Berelson, and Hazel Gaudet, *The People's Choice: How the Voter Makes Up His Mind in a Presidential Campaign* (New York: Duel, Sloan and Pearce, 1944).

[41]Paul F. Lazarsfeld, "Some Remarks on Administrative and Critical Communications Research," *Studies in Philosophy and Social Science*, 9(1): 2-16 (1941).

not at issue ... The administrative theorist is not concerned with the corporate structure of ownership and control at all, or with the corporate criteria for media content that follow from it: he or she begins with the existing order and considers the effects of a certain use of it.[42] [emphasis added]

Unlike most philosophers, some Critical Theorists and many other Marxist scholars granted some validity to positivism in terms of its power to generate knowledge.[43] But, to them, the main problem was that the knowledge was used in the wrong way — to help powerful political and economic (mainstream) elites exert their power in the marketplace and subjugate ordinary people and consumers. As British political theorist Russell Keat put it in 1981:

Scientific knowledge, positively conceived, is inherently repressive, and contributes to the maintenance of a form of society in which science is one of the resources employed for the domination of one class by another, and in which the possibilities for a radical transformation towards a more rational society are blocked and concealed ... The attempt to formulate universal laws governing social phenomena leads to the misrepresentation as eternal or natural of what should instead be seen as historically specific and alterable. Positivism ... makes scientific knowledge manipulative, the ideal basis for a system of social control exercised by a dominant class, which can present itself as making political decisions in a purely rational, scientific manner.[44]

The Postmodern Assault

The most radical assault on positivism and mainstream social science in the 1980s and 1990s came from scholars who identify with what has come to be known as "postmodernism." The term postmodern first emerged in architecture and art criticism during the 1950s and 1960s and worked its

---

[42]Gitlin, *Media Sociology*, p. 93

[43]Held, *Introduction to Critical Theory*, p. 162.

[44]Russell Keat, *The Politics of Social Theory: Habermas, Freud and the Critique of Positivism* (Chicago: University of Chicago Press, 1981), p. 2.

Allen Ginsberg (right), shown here with Bob Dylan, is often associated with beginnings of the postmodernist movement in literature. As the guiding spirit of the "Beat" movement during the 1950s and 1960s, Ginsberg questioned mainstream American middle-class values and celebrated individual liberty, self-expression and nonconformism. (*Photograph by Elsa Dorfman, released to the public domain*)

way into the social sciences in the 1970s. The initial assault was on scientific rationality and positivism. In 1979, French scholar Jean-François Lyotard declared that people in advanced capitalist systems had been living in a "postmodern world" since the early 1960s. Modernism, he argued, had failed to solve many social problems (poverty, war, genocide, etc.), and the underlying reason was simply that knowledge and truth were relative, not absolute.[45] Instead, the postmodern world is one in which imagination, dissensus, and the idea that there is no theory-neutral observation take a center stage. In some versions of postmodernism, mass media and popular culture are seen as institutions that create multiple realities as opposed to one that mirrors a so-called "objective world."

---

[45] Jean-François Lyotard, *The Postmodern Condition: A Report on Knowledge*, trans. by Geoff Bennington and Brian Massumi (Minneapolis: University of Minnesota Press, 1984; originally published in French in 1979).

There are many different conceptions of postmodernism, and adherents themselves often disagree on many points. This divergence has led many scholars to argue that postmodernism is now in decline — ironically a victim of its own relativistic conception of the world. If there is no knowledge, no truth, then how can one assert that postmodernism is true?[46] Many philosophers and humanistically oriented social scientists reject postmodernism because it contends there is no truth, no facts, and no knowledge.[47] Others point out that there isn't much evidence to support Lyotard's claim that modern societies have moved into a postmodern condition, one in which science no longer is seen as a viable institution. Whatever the failures of modern science and industry, it is clear that billions of people around the world still look to these institutions for hope in solving technical and social problems, and the vast majority of people in Western societies continue to believe in the idea of scientific progress, even during tough economic times.[48]

Attacks on Positivism Since the 1990s

The attacks on positivism continued into the 1990s and the 21st century. In 1991, sociology professor Stjepan G. Mestrovic of Texas A&M University chastised mainstream sociologists in *The Chronicle of Higher Education* for failing to predict the demise of the Soviet Union.[49] He blamed quantitative research for the problem.

---

[46]Some postmodernists even argue that we are now living in a post-postmodern world, one in which people have lost faith and trust in each other. In response, modernists assert that postmodernists have created their own illusions about the nature of society and people.

[47]See, e.g., Herbert W. Simons and Michael Billig (eds.), *After Postmodernism: Reconstructing Ideology Critique* (Thousand Oaks, CA: Sage Publications, 1994).

[48]For additional information about postmodernism, see Dominic Strinati, *An Introduction to Theories of Popular Culture* (New York: Routledge, 1995); David Harvey, *The Condition of Postmodernity: An Enquiry into the Origins of Cultural Change* (Cambridge, MA: Blackwell, 1989); Herbert W. Simons and Michael Billig (eds.), *After Postmodernism: Reconstructing Ideology Critique* (Thousand Oaks, CA: Sage, 1994); and Jürgen Habermas, *The Philosophical Discourse of Modernity: 12 Lectures*, trans. by Frederick Lawrence (Cambridge, MA: MIT Press, 1987)

[49]Stjepan G. Mestrovic, "Why East Europe's Upheavals Caught Social Scientists Off Guard," *The Chronicle of Higher Education* (September 25, 1991).

[A] century ago, the founding fathers of sociology erected their new discipline on the premise that the heart is a stronger and more important force than the mind. For them the proper subjects of study were passions, desires, the unconscious, and other irrational aspects of what was often styled a "will to life." ... Today, however, most contemporary sociologists are operating under a modernist assumption that the mind can rule the heart. The difference in our discipline then and now helps to explain why so many social scientists were caught off guard recently by the fall of Communism in the U.S.S.R. and in Eastern Europe.

At the end of the article, Mestrovic wrote:

If the West is to aid in establishing the desired, democratic scenario, it must understand the cultural forces at work in formerly Communist nations and acknowledge that they are different from those in the West. *Qualitative theories and research methods — those that seek to illuminate how different peoples make sense of their everyday, lived experiences — are the only ones that supply such knowledge.* [emphasis added]

STILL ALIVE AND KICKING

The number of humanists in the social science has grown during the last several decades. But despite the massive amount of criticism that humanists have lobbed against positivism and quantitative social science over the last six decades or so, mainstream social science research continues to rule the roost in the social sciences. A government bias of giving grant money to quantitative researchers partly explains this bias. Government bureaucracies and private foundations adore quantitative research and operate under the belief that it is more scientific. But a better reason to explain why positivism has survived, the next chapter will show, is that it adapted and changed in response to the criticism.

CHAPTER 4

THE RISE OF NEOTERIC POSITIVISM

Like most philosophy professors during the 1980s, University of Minnesota associate professor Michael Root was a vigorous advocate of free will, or human agency, and a critic of objectivity, determinism, positivism, quantitative research and mainstream social science research, or what he collectively called "liberal sciences." He incorporated these views into his classes and into a book he was writing, titled *Philosophy of Social Science*. The original draft of the book contained extensive criticism of four major 19th or early 20th century scholars — German sociologist Max Weber, French sociologist Émile Durkheim, Austrian psychiatrist Sigmund Freud, English social anthropologist Alfred R. Radcliff-Brown — and one contemporary scholar, American economist Gary Becker. Root criticized these scholars and contemporary social science researchers in general because he says they fail to recognize that all research is value-laden.

> I believe that social scientists have told themselves and their subjects a false story about the relation between science and politics, and although the story serves a purpose — namely, in supporting the scientists' claims of disinterestedness and objectivity — it offers a misleading picture of the nature of social inquiry. My aim is to question liberalism as a philosophy for the social sciences to show how the practice of social science favors some policy objectives and ends over others.[1]

[1]Michael Root, *Philosophy of Social Science: The Methods, Ideals, and Politics of Social Inquiry* (Oxford, UK: Blackwell, 1993; reprinted in 1999), p. 20.

STRAW-MAN ARGUMENTS

All of the students in Root's classes respected his arguments, which were thoughtful and reasoned. Root was an expert in his field. But he didn't go unchallenged. One student questioned whether the criticism he and other philosophers have been leveling against the social sciences was still valid, because many contemporary positivists no longer approach research with the same philosophical assumptions as the classical scholars. In fact, this "straw-man" issue had been raised a decade earlier, in 1980, when sociologist Percy S. Cohen pointed out that "what is attacked as sociological positivism is, according to certain strict philosophical criteria, not necessarily true positivism."[2] "Professor," the student said in class one day,

> some scholars might argue that your criticism is a straw-man argument. The prevailing view in mainstream sociology today doesn't reject the idea that human beings have free will, or that knowledge is derived only through an inductive empirical process, or that science is value-free. Rather, it holds that the choices people make are shaped and constrained by the opportunities or limitations they are accorded from nature, culture, social structure and their own decisions. Most mainstream sociologists no longer search for universal laws of human behavior, nor do they ignore the reasons humans give for their behavior. Rather, they look at how social structure and culture increase or decrease the probability of certain kinds of choices or behaviors. Mainstream social scientists also concede that their research is informed by values and by moral judgments, but this doesn't mean that facts don't exist or that all knowledge is relative.

Root listened and was genuinely concerned. The published version of his book in 1993 excluded the detailed attacks on the classical scholars, but

---

[2]Percy S. Cohen, "Is Positivism Dead?" *Sociological Review, 28*(1): 141-176 (February 1980), p. 141. Also see D. C. Phillips, "Two Decades After: 'After The Wake: Postpositivistic Educational Thought,'" *Science & Education 13*(½): 67-84 (February 2004).

mainstream social science still was presented as an idealized version of classical and logical positivism.

> This book describes how theories are constructed and tested, how facts are predicted or explained, data collected and categorized, causes identified, and findings presented in the social sciences, *and show how the social sciences attempt, but fail, to be liberal or value-neutral.*[3] [emphasis added]

Root's book, however, was not just another left-wing critique of mainstream social science research. At the end of the book, he also argued that critical perspectives don't have all of the answers, either. In fact, he specifically criticized Critical Theory because

> the theory relies on the judgment that some group of people is oppressed. The question of whether it is oppressed is not ... depends on knowing some facts about political and economic power that seem to fall within the empirical-analytic [or mainstream social] sciences.[4] [bracketed material added]

In other words, to make their case, critical theorists need to rely on mainstream social science empirical methods, because they have no other means of demonstrating the truth of the propositions pertaining to oppression.

Cohen said humanist critics "evade the problem of facticity."[5] Sociologist Axel van den Berg also echoed this criticism in 1980, pointing out that "on the one hand, the Frankfurt philosophers [and their descendants] hold that there is a higher truth over and beyond the verifiable 'facts' of an empiricism ... and that, furthermore, this higher truth is capable of some sort of nonpositivist verification; on the other hand, they refuse to unveil that higher truth, or the method of verification, fearing that it might

---

[3]Root, *Philosophy of Social Science,* p. xv.
[4]*Ibid.,* p. xii.
[5]Cohen, "Is Positivism Dead?"

become petrified into another elitist, and possibly oppressive, dogma."[6] Van den Berg also argued that Jürgen Habermas, the intellectual leader of the Critical Theory movement in the last half of the 20th century, was unable to solve this problem.

Root's book also criticizes Critical Theory for failing to give the subjects of research an active role in the research process. In this respect, Critical Theory (as well as mainstream research) can be accused of elitism, because even though

> a critical science is supposed to transfer authority from the expert or theorist to her subjects ... for in treating their subjects as deluded, benighted, self-deceived, or suffering from false consciousness, they give them little or no say in how the research is to be conducted. Moreover, the subjects' say on whether the theory of working-class oppression or sexual repression is acceptable is won only after appropriate discussion and reflection ...[7]

According to the Root's book, the solution to this problem is "participatory research," in which the participants actively engage in the research process and in analyzing the results. "All research aims to make someone wiser, but participatory research differs from liberal [mainstream] research in specifically aiming to make the participant subjects wiser."[8] The advantage of this approach is that it has a greater potential to lead to social change, because the participants themselves become the social change agents. Although significant difficulties would be encountered in applying participatory research on a grand scale in modern complex societies, the idea is intriguing and, as Root's book points out, has been successfully tested on a limited basis in many areas around the world.

---

[6] Axel van den Berg, "Critical Theory: Is There Still Hope?" *American Journal of Sociology, 86*(3): 449-478 (1980), p. 452.

[7] *Ibid.*, p. 240.

[8] *Ibid.*, p. 241.

RUMORS OF POSITIVISM'S DEATH EXAGGERATED

By the mid-1980s to early 1990s, many philosophers of science and many humanists were convinced that positivism was in decline and soon would be replaced with a humanist paradigm. As philosopher James Bohman put it in 1991:

> Philosophers and methodologists have tried for decades to unify the complex and diverse activities called "social science," without much success. At one extreme, naturalistic philosophers of science have demanded that the social sciences imitate the natural sciences. But the social sciences have never achieved much in the way of predictive general laws — the hallmark of naturalistic knowledge — and so have often been denied the honorific status as "sciences."[9]

Bohman and many other philosophers, neo-Marxists and humanists contended that the main problem with positivism and mainstream social science is "indeterminancy" or "open-endedness." In other words, the positivists can't explain variances in human behavior because behavior is too complex and not subject to universal laws. A good example has been the unsuccessful effort in criminology to predict which juvenile delinquents will turn into chronic adult offenders. For every three offenders social scientists identify as "chronic," only one will actually become a chronic adult offender.[10]

Humanistic approaches no doubt benefited from the inability of quantitative methods' failure to explain more variance in "deviant behavior." The number of humanist scholars was growing in the social sciences. Some mainstream social scientists were even jumping ship. However, a content of analysis of four major sociology journals from 1967 to 1990 showed that even though there was a decrease in the number of articles containing "positivistic" content, three of the four journals

---

[9]James Bohman, *New Philosophy of Social Science* (Cambridge, MA: The MIT Press, 1993, paperback edition; first published in 1991), p. vii-viii.

[10]See Chapter 5 for details.

continued to publish a large number of positivist articles. The researchers concluded:

> Is positivism dead? To appropriate Sam Clemens' felicitous phrase, the rumours of positivism's death have been greatly exaggerated. If we assume that the ASR's (*American Sociological Review*'s) editorial policy reflects the prevailing norms of scientific practice among members of the association, then it seems reasonable to infer that sociological practice among the association's membership is predominantly positivistic.[11]

In 1997, sociologist Andrew Abbott drew a similar conclusion: "Many have argued that we have entered a postpositivist age. Having swept our intellectual horizons clear of measurement, we can move forward to view social reality in its full complexity. Yet social measurement is far from dead, either intellectually or practically." Abbott added that

> even though positivist social science has been shown to be in principle impossible, the vast majority of social-science effort (and funding) is in fact spent doing it. Such research is often highly consequential, whether it be the market studies that shape consumer demand or the census figures that determine political districts. It would thus be politically foolish to ignore this research.[12]

Although humanists continued to criticize classical and logical positivism, and still do today,[13] by the late 1990s it was clear that mainstream social science was not going away any time soon. Ironically, though, many social scientists doing positivistic research didn't like to call

---

[11]C. David Gartrell and John W. Gartrell, "Positivism in Sociological Practice: 1967-1990," *The Canadian Review of Sociology and Anthropology* (May 1, 1996), p. 13.

[12]Andrew Abbott, "Of Time and Place," *Social Forces, 75*: 1149-1182 (1997). Also see Andrew Abbott, "Seven Types of Ambiguity," *Theory and Society, 26*: 357-391 (1978).

[13]Valerija Vendramin and Renata Sribar, "Beyond Positivism or the Perspectives of the 'New' Gender Equality, *Solsko Polje, 21*(1-2): 157-169 (2010) and Richard York and Brett Clark, "The Problem with Prediction: Contingency, Emergence, and the Reification of Projections," *The Sociological Quarterly, 48*(4): 713-743 (Fall 2007).

themselves positivists. The decades of relentless criticism had turned *positivism* into a dirty word. "With the notable exception of [sociologist] Jonathan H. Turner," write sociologists C. David Gartrell and John W. Gartrell, "few sociological theorists seem intent on proclaiming their positivism, at least in public."[14] This was the case even though Turner himself recognized that "within the larger sociological community, my position is still in the majority."[15]

The reluctance of some positivists to come out of the closet may have stemmed in part from their lack of training in philosophy of social science. Most quantitatively oriented graduate students take few in-depth courses that address the philosophical (ontological and epistemological) assumptions underlying their research. Consequently, few are likely to feel competent engaging in a debate with the philosophical-savvy humanists. Another possible reason is that many — maybe even most — don't even care about the debate over the validity of what they do. In the early 1990s, one Ph.D. candidate who was well aware of the criticism of logical positivism was aghast when, during an interview for a job at a major university, he was told that "all of the faculty in our program would call themselves logical positivists." These positivists apparently saw themselves as scientists, so what's to defend?

In contrast, philosophy, as a body of knowledge, has played a central role in influencing the other humanistically oriented disciplines. Humanist graduate students, whether in or out of the social sciences, take a fair number of courses that examine the nature of reality and ways of knowing it. So it's not surprising that humanists were able to take the higher ground in terms of attacks on the philosophical foundations of positivistic research. They had the intellectual training and knowledge. One wonders how history might have changed if the positivists had been just as skilled in the philosophy of social science. But regardless of the reasons why positivists were afraid to come out of the closet, positivism has survived a prolonged siege from its critics.

---

[14]Gartrell and Gartrell, "Positivism in Sociological Practice," p. 13.
[15]*Ibid.*

EXPLAINING THE PERSISTENCE OF POSITIVISM

The reason positivism has survived is simple, according to many of the humanists: positivists give governmental agencies and private business elites information and knowledge that helps them achieve their goals, legitimate their decisions, and maintain control over people. In exchange, these elite organizations and individuals give positivist researchers money to conduct research. A *quid pro quo*, as academics and lawyers are fond of saying. In contrast, critical scholarship is far less likely to be rewarded because it usually criticizes those powerful people and organizations for failing to pay more attention to the needs and concerns of disadvantaged groups and individuals and ordinary people. Governments, the humanists maintain, are not in the practice of funding scholars who criticize them.

It would be difficult to deny some validity to this "payback theory." After all, in the social sciences, most of the research grant money is spent on health-related or life-science research, which is often used by pharmaceutical companies, health insurance companies, and other private run hospitals and health organizations.

Other humanist critics attribute the persistence of positivism to the inability of the humanists to unify behind one general model. Although positivists often disagree about the nature of knowledge, such disagreements are sometimes even more pronounced in qualitative research, where the rules are less rigid and, consequently, the findings are less uniform. Georgia State University philosophy professor William Bechtel noted in 1988 that even though few philosophers of science "still affirm allegiance to the positivists' position in its original form,"

> the Positivists' picture of science remains the most comprehensive we
> have. The failure of Logical Positivism, if indeed it has failed, is
> therefore, all the more noble and it leaves a legacy. Most philosophers
> of science find it impossible to dispense totally with the Positivist
> Heritage even while recognizing various shortcomings.[16]

---

[16]William Bechtel, *Philosophy of Science: An Overview for Cognitive Science* (Hillsdale, NJ: Lawrence Erlbaum Associates, 1988), p. 49.

Although money, power and fractionalization among humanists may have contributed to the staying power of positivism, other scholars argue that a better explanation is simply that positivism adapted and changed in response to the criticism. In the late 1980s and early 1990s, sociologist Jeffrey Alexander called this new movement "postpositivism" and argued that it represented the best of both the positivist and humanist paradigms, while avoiding the extremist positions in both traditions.[17] Humanists were moving away from relativist positions and were embracing empiricism more than in the past, and contemporary positivists were placing more emphasis on theory than empirical observation and more emphasis on deductive theorizing than inductive.

Alexander and others pointed out that no explanation of phenomena can be built solely through inductive logic or tested solely on the basis of phenomenal evidence, as logical positivism had asserted.[18] Theory-neutral observation is impossible. Data are not self-explanatory. They need a logical framework to be interpreted. Alexander argues, in fact, that theorizing at a general level, without reference to particular empirical problems, is a significant and meaningful endeavor for the social sciences. Although this claim might have been more than many positivists could swallow, Alexander points out that the social sciences will always be overdetermined by theory and underdetermined by fact. What this means is that there is no single or right way to test a theory. An infinite number of studies and approaches can be used, and none will ever be sufficient to prove a theory, because a new study or method may, at any time, overturn previous studies.

---

[17]Alexander implies that post-positivism as a synthesis of humanist and positivist approaches. See, e.g., Jeffrey C. Alexander, "The New Theoretical Movement," pp. 77-101 in N. J. Smelser (ed.), *Handbook of Sociology* (Beverly Hills, Calif.: Sage, 1988) and Jeffrey C. Alexander and Paul Colomy, "Traditions and Competition: Preface to a Postpositivist Approach to Knowledge Cumulation," pp. 27-52 in George Ritzer (ed.), *Metatheorizing* (Newbury Park, CA: Sage Publications, 1992).

[18]See, e.g., Thomas Kuhn, *The Structure of Scientific Revolutions* (Chicago: University of Chicago Press, 1962) and Imre Lakatos, "Falsification and the Methodology of Research Programmes," pp. 91-196 in Imre Lakatos and A. Musgrave (eds.), *Criticism and the Growth of Knowledge* (Cambridge, England: Cambridge University Press, 1970).

Debates about the adequacy of various methodologies are endless in the social sciences. As such, logic, reason and theory ultimately become the prime arbitrators, not data. Facts are never directly interpretable. Truth claims always involve appeal to reason and logic.

> There is no clear indisputable reference for the elements that compose social science — definitions, concepts, models, or "facts." Because of this, there is not neat translatability between different levels of generality. Formulations at one level do not ramify in clear-cut ways for the other levels of scientific concern. For example, while precise empirical measurements of two variable correlations can sometimes be established, it is rarely possible for such a correlation to prove or disprove a proposition about this interrelationship that is stated in more general terms. The reason is that the existence of empirical and ideological dissensus allows social scientists to operationalize propositions in a variety of different ways.[19]

As a consequence, Alexander argues that scientific analysis involves not just explanation but also discourse. Progress comes through discourse and politics. "Discourse seeks persuasion through argument rather than prediction. Its persuasiveness is based on such qualities as logical coherence, expansiveness of scope, interpretive insight, value relevance, rhetorical force, beauty, and texture of argument."[20] Political scientist Erik Albæk extends this logic to the real world.

> To understand the complex interfaces between social science research and the political-administrative decision-making process, it is necessary to be aware that research is transferred to, and becomes part of, a discourse of action, in the philosophical as well as the everyday practical sense — a discourse in which (self)reflecting participants deliberate on and debate norms and alternatives with a view to concrete action.[21]

---

[19]Alexander, "The New Theoretical Movement," p. 81.
[20]*Ibid.,* p. 80.
[21]Erick Albæk, "Between Knowledge and Power: Utilization of Social Science in Public Policy Making," *Policy Sciences, 28*: 79-100 (1995), p. 79.

The idea that positivism and humanism could coexist and complement each other wasn't isolated to just sociology. In 1992, marketing communication scholar Timothy B. Heath wrote that "once terminological differences and methodological similarities are recognized, the differences between humanism and naturalism within consumer research are few. While arguments persist at the philosophical extremes, it appears that practicing researchers have achieved considerable reconciliation between the theories, methods, and philosophies of the two approaches."[22]

Today, most mainstream social scientists and many humanists acknowledge that science or scholarship involves an interplay between theory and data. Sociologist and mass communication professor Phillip J. Tichenor summed up the dominant approach in 1981:

> Science is neither theory alone nor pure gathering of evidence in the absence of higher-order reasoning. Science requires both, pursued in an atmosphere of rigor in logic and measures that allows others to determine whether they, using that combination of reasoning and procedure, would come to similar conclusions.[23]

Alexander's analysis implies that adaptation and change account in large part for the persistence of positivism. His use of the term "postpositivism" to refer to the changes that had taken place, however, is somewhat problematic, because it implies that positivism and its various elements have been abandoned. The term neopositivism would have been better, but that term had already been expropriated in the early 20th century to refer to revisions in classical positivism, which included Austrian-British scholar Karl Popper's concept of falsification.

---

[22]Timothy B. Heath, "The Reconciliation of Humanism and Positivism in the Practice of Consumer Research: A View from the Trenches," *Journal of the Academy of Marketing Science, 20*(2): 107-118 (Spring 1992), p. 107.

[23]Phillip J. Tichenor, "The Logic of Social and Behavioral Science," pp. 10-28 in Guido H. Stempel III and Bruce H. Westley (eds.), *Research Methods in Mass Communication* (Englewood Cliffs, N.J.: Prentice-Hall, 1981).

To avoid confusion, this book refers to the new positivist movement as "neoteric positivism."[24]

NEOTERIC POSITIVISM

Neoteric positivism retains many elements of traditional positivism. It seeks to solve social problems. It believes that the methods of the natural sciences (e.g., experimentation, quantification) can help scholars understand human behavior, even though the amount of explained variance in human behavior falls far short of the ideal. It makes a distinction between the subjective and objective. The selection of a research topic clearly involves value judgments; however, some level of objectivity in research is possible, meaning that researchers must be open to rejecting their theories or data in the face of logic or evidence to the contrary. Neoteric positivism also holds that nonobservable human phenomena — like beliefs, attitudes, intents and opinions — can be quantitatively or qualitatively measured, usually through self-reports, and that emotions, or affective components of human behavior, can be measured with medical devices or other instruments.

Neoteric positivism also embraces social constructionism. Laws, values, customs, concepts and social structures are constructed and reconstructed by people and society, who give meanings to things and ideas. Neoteric positivism rejects radical empiricism, universal laws of human behavior, the idea that fact and value can be strictly separated, and strict determinism. In terms of keeping positivism alive, the last item in this list — reconciling the conflict between free will and determinism — is the single most important, because it is a necessary condition for rejecting radical empiricism, universal laws and value-freedom. The most distinctive feature of neoteric positivism, then, is its philosophical assumptions about the nature social action, or what will be called here the Probabilistic Doctrine of Social Action (more on this subject later).

----

[24]Neoteric is derived from the Greek word *Neotericoi* ("new poets"), which refers to a period during the Hellenistic Period (323 BC+) when avant-garde poets developed a new style of poetry that turned away from classical Homeric epic poetry. In English, the word neoteric means modern, new, recent.

Soft Empiricism

Neoteric positivists subscribe to what some scholars call *soft empiricism*, or the idea that reason, or theory, should play as much or even more role in the development of knowledge as empirical observation. Soft empiricism embraces the notion that data can be important in sifting good from bad theory, but data are never a good substitute for sound logic. All other things being equal, theory takes precedence.

The notion that science should involve both formal theory and empirical observation might seem obvious or trite to many social scientists. But a fair amount of research in some of the social sciences continues to lack formal theory. Mass communication scholars W. James Potter, Roger Cooper and Michel Dupagne surveyed major mass communication journals and found that only 13 percent of the published "social scientific" studies are theory-driven — most are data-driven (inductive and quantitative).[25]

The idea that explanation should focus exclusively or more heavily on empirical observation rather than on formal theory is a major tenet of logical positivism. Logical positivism rejects formal deductive theoretical systems, preferring instead an inductive approach that seeks to understand or explain phenomena primarily through experience and the senses. Neoteric positivists reject this idea.

Not Laws, But Probabilistic Generalizations

Neoteric positivists do not seek to uncover *universal laws of human behavior*. Humans are not assumed to be subjects of invariant properties of forces of nature, because they have one thing that inanimate objects of the universe do not: the ability to act and make decisions. They have free will. This is one reason why it is so difficult to predict individual human behavior. Identifying chronic offenders is an example mentioned earlier. Only a third of juveniles who get into trouble will actually become career

---

[25]W. James Potter, Roger Cooper and Michel Dupagne,"The Three Paradigms of Mass Media Research in Mainstream Communication Journals," *Communication Theory, 3*: 317-335 (1993).

criminals. However, this doesn't mean that social scientists are unable to identify cultural, psychological or social factors that influence criminal behavior. They can estimate the percentage of the population that will become part of that group and identify aspects of the social structure (e.g., demographics) and culture (gang activity) that contributes to chronic delinquency in populations.

In other words, social scientists can search for and identify *probabilistic generalizations* that explain or predict social patterns and human behaviors among groups or populations, with varying degrees of accuracy. Armed with such knowledge, it is theoretically possible for social scientists and policymakers to alter beliefs, attitudes or structure to correct or assuage some social problems.

Not Just the Facts, But Values, Too

Neoteric positivists acknowledge that all research involves *value judgments* about good and bad. They readily acknowledge that the decision to select a topic for research involves value judgments, because their goal is to solve social or moral problems. Science cannot, and should not, be divorced from questions about what is good or bad.

Neoteric positivists also recognize that power and money can influence the research process. Sometimes this can pose ethical or moral dilemmas. In such cases, neoteric positivists refuse to engage in such research. However, on other occasions, power and money can produce research that benefits disadvantaged group in society. And even though all research involves value judgments, neoteric positivists are strongly opposed to dogmatism; they stand ready to reject even their own theories and ideas should the empirical data and logic suggest otherwise. An open mind, according to a neoteric positivist, is a terrible thing to waste.

Not Determinism, But Probabilism

Neoteric positivists begin with the assumption that people have *free will*, or the ability to choose between alternative courses of action. The question of fate is metaphysical, beyond the realm of science. But free will does not exist in a vacuum. The decisions that people make are influenced by many aspects of culture, psychology and social structure (e.g., wealth, education, values, gender etc.).[26]

In many instances, people are even unaware of the extent to which demographic characteristics and value systems influence or shape (not determine) their choices. Everyone has a choice, for example, of disobeying the rules of an organization in which they are members. However, most people follow the rules because their value systems (especially religious beliefs) encourage such behavior and the organization often rewards them with raises, promotions, awards and other perks. The probability of people conforming to those rules generally increases as the rewards increase — a generalization that can be deduced from the economic assumption that people tend to seek that which benefits them and avoid that which causes them pain or hardship.

The role of a social scientist, then, is to uncover the patterns of human activity that emerge from these differential conditions. And the search for general patterns of behavior (as opposed to invariant laws of the universe) is made possible by the "doctrine of probabilistic social action."

DOCTRINE OF PROBABILISTIC SOCIAL ACTION

Neoteric positivism didn't emerge overnight, nor did any scientist or group of scientists sit down and formally design its main features. It evolved gradually over the past seven decades. Its roots can even be traced to the late 1930s and 1940s, when classical functionalism challenged logical positivism's emphasis on inductive reasoning and radical empiricism.[27] Of course, explaining or understanding the origins of a set of ideas that change over time is no easy task. But if one single element could be identified as

---

[26]Genetics, biology, and psychology also create differential opportunities, but social scientists focus on social structure and culture.

[27]Functionalism embraced deductive logic whereas logical positivism was highly inductive.

key in the survival of positivism, it is the idea that free will and determinism are not incompatible.[28]

Social Structure vs. Agency

In the early part of the 20th century, sociologists tended to emphasize determinism over free will (they called it "structure over agency"). This is not surprising because Comte defined sociology as a discipline that looked at the impact of the social environment on human behavior (i.e., things external to the individual). If sociologists had taken a highly pro-agency or individualistic position, it might never have emerged as a discipline, because the humanities and psychology already covered those grounds. But the agency camp grew in sociology — no doubt a reaction to the hardcore determinism of early sociology — and tension between the two perspectives increased. That tension still exists today in some of the social sciences (especially communication), but it has died down substantially in sociology because the role of the structure and agency has been redefined and reconciled, at least to some degree.

Some scholars argue that the new role can be traced to sociologist Robert K. Merton, who argued in the 1950s that agency and structure were complementary. Unlike other philosophers of social science, who sometimes argued that structure took precedence under some conditions and agency under others, Merton assumed that both conditions exist side by side. As he put it, people have the power to make choices, but their choices are constrained or enabled by social, economic and political conditions and by their linkages to groups and organizations. For example, a subordinate in an organization always has the choice of deciding whether to violate organization rules, but that decision may be influenced by whether the subordinate has a family to support (needs the money), believes the rule is unfair to him or her, or sees an opportunity to gain from the

---

[28]Soft determinism is another term used to describe the idea that people can make choices in some situations but are coerced in others. The probabilistic principle of social action, however, does not draw a hard line between free will and determinism. Choice and constraints are always operating, to some degree or another.

violation (e.g., embezzle money). These are elements of the social environment that can influence, but not determine, the decision. The social actor has some freedom to decide. Of course, most people at most times obey most rules because organizations often reward them for doing that and punish them for breaking the rules.

Merton referred to this process as individuals making choices between socially structured alternatives.[29] Merton also pointed out that social control is not a one-way street: institutions place constraints on individual behavior but individuals in turn control and can change institutions — even though, it must be mentioned, elites usually have an advantage when it comes to constructing the rules and the organizations. Merton's approach might be thought of as presaging social constructionism, which gained momentum in the 1960s.

Merton's reconciliation to the agency-structure problem spread quickly in sociology, partly because this field already had a well-developed subfield specializing in the "sociology of science." By the late 1970s and early 1980s, many sociologists considered the debate between agency and structure settled. Even the fourth edition of Earl Babbie's popular methodology textbook backed off of earlier statements that all behavior was "determined."

> [T]he kind of understanding we seek as we analyze social research data inevitably involves a deterministic model of human behavior. In looking for the reasons why people are the way they are and do the things they do, we implicitly assume that their characteristics and actions are determined by forces and factors operating on them. *You do not need to believe that human beings are totally determined, nor do you have to lead your life as though you were,* but you must be willing to use deterministic logic in looking for explanations when you engage in social science research (emphasis added).[30]

---

[29]Arthur L. Stinchcombe, "Merton's Theory of Social Structure," pp. 11-33 in *The Idea of Social Structure: Papers in Honor of Robert K. Merton*, Lewis Coser, ed. (New York: Harcourt Brace, 1975), p. 12.

[30]Earl Babbie, *The Practice of Social Research*, 4th ed. (Belmont, CA: Wadsworth, 1986), p. 53.

One of the most elaborate attempts to reconcile agency and structure is Anthony Giddens' "theory of structuration."[31] Structuration contends that all human action is regulated by a set of norms and/or laws and values. Human action, thus, is partly determined by the context in which it takes place. But structure, rules and values are not fixed and permanent. They are always subject to change, because of "reflexive feedback," or the idea that social actors can alter the rules that regulate their actions. Although Giddens refers to structuration as a theory, some scholars prefer to call it a philosophical doctrine, because there is no way to test structuration. It deals with metaphysical, not empirical, phenomena.[32] As such, structuration is better conceptualized as a more in-depth extension of the classic free will/determinism debate.

Whether called a theory or a doctrine, the idea that free will and determinism could be reconciled was a big turning point for sociology and, eventually, for the other social sciences. It extended legitimacy to both positivistic and humanistic approaches. Under this new model, neither, alone, was sufficient to explain human action. Both were necessary. Pluralism of perspectives was now hip.

However, not all of the social sciences jumped on the bandwagon at the same time. Some were slower, because increasing specialization had insulated them from knowledge in other disciplines. Mass communication is perhaps the best example. While sociologists were busy in the 1980s trying to incorporate both agency and structure into their models, critical mass communication scholars were still beating up on logical positivism, which by then was already a dead horse. The delay among mass communication scholars in joining the reconciliation bandwagon might be explained by the fact that the critique of classical and logical positivism was a central element of many critical theories. In other words, reconciling free will/agency and determinism/structure meant blurring the boundaries

---

[31]Anthony Giddens, *Central Problems of Social Theory* (Berkeley: University of California Press, 1979) and Anthony Giddens, *The Constitution of Society Constitution of Society: Outline of the Theory of Structuration* (Berkeley: University of California Press, 1984).

[32]John Castel, *The Group in Society* (Thousand Oaks, CA: Sage, 2010), p. 49, see footnote 13.

REFLEXIVITY IN BANDURA'S SOCIAL COGNITIVE THEORY

The work of social psychologists is sometimes criticized for failing to account for human agency, or free will. But in the 1970s, some of them were already moving already introducing revisions to their theories to incorporate both determinism and agency. One of them was Albert Bandura, well known for his social cognitive theory. The theory basically holds that humans imitate and copy the behavior of others. They learn from others. Humanist critics are quick to associate this kind of analysis with simple stimulus-response behavior (a deterministic perspective).

But in 1977 and 1978, possibly under pressure from critics, Bandura introduced the concept of "reciprocal determinism," which grants a measure of free will to human behavior. Reciprocal determinism, he writes, holds that "behavior — cognitive, biological, and other personal factors — and environ-mental events all operate as interacting determinants that influence each other bidirectionally ... Reciprocal causation provides people with opportunities to exercise some control over events in their lives, as well as set limits of self-direction. Because of the bidirec-tionality of influence, people are both products and producers of their environment."

He adds that "to say that a major distinguishing mark of humans is their endowed plasticity is not to say they have no nature or that they come structureless ... The plasticity, which is intrinsic to the nature of humans, depends on neurophysiological mechanisms and structures that have evolved over time. These advanced neural systems for processing, retaining, and using coded information provide the capacity for the very characteristics that are distinctly human — generative symbolization, forethought, evaluative self-regulation, reflective self-conscious-ness, and symbolic communication."

In short, Bandura is not suggesting that humans do not have free will or the ability to make choices; rather, he is arguing that those choices are constrained by neurophysiological systems and processes. In other words, certain limits are placed on the ability of the human mind to perceive stimuli, acquire information or understand a message. These limits are not the same from person to person, but they are real and are attributed to neurophysiological processes as well as the environment.

Albert Bandura (1994). Social cognitive theory of mass communication, pp. 61-90 *in* J. Bryant and D. Zillmann, *Media Effects: Advances in Theory and Research* (Hillsdale, NJ: Lawrence Erlbaum Associates), pp. 61-62.

between the positivist and humanist camps, which could have created an intellectual crisis for some critical scholars.

The Doctrine

The doctrine of probabilistic social action asserts that neither deterministic nor free will models are sufficient for understanding human actions and mental processes. The free-will model imparts too much choice to social actors; it fails to recognize that social structures and cultural values, in particular, limit or enhance choices. In many cases, social actors are even unaware of the extent to which their choices are limited. Social institutions and dominant groups also resist change and often have the power to control or contain change. The deterministic perspective, on the other hand, fails to recognize that people are not simply passive recipients of social and political laws, like a ball dropped from a roof. Social actors have the power to choose between alternative courses of action; they have free will. But, again, those choices are not limitless; they are constrained or enabled by social roles, values, norms and other phenomena. And the probability of any particular action increases or decreases depending upon the constraints or opportunities of the situation.

More formally, these constraints or enablements may be classified into five levels of analysis (see Figure 1): physiological, organic, psychological, social and cultural. At the physical level, the focus is on natural laws that constrain or affect human action or communication. Here one can talk about law-like propositions, as is often the case in the natural sciences. Laws of physics are an example. Natural scientists work primarily at the physical level of analysis, studying phenomena such as forces, atoms, chemical processes, mathematics, and molecules. In the human realm, aspects of the physical environment also can constrain choices. As much as two people might want to talk to each other personally, interpersonal communication cannot exist if they are a mile apart and have no access to long-distance communication devices (e.g., telephones, telegraph, smoke-signals, drums) or means of travel (car, train, boat, horse, etc.). The physical properties of the environment (and/or biological limitations of the

FIGURE 1. FORM OF EXPLANATION BY LEVEL OF ANALYSIS

Form of Explanation	Level of Analysis	Academic Discipline[a]	Examples of Phenomena Studied[a]
Probabilistic Generalizations	Culture	Communication, Law, Philosophy, History, Linguistics, Sociology, Literature	Values, Rituals, Language, Laws, Public Opinion, Norms, Technology
	Social	Communication, History, Sociology, Economics, Political Science, Social Anthropology	Status, Roles, Power, Organizations, Institutions, Groups, Social Interaction
	Psychological	Communication, History, Psychology, Psychiatry Social Psychology, Cognitive Psychology	Attitudes, Beliefs, Individual Values Cognitions, Personality
	Organic	Biology, Medicine, Physical Anthropology, Psychobiology, Cognitive Pyschology, Sociobiology	Cells, Organs, Tissues, Nerves, Diseases, Drives
Law-Like Propositions	Physical	Physics, Chemistry, Mathematics	Forces, Motion, Atoms, Molecules

[a]Illustrative, not a comprehensive listing.

human body) prohibit interpersonal communication under such conditions. There is no choice; it is determined. However, as one moves from the physiological to the cultural level of analysis, it is less useful to talk about determinism and invariant laws and more useful to talk about constraints in terms of probabilistic generalizations.

At the organic level, the focus is on the biological features of human life. Thus, a person who was born without sight will not be able to watch television because blindness is a constraining factor. However, the fact that other people can see does not necessarily mean they will all choose to watch television or to watch the same program. Choices often differ and are shaped by other phenomena, especially at the psychological, social and cultural levels. Organic structure also places constraints on human perceptions. For example, cognitive psychologists have found that the amount of time it takes for an individual to visually recognize a pattern between two or more motionless stimuli increases as the time interval between them increases: accuracy declines about 40 percent in 600 milliseconds.[33] This parameter varies from person to person, but there are certain constraints beyond which no individual may perceive the pattern. Thus, at the organic level, one can also talk about law-like propositions, but the parameters are more variable than at the physical level of analysis. Behavior modification research that treats the mind as a "black box" (ignores it) also would fit at this level.

At the level of the psychological, the focus is on the mental characteristics of human life, or the conscious mind or personality. Loneliness, for example, generally increases the probability of watching television, because television may serve as a crude functional substitute for companionship. But loneliness does not automatically lead to television viewing, because most people have other options or choices available to them, such as calling a friend, reading a book, going for a walk in a park, or joining a club. The decision will be affected in part by the availability of other resources in the individual's environment. At this level it is even less feasible to talk about law-like propositions. The preferred terminology, at the risk of sounding redundant, is probabilistic generalization; that is, under certain psychological conditions (or constraints), the probability of engaging in a certain action increases or decreases.

At the social level, the focus is on the interpersonal or intergroup relationships, wherein the social actor is viewed as a member of some social group or is acting in a particular role. Social actor is defined here as any individual or group whose action is aimed at achieving some goal or objective. Thus, it comes as no surprise that business people spend more time watching business-oriented television programming, such as Bloomberg Television, than nonbusiness people. Their roles in and social

---

[33]Stephen K. Reed, *Cognition: Theory and Applications* (Monterey, CA: Brooks/Cole Publishing, 1982), p. 16.

linkages to organizations or the social system as a whole often require that they keep abreast of the latest developments. But such constraints are not deterministic. Business people have other options available to them. They may choose to read a newspaper or a magazine to obtain similar information, or they may go uninformed. And each of these choices, in turn, has consequences. A business executive who does not follow the news, for example, runs the risk of making some bad business decisions. The probability that social actors will choose a particular course of action will vary in part to the extent that they perceive these consequences as contrary to or in line with their professional or personal interests or goals.

At the level of culture, the focus is on the symbolic meanings in human life, such as language, values, beliefs and norms. Individuals and groups are primarily viewed as carriers of shared values and ideas. Certain values may increase or decrease the probability of watching certain types of television programs. Among high-status groups, television viewing is often viewed as a waste of time and culturally profane. Regardless of whether this is true, the existence of such a value or belief can have powerful effects. This does not mean those holding that value will never watch television — many do and some avoid being stigmatized by keeping knowledge of such activity to themselves or reporting on only those programs that are socially acceptable (e.g., news). But, *ceteris paribus,* the negative stigma attached with viewing television decreases the probability of viewing.

In sum, the ability to explain or predict action using deterministic formulas or causal laws decreases as one moves from the physical to the cultural level. Social structures and value systems, in other words, are not simply the outcome of some law-like process — rather, they are created by people to solve certain problems or to control other social actors. Thus, social action and cultural phenomena at the social and cultural levels are relatively autonomous from the physical and organic levels. This does not mean that the higher levels of analysis are independent of the lower levels. In fact, each level encompasses the levels below it. That is, the psychological cannot exist without the organic (cells, tissue, brain) as well as the physical levels; the social cannot exist without the interaction of two or more individuals (or personalities); and the cultural is an outgrowth of social activities. Each successively higher level of analysis, in other words, develops out of the lower level and is dependent to some extent on all of the lower levels. However, even though each level is emergent from those below it, that level is not reducible to lower levels. Phenomena at each level possess some degree of autonomy that is not fully determined or constrained by the lower levels. A personality, for example, is more than just a living organism. Furthermore, each higher level, even though it emerged from a lower level, may influence the levels below it. Social psychologists, in particular, study not only the impact of the personality on the group but the effect of the group on the individual.

It is also important to point out that the goal of research under the probabilistic model being offered here is not to explain 100 percent of the variance in human behavior or mental states (attitudes, beliefs, etc.). In fact, this is rarely possible, because the model assumes that the behavior or decisions of any single social actors cannot be fully predicted or explained under most conditions. At the same time, however, the actions and decisions of people are not completely random. The proportion of the population that watches television at a particular hour on a particular day is very stable over time. These regularities are partly a function of the physical, organic, psychological, social and cultural constraints in which people live and work. They set powerful boundaries on human activity.

Within this general framework, the goal of quantitative research and some qualitative research is to explain and predict how populations of social actors will act under the various constraints at the different levels of analysis. This approach does not deny the existence of the individual and idiosyncratic decisions. The actions of any single actor, in fact, are usually quite difficult to explain or predict using quantitative research methods. Instead, this is where qualitative and interpretive research methods are valuable. They can focus in on one social actor or a small number of cases and examine in-depth the reasons, as opposed to the causes, for an action. In contrast, the goal in quantitative research usually is to create models which estimate the probability that populations of social actors will engage in a particular action or behavior based upon the constraints or enablements in the five levels of analysis mentioned above. This means that quantitative research studies populations of social actors (at least two or more) and/or their interactions, rather than the individual. There is, therefore, no necessary conflict between quantitative, qualitative and interpretive methodologies. In most cases, they are answering different though often complementary questions.

RECONCILIATION

This chapter has examined the criticism against positivism and mainstream social science research. The analysis showed that positivism has been the target of many attacks from humanists. Some of the criticism has merit. Some is based on straw-man arguments, because contemporary positivism is quite different from classical positivism and neopositivism. But those practicing positivism responded to these attacks and adopted new ontological assumptions that have reduced the intellectual distance between them and humanists.

Action and mental processes need not be considered as either a function of deterministic forces or voluntaristic (free will) actions, in the traditional sense of these terms. Rather, individuals and groups should be viewed as having the ability to make choices within certain physiological, organic, psychological, social and cultural constraints or enablements. There is no inherent conflict between quantitative, qualitative and interpretive research method. Each makes a contribution. And positivism and quantitative research also are capable of generating empirical evidence that criticizes the status quo.

A good, though overused, metaphor is the landscape oil painting. Artists usually begin with broad-brush strokes, applying paint or water color to a large area such as the sky, the forest or the earth. These background colors may be likened to quantitative research, which typically searches for very general propositions that explain the actions of large populations. The leaves and the blades of grass, on the other hand, are the qualitative and interpretive studies, which focus heavily on individual agency. Which is a more accurate picture of reality? Neither. Both are necessary to develop a comprehensive understanding of the landscape of the human mind.

CHAPTER 5

CRIMINOLOGY AND THE
CRIME PROBLEM

The white-haired professor stared at his class of four dozen criminology students, pausing briefly to transition to a new topic.

"During the nineteen-fifties and nineteen-sixties, OSU criminologist Walter Reckless conducted studies on the behavioral patterns of nondelinquent boys who live in high-delinquency neighbor-hoods," Simon Dinitz said.[1] "He concluded that a good self-concept insulates these boys from the social and personal pressure to engage in delinquent behavior. In the late 1960s, Reckless and I conducted a series of field experiments that were designed to instill a higher level of self-esteem in seventh-grade boys.[2] Boys who had delinquent backgrounds were placed in special classrooms, where they were exposed to instruction that

Simon Dinitz in 1981 *(Photograph courtesy of Risa Dinitz Lazaroff)*

---

[1]Walter Reckless conducted observational studies of crime in Chicago with sociologists Robert Park and Ernest Burgess. His 1925 dissertation was published in 1933 under the title *Vice in Chicago* and was a landmark sociological study of crime. In 1932, he and Mapheus Smith published the first book on juvenile delinquency. He began teaching at Ohio State in 1940. Reckless retired in 1969 and died in 1988 at age 89.

[2]Walter C. Reckless and Simon Dinitz, *The Prevention of Juvenile Delinquency: An Experiment* (Columbus: Ohio State University Press, 1972).

contained positive role models and positive self-image concepts. The so-called 'good' boys had standard instruction. The hope was that improving the self-image of the 'bad' boys would reduce their chances of being arrested again."[3]

"But after two years of treatment and four years of follow-up, the program had no appreciable effect on arrest rates," Dinitz added, waving his left hand through the air to emphasize the point. "Boys who went through the program had the same recidivism rates as those who did not. Our study supported much of the literature up to that point in time, which basically concluded that social intervention did not seem to have much impact. In fact, several years later one criminologist who reviewed more than 200 intervention and rehabilitation programs reached a similar conclusion."

"Dr. Dinitz," one student in the third row interrupted. "Are you saying that rehabilitation programs are ineffective?"

"That's precisely what the researcher concluded," Dinitz responded, looking down at his notes, something he rarely needed to do. "He examined 231 correctional evaluation studies undertaken between 1945 and 1967. A summary of his analysis was published in *The Public Interest* magazine in 1974. Here is a direct quote":

> With few and isolated exceptions, the rehabilitative efforts that have been reported so far have had no appreciable effect on recidivism ... [Our present strategies ... cannot overcome, or even appreciably reduce, the powerful tendencies of offenders to continue in criminal behavior.[4]

---

[3]During the 1960s, Reckless developed "containment theory," which contended that people have inner and outer forces that restrain them from committing crimes. The inner forces stem from moral and religious beliefs whereas the outer forces come from family members, teachers and others. He believed that the effectiveness of containment forces can be influenced by effective supervision and by internal factors such as a good self-concept.

[4]Robert Martinson, "What Works? Questions and Answers about Prison Reform," *The Public Interest*, *35*: 22-54 (Spring 1974), p. 25 (first sentence) and p. 49 (second sentence). The full report was published as a book a year later. Douglas Lipton, Robert Martinson and Judith Wilks, *The Effectiveness of Correctional Treatment: A Survey of Treatment Evaluation Studies* (New York: Praeger, 1975).

Dinitz added that other scholars had reached the same conclusion — that rehabilitation programs were not very effective in reducing recidivism rates.[5] But those reports had little direct impact on public policy because they had been published in obscure scientific journals, which were read only by scholars. In contrast, nearly 10,000 policymakers, journalists and citizens read *The Public Interest*. No article in the history of criminology has had more political impact, Dinitz said, quoting other scholars.[6]

"In fact, within one year many scholars and policymakers completely abandoned the rehabilitation model," Dinitz said. "Conservatives, in particular, seized upon the 'nothing-works' conclusion to justify closing down rehabilitation programs and passing laws that increased the severity of punishment. Capital punishment was reinstated in the United States in 1976. This was the case even though other research had shown that capital punishment as well as increasing the severity of punishment for many other violent crimes had little impact on crime rates."

"So, Professor Dinitz, are you saying that policymakers failed to take the research evidence into account?" another student asked.

"Since when have public policymakers based their decisions mostly upon scientific evidence?" he responded as the bell rang. "More truth next time."

Professor Dinitz always ended his formal lectures with that "more-truth-next-time" remark, which could have sounded pompous coming from

---

[5]See, e.g., Walter C. Bailey, "Correctional Outcome: An Evaluation of 100 Reports," *Journal of Criminal Law, Criminology and Police Science, 57*: 153-160 (1966); William C. Berleman and Thomas W. Steinburn, "The Value and Validity of Delinquency Prevention Experiments," *Crime & Delinquency, 15*: 471-478 (1969); and James Robison and Gerald Smith, "The Effectiveness of Correctional Programs," *Crime & Delinquency, 17*: 67-80 (1971).

[6]Two years after the article was published, criminologist Stuart Adams wrote that the work had "shaken the community of criminal justice to its root." Stuart Adams, "Evaluation: A Way Out of Rhetoric," pp. 75-91 in Robert Martinson, Ted Palmer and Stuart Adams (eds.), *Rehabilitation, Recidivism, and Research* (Hackensack, NJ: National Council on Crime and Delinquency, 1976).

anyone else. But Dinitz never failed to impress students and faculty as well. He won many research, teaching and service awards during his career.[7]

NOTHING WORKS REVISITED

The year was 1982. In a subsequent lecture, Dinitz elaborated on the "nothing-works" article and its political fallout. Robert Martinson, a City College of New York sociologist, had written the article after he and two other colleagues had conducted a comprehensive literature review of studies of rehabilitation. The research project was already well underway when Martinson joined lead researcher Douglas Lipton and Judith Wilks in the late 1960s. The project was finished in 1970, but a lengthy book they wrote about it would not be published until 1975.[8] That book was cautious in its conclusions, stating that "the field of corrections has not as yet found satisfactory ways to reduce recidivism by *significant amounts*."[9]

However, a year before the book was published, Martinson, without consulting his two colleagues, wrote the article for *The Public Interest*, a right-leaning magazine, implying that rehabilitation had "no appreciable effect on recidivism." He also wrote a four-part series for *The New Republic*, a left-leaning magazine, and he appeared on CBS's *60 Minutes* in August 1975. The segment was titled, "It Doesn't Work," and *60*

---

[7]Dinitz was a recipient of the Society's Edwin H. Sutherland Award in 1974. In 1981, criminology scholars across the country wrote a book in honor of him. I. Barak-Glantz and C. Ronald Huff (eds.), *The Mad, the Bad, and the Different: Essays in Honor of Simon Dinitz* (Lexington, MA: D.C. Heath, 1981). Dinitz had written or co-written more than two dozen scholarly books and 120 scientific articles. He had advised more than three dozen Ph.D. recipients. He had lectured at universities around the world, including Israel, where he was widely respected and popular. He had won many awards for his research and service, including the prestigious Donald Sutherland Award from the American Society of Criminology. At OSU, Dinitz was honored as the first faculty member in history at OSU to deliver a Commencement Address. He served as president of the American Society of Criminology and was former editor of *Criminology* (then *Criminologica*). But the greatest distinction he would achieve was to become the only professor in the history of OSU to earn all three of the highest honors that could be bestowed on faculty — Distinguished Teaching (1970), Distinguished Research (1979) and Distinguished Service (1996). This was no small feat given that OSU employed more than 3,400 professors.

[8]Lipton, Martinson and Wilks, *The Effectiveness of Correctional Treatment*.

[9]*Ibid.*, p. 627. [emphasis added]

The visitors entrance to Utah State Prison's Wasatch facility. *(Photograph by Douglas Rahden Chupper; used with permission)*

Minutes host Mike Wallace announced that Martinson's research "findings are sending shockwaves through the correctional establishment."[10] Martinson told Wallace that treatment approaches have "no fundamental effect on recidivism" and that psychological counseling may be a "good way to pass the time" but it "has no effect."[11]

The timing of these media events couldn't have been better for critics of rehabilitation and proponents of the get-tough-on-crime model. They and the public had been losing faith in the ability of social scientists to solve the crime problem. The murder rate had doubled from 1963 to 1973, going from 4.5 per 100,000 U.S. residents to 9.1.[12] Assaults rose from 91 to 194; robbery from 62 to 178; and theft from 1,129 to 2,432.

"The idea that this explosion of street crime must be due to an attitude of permissiveness was particularly appealing," government crime

[10]CBS Television Network, *60 Minutes: It Doesn't Work* (Transcript), 7: 2-9 (August 24, 1975), p. 3.

[11]*Ibid.*, p. 4.

[12]Jerome G. Miller, "The Debate on Rehabilitating Criminals: Is It True that Nothing Works?" *The Washington Post* (March 1989), retrieved October 3, 2009, from <http://www.prisonpolicy.org/scans/rehab.html>.

researcher Jerome G. Miller wrote in the late 1980s. "Barry Goldwater tried unsuccessfully to make crime an issue in the 1964 campaign. But as the crime rates rose, Richard Nixon elevated the matter to a high art. The 1968 campaign made crime a major issue ... The implication was that the criminal justice system, and in particular, corrections, had grown soft by over-relying on such vague concepts as 'rehabilitation.'"[13]

Ironically, though, Miller pointed out that the rehabilitation model had never been fully implemented anywhere in the U.S. correctional system. In fact, few correctional systems employed trained psychiatrists, psychologists, or social workers. The vast majority of taxpayer monies spent on corrections went to salaries of guards and to prison or juvenile detention operations. Little money was spent on rehabilitation or intervention programs. "What looked to outsiders like permissiveness was more often neglect and chaos in a system overcome with an explosion of 'baby-boomers,'" Miller wrote.

Years later, University of Cincinnati criminology professor Francis Cullen would write that Martinson's message "confirmed what critics 'already knew' and gave them a weapon — scientific data — to back up their attack on correctional treatment."[14]

> In this context, Martinson's research was soon reified[15] — with no dispute on his part — into the "Nothing Works Doctrine."... For criminologists, being against rehabilitation — rejecting it as a case of good intentions corrupted for sinister purposes — became part of the discipline's professional ideology, an established, unassailable truth that required no further verification.[16]

---

[13]*Ibid.*

[14]Francis T. Cullen, "The Twelve People Who Saved Rehabilitation: How the Science of Criminology Made a Difference — The American Society of Criminology 2004 Presidential Address," *Criminology* 43(1):1-42 (2005), p. 8.

[15]*Reified* is defined here as the process of considering an abstract concept to be real.

[16]Cullen attributes this comment to Francis T. Cullen and Paul Gendreau, "From Nothing Works to What Works: Changing Professional Ideology in the 21st Century," *The Prison Journal, 81*: 323-338 (2001).

In 1976, a Panel on Research on Rehabilitative Techniques from the National Academy of Sciences reviewed the Lipton, Martinson and Wilks' 1975 book and concluded the authors "were ... accurate and fair in their appraisal of the rehabilitation literature." However, the panel indicated that Martinson's articles had exaggerated the lack of effects of rehabilitative efforts.[17] In fact, psychologist Ted Palmer reanalyzed 82 studies cited in one of Martinson's articles and found that 48 percent of them yielded "positive or partly positive results." In 1978, Palmer wrote that "a cup half empty is also half full. That is, one should not overlook the fact that many programs *have* reduced recidivism and have provided personal assistance to a sizable portion of the offender population" [emphasis in original].[18]

Martinson began to backpedal in 1977. By 1978, he wrote that "some treatment programs do have an appreciable effect on recidivism" and that "startling results are found again and again in our study, for treatment programs as diverse as individual psychotherapy, group counseling, intensive supervision, and what we have called individual/help (aid, advice, counseling)."[19] Miller, reflecting back in 1989 on Martinson's role, wrote that

> In the course of debate, the man who started it all had come full circle. But by now, no one was listening. He had served his purpose and his own issue was wrested from his grasp.[20]

The national media ignored Martinson's change of heart. No followup stories were written. Then, adds Miller:

---

[17]L. Sechrest, S. White, and E. Brown, E. (eds), *The Rehabilitation of Criminal Offenders: Problems and Prospects* (Washington DC: National Academy of Sciences Press, 1979), p. 5.

[18]Ted Palmer, *Correctional Intervention and Research: Current Issues and Future Prospects* (Lexington, MA: Lexington Books, 1978), p. xxi.

[19]Robert Martinson, "New Findings, New Views: A Note of Caution Regarding Sentencing Reform," *Hofstra Law Review, 7*: 243-258 (1978), pp. 244 and 255, respectively.

[20]Miller, "The Debate on Rehabilitating Criminals."

Late one gloomy winter afternoon in 1980, New York sociologist Robert Martinson hurled himself through a ninth floor window of his Manhattan apartment while his teenage son looked on from across the room. An articulate criminologist, Martinson had become the leading debunker of the idea we could "rehabilitate" criminals. His melancholy suicide was to be a metaphor for what would follow in American corrections.[21]

By 1982, many criminologists had concluded that the "nothing works" thesis was more of a "law" than a "hypothesis." Harvard University criminologist Walter Miller told *The New York Times* that "youth crime is an extremely serious problem in the United States and by and large we're baffled about it. Amazing as it may seem to outsiders, that's the reality. We really do not know what to do." The newspaper also quoted Franklin E. Zimring, director of the Center for Studies in Criminal Justice at the University of Chicago: "Nothing that we are doing right now demonstrably works. If anyone has a program for juvenile crime that he says will make a statistical dent in the problem, he is operating on sheer faith. There are no panaceas nor any general theory that bears endorsement."[22]

THE ECONOMETRIC CRIME MODEL

The election of Republican Ronald Reagan as president in 1980 assured the country that the rehabilitation model would be put into the equivalent of public policy hibernation. Conservatives were now in control, and the emphasis was on punishment, retribution and deterrence.

Dinitz referred to this approach as "econometric model" of crime fighting.[23] The premise is simple: "Individuals engage in criminal activity

---

[21]*Ibid.*

[22]Philip M. Boffey, "Youth Crime Puzzle Defies a Solution," *The New York Times* (March 5, 1982), retrieved September 5, 2008, from <http://query.nytimes.com/gst/fullpage.html?res=9F00EFDE153BF936A35750C0A964948260&sec=health&spon=&pagewanted=all>.

[23]Other criminologists call it the rational choice model. See D. Cornish and R. Clark (eds.), *The Reasoning Criminal* (New York: Springer-Verlag, 1986).

to the extent that it is profitable."[24] Profit is the perceived difference between cost and benefit. In other words, the best way to combat crime is to increase the certainty of punishment (e.g., hire more police officers or increase patrols) and increase the severity of punishment for various crimes (e.g., longer prison sentences).[25] The assumption underlying the econometric model is that people rationally calculate the costs and benefits of engaging in various types of behaviors. But this assumption, which is accepted at face value by some economists and many policymakers, doesn't always work, Dinitz told his class. For example, a drug addict who needs the next fix may not rationally calculate the odds of getting caught in a robbery. He needs that fix no matter the risks. Many murders also are committed in a "heat of passion," where the offenders do not calculate the costs of getting caught as well as the punishment.

The principle that punishment can deter criminal behavior has a long history in America. But even after eight decades of research, criminologists still disagree about whether, when and how it works.

A Brief History of Deterrence Research

In 1705, John Campbell, publisher of the *Boston News-Letter*, told readers that his newspaper was carrying an account of a man who was severely whipped for selling tar mixed with dirt "only ... to be a caveat to others, of doing the like, least a worse thing befal (sic) them."[26] This is called *general deterrence* — punishing some offenders serves to deter others from committing crimes. *Specific deterrence* refers to the effect of punishment on the individual sanctioned (i.e., Does she or he decrease the

---

[24]Jack P. Gibbs, *Crime, Punishment, and Deterrence* (New York: Elsevier, 1975), p. 204.

[25]A third factor, the celerity of punishment (or how fast an offender is punished once caught), has received relatively little empirical treatment in the literature, primarily because most criminologists believe it has little effect compared with the certainty and severity of punishment.

[26]The incident appeared in the October 1-8, 1705, issue. Cited in Willard Grosvenor Bleyer, *Main Currents in the History of Journalism* (New York: Houghton Mifflin, 1927), p. 50.

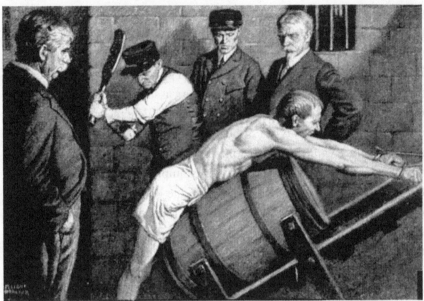

A 1912 illustration of an inmate in a prison being "paddled," a form of punishment used in some state prisons in the early part of the 19ᵗʰ century *(Illustration by Julian Leavitt for "The Man in the Cage,"* The American Magazine, *February 1912).*

behavior?).

Many of the earliest studies focused on specific deterrence. One involved three five-year follow-ups of 500 convicted offenders. The study was conducted by Sheldon and Eleanor Glueck and published in book form in 1943. They found high rates of recidivism (88 percent after 15 years) and concluded that "prevention of recidivism as the chief aim of punishment has, under existing methods and regimes, miserably failed."[27] Another study, still widely cited today, examined 320 prisoners in Delaware who were whipped between 1900 and 1942 for a variety of statutory offenses. Sixty-two percent were again convicted of some crime after their first whipping, and 65 percent were convicted after a second whipping. Robert G. Caldwell, the researcher, concluded that whipping of criminals did not

---

[27]Sheldon Glueck and Eleanor Glueck, *Criminal Careers in Retrospect* (New York: The Commonwealth Fund, 1943), p. 289.

effectively deter them from committing a crime after release from prison.[28]

During the 1950s, social scientists began conducting research that explored general deterrence in more depth. Evidence continued to accumulate that capital punishment[29] and increasing the severity of punishment for noncapital crimes[30] were ineffective in deterring criminal behavior. For example, a comprehensive review of 1978 by Alfred Blumstein, Jacqueline Cohen and Daniel Nagin found no relationship between murder rates and capital punishment.

> Despite the intensity of the research effort, the empirical evidence is still not sufficient for providing a rigorous confirmation of the existence of a deterrent effect. Perhaps more important, the evidence is woefully inadequate for providing a good estimate of the magnitude of whatever effect may exist.[31]

In the 1960s and 1970s, researchers spent more time studying noncapital crimes. The debate often was heated. One group of researchers would find support for the deterrence hypothesis,[32] and another would

---

[28]Robert G. Caldwell, "The Deterrent Influence of Corporal Punishment upon Prisoners Who Have Been Whipped," *American Sociological Review 9*: 171-177 (April 1944).

[29]Thorsten Sellin, *The Death Penalty* (Philadelphia: American Law Institute, 1959); Karl F. Schuessler, "The Deterrent Influence of the Death Penalty," *The Annals of the American Academy of Political and Social Science, 284*: 54-63 (November 1952); and Leonard D. Savitz, "A Study of Capital Punishment," *Journal of Criminal Law, Criminology and Police Science, 49*: 338-341 (December 1958).

[30]Frederick K. Beutel, *Some Potentialities of Experimental Jurisprudence as a New Branch of Social Science* (Lincoln: University of Nebraska Press, 1957) and Carol Crother, "Crimes, Penalties and Legislatures," *The Annals of the American Academy of Political and Social Science, 381*: 147-158 (January 1969).

[31]Alfred Blumstein, Jacqueline Cohen and Daniel Nagin (eds.), *Deterrence and Incapacitation: Estimating the Effects of Criminal Sanctions on Crime Rates* (Washington, D.C.: National Academy of Sciences, 1978), p. 135.

[32]Studies providing support for the deterrence hypothesis include Charles R. Tittle and Charles H. Logan, "Sanctions and Deviance: Evidence and Remaining Questions," *Law and Society Review, 7*: 371-392 (Spring 1973); Jack P. Gibbs, "Crime, Punishment, and Deterrence," *The Southwestern Social Science Quarterly, 48*: 515-530 (March 1968); Charles H. Logan, "Legal Sanctions and Deterrence from Crime," unpublished Ph.D. Dissertation (Indiana University, 1971); William C. Bailey, Louis N. Gray and David J. Martin, "On Punishment and Crime (Chiricos and Waldo, 1970): Some Methodological

challenge those findings.[33] Although most of the studies found a moderate inverse relationship between crime rates and certainty of punishment, correlation does not mean causation. Even researchers whose studies had found such correlations, such as Jack P. Gibbs, were skeptical. In 1975, he published a book in which he called for a moratorium on deterrence research until "evidential" problems are worked out.

> Consider an individual contemplating an act and assume that the individual (1) views the act as contrary to a law, (2) knows the prescribed punishment, (3) perceives the punishment as severe, (4) estimates the actual imposition of the punishment as certain. If the individual commits the act, then the threat of punishment clearly did not deter him or her. However, even if the individual refrains, the omission could be attributed to (1) the dictates of personal conscience, (2) the individual's recognition of and respect for the social (extralegal) condemnation of the act, and/or (3) the fear of some extralegal consequence (e.g., stigma). So we have a paradox — regardless of what the individual does (commits or omits the act), it is not evidence of deterrence.[34]

By 1981, researchers couldn't agree on whether punishment had general or specific deterrent effects. As sociologist Philip J. Cook put it:

Commentary," *Social Problems, 19*: 284-289 (1971); Charles H. Logan, "General Deterrent Effects of Imprisonment," *Social Forces, 51*: 64-73 (1972); L. N. Gray and D. J. Martin, "Punishment and Deterrence: Another Analysis of Gibbs' Data," *Social Science Quarterly, 50*: 389-395 (1969); Charles H. Logan, "Arrest Rates and Deterrence," *Social Science Quarterly, 56*: 366-389 (1975-76); Charles R. Tittle and Alan R. Rowe, "Certainty of Arrest and Crime Rates: A Further Test of the Deterrence Hypothesis," *Social Forces ,52*: 455-462 (June 1974); and Harold G. Grasmick and George J. Bryjak, "The Deterrent Effect of Perceived Severity of Punishment," *Social Forces, 59*: 471-491 (December 1980).

[33]Studies that failed to find support for the deterrence hypothesis or criticized studies that did find support include Theodore G. Chiricos and Gordon P. Waldo, "Punishment and Crime: An Examination of Some Empirical Evidence," *Social Problems, 18*: 200-217 (Fall 1970) and Gordon P. Waldo and Theodore G. Chiricos, "Perceived Penal Sanction and Self-Reported Criminality: A Neglected Approach to Deterrence Research," *Social Problems, 19*: 522-540 (Spring 1972).

[34]Jack P. Gibbs, *Crime, Punishment, and Deterrence* (New York: Elsevier Scientific Publishing Co., Inc., 1975), p. 12.

The empirical literature on the preventive effects of punishment is highly uneven. Rehabilitation and other specific effects of punishment lend themselves to systematic experimentation in a way that general preventive mechanism do not ... The correlational studies of the simple deterrence mechanism, while in some cases sophisticated and carefully done, have, in my judgment, contributed very little to our fund of knowledge concerning this important mechanism.[35]

Although there were doubts about whether deterrence worked, especially for violent crimes, most criminologists did agree with criminologist Jackson Toby that "the socialization process prevents most deviant behavior. Those who have introjected the moral norms of their society cannot commit crimes because their self-concepts will not permit them to do so."[36] But socialization — defined here as the inculcation of dominant norms and values — may be less effective for nonviolent crimes.

Socialization works well for what criminologists call crimes *mala in se,* a Latin phrase meaning wrong or evil in itself. Murder, robbery, rape, theft and assault are examples. Punishment is not necessary to deter most people. Even without punishment, most people, for example, won't kill other people, because they have been socialized into the belief that human life is sacred and that killing is wrong (and violates such norms as the Ten Commandments).

Socialization may also deter people from committing crimes *mala prohibita,* which are those that are wrong because someone says they are wrong. They are not perceived as evil in themselves. Examples include speeding, illegal parking and failing to file a tax return. Socialization can certainly play a role in diminishing crimes *mala prohibita.* But punishment can also be very effective, perhaps even more effective. Illegal parking is a major problem at universities, but it is relatively easy to control through

---

[35]Philip J. Cook, "Punishment and Crime: A Critique of Current Findings Concerning the Preventive Effects of Punishment,"*Law and Contemporary Problems, 41*: 200-208 (Winter 1977), pp. 203-204.

[36]Jackson Toby, "Is Punishment Necessary?" *Journal of Criminal Law, Criminology, and Police Science, 55*(3): 332-337 (September 1964), p. 333.

strict enforcement (increase the certainty of punishment) and big fines (increase the severity of punishment).[37]

Instrumental vs. Expressive Crimes

In his lectures, Dinitz formalized the deterrence issue even more, dividing crimes into two categories, "instrumental" and "expressive." Instrumental crimes are purposive and planned. Robbery, larceny, burglary, shoplifting, embezzlement, illegal parking and forgery are examples. These acts require some contemplation and forethought by the perpetrator and, thus, may be deterred by increasing the certainty or severity of punishment. One British researcher found, for example, that the prevalence of drunken driving may be reduced by punishment.[38]

Expressive crimes, on the other hand, are committed during a state of passion, anger, rage, impulsiveness, or during a "general loss of control," Dinitz pointed out. Crimes that have been called expressive include murder, rape and aggravated assault. One U.S. researcher found no evidence that rape, for example, could be deterred by the possibility of punishment.[39] Dinitz also pointed out that about three-fourths of all murders are committed in a "state of passion," in which the offender is angry and judgment is often impaired by the influence of drugs or alcohol.

Dinitz's ideas on deterrence were elaborated upon in a proprietary report[40] he and a student produced in June 1983 under contract to the Battelle Memorial Institute, which is headquartered in Columbus. The U.S.

---

[37]William J. Chambliss, "The Deterrent Influence of Publishment," *Crime and Delinquency, 12*: 70-75 (January 1966).

[38]H. Laurence Ross, Donald T. Campbell and Gene V. Glass, "Determining the Social Effects of a Legal Reform: The British 'Breathalyser' Crackdown of 1967," *American Behavioral Scientist, 13*(4): 493-509 (March/April 1970).

[39]Barry Schwartz, "The Effect in Philadelphia on Pennsylvania's Increased Penalties for Rape and Attempted Rape," *Journal of Criminal Law, Criminology, and Police Science, 59*(4): 509-515 (December 1968).

[40]Simon Dinitz and David K. Demers (1983), "Money: Is It Real or Is It Reprographed?" Proprietary paper prepared for the Battelle Memorial Institute, Columbus, Ohio, under contract to the U.S. Department of Treasury, Columbus, OH.

Department of Treasury was concerned about the impact that increasingly sophisticated reprographic machines (or what we now call copy machines) would have in terms of counterfeiting. Treasury wanted estimates of the number of people who might use color copy machines to counterfeit money. The proprietary report provided such estimates as well as strategies for prevention and deterrence, which included target hardening measures (e.g., embedding a material or compound that prevents copy machines from reproducing money with precision) as well as legal, law enforcement and prosecutorial strategies.

In the Battelle report, Dinitz also provided a list of generalizations that he saw as emerging from the deterrence literature. They include:

- The more instrumental the crime, the greater the potential deterrence effects of punishment.
- Crimes of opportunity are the most difficult of the instrumental crimes to deter, because they require no skill, no planning, or no identification with a criminal subculture.
- The more immediate the gratification from the criminal act, the more difficult the act is to deter.
- The more certain the punishment, the less severe need be the sanction.

Thus, for Dinitz and many other criminologists, the question wasn't whether deterrence worked, but *under what conditions does it work?* This nuanced approach to the deterrence issue made a lot of sense. But in the 1980s, policymakers were not interested in generating public policy that could take these or other nuances into account. In fact, many critics argued that public policy was driven more by the ideology of a political party than by science or facts.

THE END OF REHABILITATION

By the end of the 1980s, two generalizations seemed certain in the field of criminology. The first was that although no treatment or rehabilitation programs on juveniles or adults were able to reduce recidivism rates by large amounts, some had been shown to have modest effects. The second was that although increasing the severity of punishment may have some modest effect on reducing instrumental crimes, there was no strong evidence to suggest that it could deter many expressive crimes, such as murder.

Thus, from a public policy standpoint, the logical thing to do would have been to (1) pour more money and resources into refining and expanding treatment programs that worked; (2) stop using the deterrence argument to justify the passage of capital punishment statutes (although this didn't preclude using retribution or other arguments to justify such statutes); and (3) pass more laws increasing the severity of punishment for instrumental crimes. At the time, public policymakers essentially ignored the first two recommendations but did implement some aspects of the third.

The "end of rehabilitation" was affirmed formally in February 1989, when the U.S. Supreme Court handed down its decision in *Mistretta v. United States*. They upheld federal "sentencing guidelines" and essentially removed rehabilitation from serious consideration when sentencing offenders.[41] According to Miller, "Defendants will henceforth be sentenced strictly for the crime, with no recognition given to such factors as amenability to treatment, personal and family history, previous efforts to rehabilitate oneself, or possible alternatives to prison." The high court cited a U.S. Senate Report that "referred to the 'outmoded rehabilitation model' for federal criminal sentencing and recognized that the efforts of the criminal justice system to achieve rehabilitation of offenders had failed." This was the case even though in 1988 an extensive survey of more than 200 studies on rehabilitation from 1981-1987 had concluded:

> Our reviews of the research literature demonstrated that successful rehabilitation of offenders had been accomplished, and continued to be accomplished quite well ... reductions in recidivism ... had been achieved in a considerable number of well-controlled studies. Effective programs were conducted in a variety of community and (to a lesser degree) institutional settings, involving pre-delinquents, hard-core

---

[41]*Mistretta v. United States,* 488 U.S. 361 (1989).

adolescent offenders, and recidivistic adult offenders, including criminal heroin addicts. The results of these programs were not short-lived; follow-up periods of at least two years were not uncommon, and several studies reported even longer follow-ups.[42]

Miller, like thousands of other criminologists across the country, was outraged by the Supreme Court's decision. "Rehabilitation is, for the most part, now absent from contemporary American corrections," he wrote in 1989. "Harsher sentences, warehouse prisons, and corrections establishment which militantly rejects the idea of salvaging offenders has become the rule of the land. We must now wait for the swing of the pendulum. I fear it will be a long wait."

Miller's fears were not exaggerated. During the 1980s, many states and the federal government began passing more laws that increased the penalty for committing various crimes, especially violent crimes like robbery, assault and rape. Usually this meant longer prison sentences. The states also took some discretionary power away from judges and began imposing minimum sentences for many crimes. The rationale was that some judges had been too lenient on offenders.

In the early 1990s, proponents of the get-tough approach to crime also began focusing on chronic offenders — individuals who have long histories of criminal activity. If these offenders could be identified and "put away" for long periods of time, they reasoned, then perhaps crime would decline. The only problem with that approach, Dinitz pointed out in various lectures as early as 1982, was that efforts to identify these offenders when they were juveniles had not been very successful. Consequently, for every three juveniles identified as "chronic offenders," only one would actually "turn into one." This, in turn, created a moral dilemma: "Can the government justify wrongly incarcerating two people for the crimes of one?" Dinitz would ask his students.

Policymakers skirted the question. They never implemented a plan to try to identify chronic offenders at an early age. Instead, they created

---

[42]Paul Gendreau and R. R. Ross, "Revivification of Rehabilitation: Evidence from the 1980s," *Justice Quarterly, 4*(3): 349-407 (1987), pp. 350-351.

"three-strikes-and-you're-out laws," which essentially meant that if an individual committed three felonious crimes, he or she could be imprisoned for long periods of time (25 years or more) or even for life. In 1993 Washington state became the first to pass such a law. By 2004, more than two dozen states and the federal government had enacted habitual offender laws.

The get-tough approach to the crime problem worked in terms of filling prisons. The rate of incarceration soared in the United States in the late 1900s, doubling from 1980 to 1990 and quadrupling from 1980 to 2000. In 1980, for every 100,000 people, 139 of them were in prison at the end of the year, compared with 297 in 1990 and 478 in 2000.[43] At the time, the United States was incarcerating more people per population than any country in the world except South Africa and Russia. During the early 2000s, the United States took over the No. 1 spot. By 2007, the incarceration rate was 509 per population. Most of the offenders sentenced under the three-strikes laws were felony drug users.

The hope, of course, was that the get-tough approach would reduce the crime rate. However, the official statistics provided no clear evidence of effect. From 1980 to 1992, the rate of violent crime (murder, robbery, rape, assault) actually increased, going from 597 to 758 per 100,000 population, even though the imprisonment rate during that time period had more than doubled. The property crime rate remained relatively stable, dropping slightly from 5,353 to 4,903 per 100,000 population.

Then, in 1994, something happened that surprised everyone: The crime rate began to fall. The violent crime rate dropped from 747 in 1993 to 463 in 2004. The rate has remained stable since then. Over the same time period, the property crime rate dropped from 4,738 to 3,514, and since then it has continued to decline, though at a slower pace. The declines took criminologists by surprise.

---

[43]U.S. Bureau of Justice Statistics, *Prisoners in State and Federal Institutions on December 31,* annual, and *Correctional Populations in the United States,* annual. Retrieved October 20, 2008, from <http://www.ojp.usdoj.gov/bjs/prisons.htm>.

"Nobody predicted the decline in the 1990s," criminologist Franklin Zimring, author of the *Great American Crime Decline*,[44] declared during a National Public Radio broadcast on Feb. 16, 2007.[45] "Nobody called this decline before it happened." Zimring was one of five guests of "Talk of the Nation," hosted by NPR's Ira Flato. The title of the show was "Mining the Crime Drop in the 1990s for Social Clues."[46]

Throughout the 1990s, proponents of get-tough laws tried to argue that the decline in the violent crime rate in the 1990s stemmed from the passage of tougher laws. But the panelists didn't give that theory much credence. For one, the violent crime rate continued to increase until 1993, even while states were incarcerating more and more people, and the decline in crime began in 1994, well before the three-strikes-you're-out laws were widely adopted. Also, Canada didn't change its criminal laws during the 1980s and 1990s, but it, too, also saw a drop in crime during the 1990s. "Our prison rate went up, theirs went down," Zimring said. "We hired more cops, they hired less." And Canada's crime rate still dropped.

Most of the panelists attributed the decline in crime partly to a "boom in the economy" in the 1990s and to a lower percentage of young people — the most crime-prone group in the population. They also attributed some of the decline in murder rates to a large drop in crack-cocaine usage, which meant fewer turf wars among drug dealers. One panelist also said "community policing" may have contributed to lower rates. Community policing focuses on increasing interaction with citizens through prevention programs and foot or bike patrols that give officers more direct contact with

---

[44]Franklin E. Zimring, *The Great American Crime Decline* (New York: Oxford University Press, 2006).

[45]A audio recording the entire program is available at National Public Radio's website: <http://www.npr.org/templates/story/story.php?storyId=7453416>.

[46]The other guests included William G. Simon, professor of law and Wolfen Distinguished Scholar at the Boalt Hall School of Law of the University of California, Berkeley; Richard Rosenfeld, professor of criminology at the University of Missouri-St. Louis; Janet Lauritsen, professor of criminology at the University of Missouri-St. Louis; and Alfred Blumstein, director of the National Consortium on Violence Research at the Heinz School of Public Policy & Management at Carnegie Mellon University in Pittsburgh. The guests were interviewed in San Francisco, which was hosting the annual meeting of the American Association for the Advancement of Science.

people. Another panelist said citizens also were "more willing to call police" and report crime. However, none of these factors, taken alone or together, could explain the dramatic decline.

Some of the panelists disputed another, highly controversial explanation for the radical drop in crime: legalized abortion. In the late 1990s, University of Chicago economist Steven Levitt and Stanford University law professor John J. Donohue III suggested that legalization of abortion in 1973 was responsible for 50 percent of the decline in crime rate in the 1990s.[47] They theorized that women who were at risk of giving birth to children who later would become delinquent — such as teenagers, poor women or those with unwanted pregnancies — opted for abortion instead.[48]

Of course, as is almost always the case with controversial studies, the findings did not go unchallenged.[49] Other scholars claimed the Levitt and Donohue study was flawed methodologically. Some studies since then have even argued the opposite: that abortion has actually increased the murder rate by 7 percent.[50] In 2008, Donohue and Levitt wrote another paper defending their use of statistics.[51] The debate goes on.

---

[47] Amy Rust, "Chicago Economist Links Abortion to Falling Crime Rates," *University of Chicago Chronicle, 18* (August 12, 1999), retrieved November 6, 2008, online at <http://chronicle.uchicago.edu/990812/abortion.shtml>.

[48] Their research was published two years later. See John J. Donohue III and Steven D. Levitt, "Impact of Legalized Abortion on Crime," *Quarterly Journal of Economics,* 116(2): 379-420 (May 2001).

[49] John R. Lott Jr. and John E. Whitley, "Abortion and Crime: Unwanted Children and Out-of-Wedlock Births," Yale Law & Economics Research Paper No. 254, University of Maryland Foundation, University of Maryland and University of Adelaide School of Economics, posted May 16, 2001 to the Social Science Research Network, available at <http://papers.ssrn.com/sol3/results.cfm?RequestTimeout=50000000>; Christopher L. Foote and Christopher F. Goetz, "The Impact of Legalized Abortion on Crime: Comment," *Quarterly Journal of Economics, 123*(1): 407-423 (2008); Theodore J. Joyce, "A Simple Test of Abortion and Crime," *Review of Economics and Statistics* (2008) available at SSRN: <http://ssrn.com/abstract=1011168 >; and Leo Kahane, David Paton and Rob Simmons, "The Abortion-Crime Link: Evidence from England and Wales," *Economica, 75*(297): 1-21 (2008).

[50] John R. Lott Jr. and John E. Whitley, "Abortion and Crime: Unwanted Children and Out-of-Wedlock Births," *Economic Inquiry, 45*(2): 304-324 (April 2007).

[51] John J. Donohue and Steven D. Levitt, "Measurement Error, Legalized Abortion, and the Decline in Crime: A Response to Foote and Goetz," *Quarterly Journal of Economics, 123*(1): 425-440 (2008).

THE CRISIS OF RELEVANCE IN CRIMINOLOGY

By the late 1980s and early 1990s, even before crime rates began to fall and before criminologists would have trouble explaining that trend, disillusionment was no longer a scarce commodity in the field of criminology. Many criminologists felt that they and their research had very little impact on public policy — policymakers were ignoring them.

Criminologist Joan Petersilia understood how they felt. But to her, the problem wasn't the inability to generate knowledge, or the idea that rehabilitation didn't work. Rather, the problem was that social scientists were failing to make themselves and their research relevant. They had, in essence, retreated into the ivory tower.

"Part of our stated mission is to be a forum for the exchange of practical information between researchers and the field — those who set policies and those who make them work," Petersilia wrote in her 1990 presidential address to the American Society of Criminology. She added:

> That seems especially compelling at a time when crime is a major public concern and the criminal justice system is, quite literally, in crisis. In the early days, the link between research and the system was virtually embodied in the faculty and students, and the influence went both ways. But since the academic has largely replaced the practitioner in the classroom and in research, the link has grown weaker and, with it, that kind of immediate influence.[52]

Drawing on criminologist Albert Morris' brief history of criminology,[53] Petersilia pointed out that most of the faculty teaching criminology courses in the late 1930s and the 1940s were former policemen "who wanted to help develop a special curriculum for students who would enter policing and to bring practical experience to bear on what the university taught." The discipline and ASC, Petersilia wrote, "were

---

[52]Joan Petersilia, "Policy Relevance and the Future of Criminology — The American Society of Criminology 1990 Presidential Address," *Criminology* 29(1):1-15 (1991), pp. 3-4.

[53]Albert Morris, "The American Society of Criminology: A History, 1941-1974," *Criminology, 13*(2): 123-166 (1975).

strongly grounded in practical concerns
of the criminal justice system." However,
she pointed out that this approach "didn't
get much scholarly or scientific respect in
academic circles." Consequently, as the
years passed, the practitioners
increasingly were replaced with Ph.D.
social scientists, who conducted
sophisticated research studies.

Petersilia didn't argue that this
transition was bad. In fact, she
acknowledged that the transition from
practitioner to Ph.D. professors
contributed to the growth of knowledge

Joan Petersilia*(photograph used with permission)*

about crime. She also didn't lock arms with criminologists who often feel
"that policymakers and practitioners largely ignore our findings or, worse,
sometimes act counter to what our best science tells us about the system."[54]
Citing the research of law and political science professor Robert F. Rich
(see Chapter 1),[55] she said the best way to gauge the impact of social
science research on public policy isn't whether a law has been passed or a
practice changed; rather, it's whether the research "influences how
policymakers think about issues, problems, and the range of variable
solutions. It works more on the conceptual than on the instrumental level."
Measuring this kind of impact, however, is difficult, she pointed out, and
so it's not surprising that "over the past 10 years at ASC and other
professional meetings, formal and informal, I have repeatedly heard
criminologists say that our research and analysis does not affect policy and
practice. That belief was implied by the past five ASC presidents, who said
in their statements that, if elected, one of their highest priorities would be

[54]Petersilia, "Policy Relevance and the Future of Criminology," p. 4.
[55]Robert F. Rich, *Social Science Information and Public Policy Making* (San
Francisco: Jossey-Bass Publishers, 1981). See Chapter 6 for more information about Rich.

to bring the prestige of our organization to bear on national and state policy making."[56]

But Petersilia did argue that criminologists could and should be having much more impact on public policy. "The potential for policy 'irrelevance' is inherent in the scientific advancement of which we are justly proud," she wrote. To many policymakers, the increasing complexity of research and its methods seems "like unnecessary complication of issues." She added that the way in which criminologists are trained may also encourage policy irrelevance.

> I recruit and interview researchers for RAND's Criminal Justice Program, and I am impressed by the increasingly strong analytic skills of many applicants. They can go on at length about beta coefficients, log-normal distributions, and whether their data are appropriately analyzed using probit or logit regressions. But ask them about the policy implications of their findings, how their "solutions" might be constrained by politics or resources, or even who in the world should be interested in their research — and they often come up blank.[57]

She also pointed out that when it comes to disseminating scientific information, academic researchers think mostly of publishing in academic journals. But even when policymakers are aware of these journals, they rarely consult them, she said. More often than not, policymakers don't understand the relevance of the research to public policy. Policymakers often tell her that criminologists "'are more interested in impressing their colleagues than informing policy or practice.'" She placed part of the blame for this situation on the "reward structure" in academia.[58] Academics are rewarded for publishing in scientific journals, not for impacting public policy or solving social problems. "[J]ournal publication is the surest route to professional recognition — including tenure."

---

[56]*Ibid.*

[57]*Ibid.*, p. 9.

[58]Some writers prefer the word "academe" to "academia." One writer to an online bulletin board said academe "seems more pretentious to me. And besides, you can't use it if you want to refer to 'academia nuts.'"

Policymakers, such as the U.S. Senators and Congressmen shown here, often ignore social science research and criticize social scientists for not producing research that helps solve social problems. *(U.S. government photograph in the public domain)*

To increase the relevance of research in the real world, Petersilia offered four suggestions: (1) establish a collaborative framework among researchers, policymakers and practitioners; (2) report and disseminate research more effectively; (3) define the mission of criminology to include assistance in the field, and (4) tailor the academic model (e.g., tenure process) to accommodate the mission of criminal justice research (e.g., reward researchers who conduct applied research).

In response to her presidential address, one scholar criticized her for placing too much emphasis on applying research to the real world. "One of the two (respondents) didn't want research to ... connect too closely to the policymaking world," she said in 2008, adding that the respondent told her: "'We, as academics, are here to produce knowledge. That's where our role stops ... If we defined our jobs as doing that (solving real world problems), we would give up the objectivity of what we do.'"[59]

---

[59]Telephone interview with Joan Petersilia, October 16, 2008.

Petersilia disagreed.

"I believe just the opposite. If you build a knowledge base, you have an obligation to transfer that to the real world."

She added that "if academics don't become more relevant, we'll be out of business ... I think the public believes academia is out of touch ... We tend to find the things that don't work rather than those that do work ... So I think our history is ... that we haven't delivered ... Academics are very soft and very comfortable in their roles. It takes a lot to affect public policy ... and we are not very good at that."

IMPACT OF CRIMINOLOGY

Dinitz retired from The Ohio State University in 1991. One of his colleagues, Joseph E. Scott, took early retirement from OSU in 1994, partly because he felt he had limited impact as a criminologist. Today he runs a successful criminal defense law practice in Columbus.

"Criminology has made so little progress in the last 30 and 40 years," Scott said in fall 2008. "Policymakers pay no attention to it. The impact of criminological research has been minimal. That's the one nice thing about being out of it (the university environment). It's nice to have impact [as an attorney]."

Scott softened that criticism a bit when asked if all of the research in the field was insignificant in terms of influencing public policy. He said Dinitz was an exception to the rule. In 1993, for example, the Ohio governor selected Dinitz to head a committee to conduct a comprehensive evaluation of all reports and information pertaining to the 1993 prison riot at Lucasville, Ohio, where one guard and nine inmates were killed.[60] Dinitz said he was proud to be associated with such a project. However, he later expressed some ambiguity about the impact it had on public policy. In an

---

[60]A summary of events surrounding the riots is contained in Reginald A. Wilkinson and Thomas J. Stickrath, "After the Storm: Anatomy of a Riot's Aftermath," *Corrections Management Review* (Winter 1997), pp. 1-8.

"oral history" interview he gave at The Ohio State University in 2005,[61] Dinitz said that even though the Legislature adopted many of the suggestions offered by the committees examining the riots, most "were the easy ones" to adopt. The state did not implement suggestions that required substantial changes to the structure of the prison system.[62] He added:

> I've had some influence in the political realm, but only because — I never kid myself — they [policymakers] wanted the changes to be made, or they wanted a "cover" [someone to blame if something went wrong]. *You use task forces as a cover, right?* [If] you want to go get more money, you bring a task force in to tell you that we're not doing well enough. That's what they do. [bracketed material added for clarification; italics added for emphasis][63]

In summer 1999, Dinitz took two scholars out to lunch at the OSU Faculty Club. One of the scholars asked him whether much had changed in criminology research since the 1980. "Have any new solutions to the crime problem been developed?" He conceded that there had been no major breakthroughs.

"How does that make you feel?"

"You do the best you can," Dinitz said.

Eight years later, on March 3, 2007, Dinitz died of complications from cardiovascular disease. He was 81.

There is no question that Dinitz did his best. But what if doing one's best doesn't help solve social problems? Can social science sustain or justify itself on this principle alone?

---

[61]Oral history transcript of Simon Dinitz conducted by Adrienne Chafetz (November 8, 2005), retrieved September 18, 2008 from <https://kb.osu.edu/dspace/handle/1811/29289>.

[62]Dinitz did not elaborate on those major changes.

[63]*Ibid.*

CHAPTER 6

MEDIA VIOLENCE, CHOMSKY AND ANOTHER PLENARY

Like most kids, 14-year-old Ronny Zamora liked television. He watched about five hours a day, slightly more than the typical adolescent. He preferred crime shows, especially "Kojak," which starred the late Telly Savalas.

However, unlike most kids, a year later Ronny found himself in a real-life crime drama. He and a friend confessed that they had shot and killed Elinor Haggart, 82, a Miami Beach widow, after she discovered them burglarizing her home.

Ronny pleaded not guilty by reason of insanity. Television, his attorney argued before a Florida jury, had "brainwashed" Ronny. Psychiatrists also testified that Ronny was living in a "television fantasy world." One attorney told *Newsweek*: "He's watched thousands of shootings, and in these shootings there have been no consequences. He didn't know the consequence and nature of the act when he pulled the trigger."

The jury disagreed. In October 1977, Ronny was convicted of murder and sentenced to life in prison. He was paroled in 2004 and deported to Costa Rica, his home.

A number of criminal defendants in the United States have tried to use "television intoxication" as a defense for their crimes. None so far has been able to convince a jury.

But are the juries wrong? Can violent images and messages in the media — especially television and the movies — make people violent? Or can they compel people into a life of crime? Has the empirical research in this area prompted significant social changes limiting children's exposure to violent content?

RESEARCH ON VIOLENT PROGRAMMING

The idea that violent images or messages may promote violent behavior is nothing new. During the 19th century, many newspapers refrained from publishing information about crimes because they worried such stories would corrupt the morals of young people.[1] During the 1920s, the motion picture industry came under assault for producing too many movies that contained scenes of violence, crime, sex and love. The first major scientific study of a mass communication medium, in fact, suggested that movies had powerful impacts on children.[2] And during the 1950s and onward, some psychiatrists and others argued that comic books and violent movies could contribute to juvenile delinquency.[3]

About 80 percent of all prime-time programs on the national networks contain some violence. A typical program contains about six violent acts. Programs broadcast on weekends during daytime hours, when children frequently are watching, contain even more violence (93%) than prime time shows (80%). In fact, programming for children on Saturday mornings

---

[1] Typical of that view is the following excerpt in 1828 from the *New York Statesman*, which criticized the imitators of the *London Morning Herald*'s style of reporting: "The question is asked us by a correspondent, why we do not, like a few of our contemporaries of late, keep a regular chronicle of trials before the police, for the amusement and instruction of our readers? We have to reply, that it is a fashion which does not meet with our approbation, on the score of either propriety or taste." Quoted in Willard Grosvenor Bleyer, *Main Currents in the History of Journalism* (New York: Houghton Mifflin, 1927), p. 157.

[2] The research is known as the Payne Fund Studies. See Chapter 2 in Shearon A. Lowery and Melvin L. DeFleur, *Milestones in Mass Communication Research*, 2nd ed. (New York: Longman, 1988). The methodologies of some of these studies have been criticized, but the conclusions in general continue to receive support in the literature.

[3] Frederic Wertham, *Seduction of the Innocent* (New York: Rinehart, 1954) even argued that Batman and Robin comic books were turning young boys into homosexuals and that Superman was teaching children that the stronger should dominate the weaker. David Allen Walsh, *Selling Out America's Children: How America Puts Profits Before Values and What Parents Can Do* (Minneapolis: Deaconess Press, 1994) hypothesized that violent movies drive children into delinquency.

contains about three times as much violence per hour as prime-time programming (21 vs. 7 per hour). Of all the different types of programming, cartoons are clearly the most violent, with about 22 acts of violence per hour.[4] Scientists estimate that by age 14, the typical child will have watched 13,000 murders on television.[5]

Critics of violent programming often use anecdotes similar to the Ronny Zamora story to back up their argument. For example, in the 1980s, four teenage boys raped two young girls playing on a beach after seeing a movie four days earlier that contained a similar scene; after watching the movie "The Deer Hunter," which contained a Russian roulette Saigon gambling scene, 29 people shot themselves in separate incidents; and serial killer Ted Bundy claimed before he went to the electric chair that pornographic magazines inspired him to stalk and kill women. The empirical research doesn't support the idea that watching a program can have such dramatic effects. However, it clearly shows that children who watch violent programming have an increased probability of engaging in aggressive or antisocial behavior.[6]

Social scientists have used a number of different approaches to study the effects of violent programming. The most interesting, however, were the Bobo Doll experiments. The design was relatively simple. Preschool and elementary school children were divided into two groups, one

---

[4]Nancy Signorielli, "Television's Mean and Dangerous World: A Continuation of the Cultural Indicators Perspective," pp. 85-106 in Nancy Signorielli and Michael Morgan (eds.), *Cultivation Analysis: New Directions in Media Effects Research* (Newbury Park, CA: Sage, 1990). For a recent review, see George Gerbner, Larry Gross, Michael Morgan, and Nancy Signorielli, "Growing Up With Television: The Cultivation Perspective," pp. 17-42 in J. Bryant and D. Zillmann (eds.), *Media Effects: Advances in Theory and Research* (Hillsdale, NJ: Lawrence Erlbaum Associates, 1994).

[5]T. M. Williams (ed.), *The Impact of Television: A Natural Experiment in Three Communities* (Orlando, FL: Academic Press, 1986).

[6]A typical child over the age of three watches 15 to 30 hours per week, or about two to four hours a day. Television is the No. 1 leisure time activity among both children and adults. About a third to half of all children over age five spend more time watching television than they do in school. Estimates of television watching vary from study to study. The estimates here are based on a review of the literature by G. Comstock, S. Chaffee, N. Katzman, M. McCombs and D. Roberts, *Television and Human Behavior* (New York: Columbia University Press, 1978), pp. 177-178. Also see Signorielli, "Television's Mean and Dangerous World."

"experimental" and the other "control." The experimental groups watched
a film showing an adult or child punch, kick or sit on the Bobo Doll, while
the control groups watched the adult or child engage in innocuous,
nonviolent behaviors. Later, the children were allowed to play in a room
that contained a number of toys, including a Bobo Doll. Trained observers
then recorded the children's behavior.

The results: Children who watched the attack on the Bobo doll were
far more likely to behave aggressively toward the doll than children who
had not seen the attack.[7] In addition, children who had seen the attack also
became more aggressive toward adults and other children in the room —
sometimes hitting or pushing them. Additional experiments revealed that:

- Cartoons produced about the same level of aggression as filmed
  adults. This finding refuted claims from television executives that
  children could distinguish between reality and cartoons.
- Children were more likely to be aggressive when they saw the
  attackers being rewarded rather than being disciplined.
- Although children who saw the aggressor being disciplined were less
  likely to behave aggressively than those who were rewarded, they
  still were more likely to behave aggressively than those who did not
  see the aggressive behavior.

These findings and those from many other studies of television's
effects were reviewed and summarized in two major research projects
commissioned by the U.S. Surgeon General and the National Institute of
Mental Health. The first project, which was conducted in the late 1960s and
early 1970s, concluded that the evidence strongly supports the notion that
television violence promotes aggressive behavior in many children.[8] The
second project, commissioned in the early 1980s, reached a stronger
conclusion. After reviewing more than 3,000 scientific studies, the project

---

[7]Albert Bandura, *Aggression: A Social Learning Analysis* (Englewood Cliffs, N.J.:
Prentice-Hall, 1973).

[8]Surgeon General's Scientific Advisory Committee on Television and Social Behavior,
Television and Social Behavior, Vols. 1-5 (Washington, D.C.: U.S. Department of Health,
Education and Welfare, U.S. Government Printing Office, 1972).

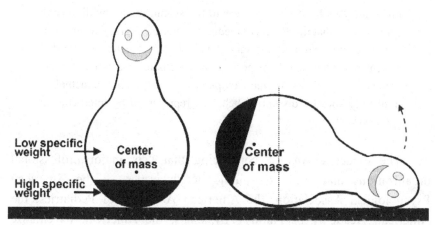

When struck, an inflatable Bobo Doll falls to the ground but returns to its upright position because of the weigh is heavier at the bottom. *(Photograph by DMY; released to the public domain)*

leaders concluded that both laboratory and field experiments overwhelmingly support claims that television violence increases aggressive behaviors in many children.[9]

As might be expected, television executives condemned the reports. They argued that violent programming should have no harmful effects, because the "bad guys" in television shows are usually punished for the violent crimes they commit. However, the TV executives had no hard evidence to refute the key findings.[10] And since then the evidence of aggressive effects has continued to pile up. One study that reviewed seven other major reviews of the literature on violent programming — which are themselves called "meta-analyses" — concluded:

[9]D. Pearl, L. Bouthilet, and J. Lazar (eds.), *Television and Behavior: Ten Years of Scientific Progress and Implications for the Eighties,* Vols. I & II (Washington, D.C.: U.S. Government Printing Office, 1982).

[10]The evidence was so convincing, in fact, that since its release many scientists have shifted their focus of research into other areas (Lowery and DeFleur, *Milestones in Mass Communication Research*, pp. 383-384). For a more recent review of the literature on media's effects, see Barrie Gunter, "The Question of Media Violence," pp. 163-212 in J. Bryant and D. Zillmann (eds.), *Media Effects: Advances in Theory and Research* (Hillsdale, NJ: Lawrence Erlbaum Associates, 1994) and Douglas A. Gentile (ed.), *Media Violence and Children: A Complete Guide for Parents and Professionals* (Westport, CT: Praeger, 2003).

Meta-analyses have made it clear to the scientific and public health communities that the effects of media violence on aggressive and anti-social behavior are real and important ... [T]he evidence asserts that violent television and film portrayals contribute to acts of extreme violence as well as to the comparatively minor but nonetheless frequently socially disruptive behavior represented by interpersonal aggression.[11]

The evidence was so convincing that "six major professional organizations that focus on public health issues — the American Psychological Association, the American Academy of Pediatrics, the American Academy of Family Physicians, the American Psychiatric Association, the American Media Association, and the American Academy of Child and Adolescent Psychiatry — recently signed a joint statement attesting to the dangers of media violence for children."[12] In short, critics of violent programming have a lot of ammunition to support their position. But has it had any effect on reducing the amount of violence on television or on reducing the amount of violence programming that children watch?

IMPACT OF RESEARCH ON PUBLIC POLICY

Psychologist Douglas A. Gentile and his colleagues assert that the greatest public policy success of research on media violence was the creation of various media content rating systems.

---

[11]George Comstock and Erica Scharrer, "Meta-Analyzing the Controversy over Television Violence and Aggression," pp. 205-226 in Douglas A. Gentile (ed.), *Media Violence and Children: A Complete Guide for Parents and Professionals* (Westport, CT: Praeger, 2003).

[12]Bruce D. Bartholow, Karen E. Dill, Kathryn B. Anderson and James J. Lindsay, "The Proliferation of Media Violence and Its Economic Underpinnings," pp. 1-18 in Douglas A. Gentile (ed.), *Media Violence and Children: A Complete Guide for Parents and Professionals* (Westport, CT: Praeger, 2003), pp. 4-5. Also see Douglas A. Gentile, Muniba Saleem and Craig A. Anderson, "Public Policy and the Effects of Media Violence on Children," *Social Issues and Policy Review, 1*(1): 15-61 (2007), p. 23.

Perhaps the most successful set of U.S. public policy initiatives to date have been the Congressional hearings that preceded and motivated the creation of the various media rating systems. The movie, music, video game, and television industries all currently have rating systems (for a review, see Gentile, 2008). Each of these systems was created "voluntarily" after Congressional pressure brought to bear on each industry. Perhaps the most interesting of these was the manner in which the television ratings were created. The Telecommunications Act of 1996 mandated that televisions be manufactured with "V-chips" in them ... The television industry was given 1 year to create its own system for rating violent, sexual, and other sensitive content. If the system was not judged to be "acceptable" to the Federal Communications Commission, then the FCC would appoint an advisory committee to create the system.[13]

So research clearly can have an impact on public policy. But the celebration is muted by another unanticipated event: few parents are actually using the V-chip, which is a device built into TV sets that allow them to control what their children watch. Moreover, despite all of the research that has documented the adverse effects of violent programming, the amount of violent content actually has steadily increased, not decreased, over the past 30 years!

Research reports published in the early 1970s indicated that by age 14, the average child had witnessed more than 11,000 murders on television.[14] This figure has dramatically increased, with more recent reports indicating that the average American child now witnesses more than 10,000 violent crimes (e.g., murder, rape, and assault) *each year*

---

[13]Gentile, Saleem and Anderson, "Public Policy and the Effects of Media Violence on Children," pp. 47-48.

[14]For these figures, the researchers cite G. Looney, "Television and the Child: What Can be Done?" paper presented at the meeting of the American Academy of Pediatrics (Chicago, October 1971).

on television — about 200,000 total violent crimes by the time they are in their teens.[15] [emphasis added]

The lack of impact of mass communication research is not limited to research on violence. In 2003, Massachusetts Institute of Technology Press published an edited volume titled *Communication Researchers and Public Policy*. Edited by mass media scholar Sandra Braman, the book contained 26 chapters that examined the impact and potential impact of mass communication research on public policy. The articles included works submitted specifically for the volume as well as articles previously published. And like most of the other books written on the topic, the overall conclusion was that mass communication research has had relatively little impact on public policy. Here's a sampling:

- "Social research in the twentieth century has had, at best, an indirect relationship to government policies toward mass communication," according to mass media scholars Byron Reeves and James L. Baughman. "Although recent considerations of the FCC, FTC, and Congress have included testimony from selected academics, the crucial political decisions have largely ignored mass communication scholarship."[16]

- "[R]ecent efforts toward the formation of policy regulating or deregulating pornography have gone wrong on many counts. One of them is social-science input, which simply proved inconsequential for policy recommendations and, hence, legislation."[17]

---

[15]For these figures, the researchers cite Nancy Signorielli, George Gerbner and Michael Morgan, "Violence on Television: The Cultural Indicators Project," *Journal of Broadcasting and Electronic Media, 39*: 278-283 (1995).

[16]Byron Reeves and James L. Baughman, "'Fraught with Such Great Possibilities': The Historical Relationship of Communication Research to Mass Media Regulation," pp. 529-571 in Sandra Braman (ed.), *Communication Researchers and Policy Making* (Cambridge, MA: MIT Press, 2003), p. 529.

[17]Dolf Zillman, "Pornography Research and Public Policy," pp. 145-164 in Sandra Braman (ed.), *Communication Researchers and Policy Making* (Cambridge, MA: MIT Press, 2003), p. 159.

- Although citizens and some scholars tried to shape the Telecommunications Act of 1996, corporations played the lead role and research provided very little input.[18]

- In a chapter titled "Communication Research on Children and Public Policy," mass media scholar Ellen Wartella opens her article with "one argument: Both the historical record and current events demonstrate that communication research and scholarship can make a difference in children's media, but that they usually do not."[19] She placed some of the blame on the fact that mass communication scholars are often "ignorant of how to act as public intellectuals and advocates for a particular point of view."[20]

In defense of the field of mass communication, some scholars correctly point out that the First Amendment is partly to blame for the lack of controls over violent content. Media executives often use the First Amendment as a shield to protect their medium's content from critics. The "don't-censor-us mantra" resonates very well with many policymakers and citizens.

But the First Amendment does not preclude society from regulating the time, place and manner of violent programming.[21] The courts have never held that anyone can broadcast anything at any time. The Federal Communications Commission restricts nudity and bad language on over-the-air broadcast television, and the courts have upheld their right to do that. Is there any reason why all violent programming couldn't be restricted

---

[18]Sandra Braman, "Introduction," pp. 1-9 in Sandra Braman (ed.), *Communication Researchers and Policy Making* (Cambridge, MA: MIT Press, 2003), p. 6. Braman cites Patricial Aufderheide, *Communications Policy and the Public Interest: The Telecommunications Act of 1996* (New York: Guilford, 1998), as her source for this statement.

[19]Ellen Wartella, "Communication Research on Children and Public Policy," pp. 359-373 in Sandra Braman (ed.), *Communication Researchers and Policy Making* (Cambridge, MA: MIT Press, 2003), p. 359.

[20]*Ibid.*, p. 370.

[21]U.S. courts have ruled that content in over-the-air broadcast media can be regulated because of the limited right of access to airwaves. But cable television, like print media in general, is not under such constraints.

to certain parts of the day or night?[22]

The real problem, some critics say, is that mass communication researchers in particular and social scientists in general are politically impotent. In response, the researchers point out that political involvement is a two-edged sword. If social scientists get more involved in the political realm, then their research might be perceived as more biased. Policymakers and the public will no longer see them as objective purveyors of truth. However, the critics then point out that if social scientists don't become more involved, then policymakers may make bad decisions, which could harm people or society. One could then accuse the social scientists of shirking a moral obligation to help prevent harms.

"So we social scientists are damned if we do and damned if we don't."

"Yes, but would you rather go to hell because you looked biased or because you allowed policymakers to harm people?"

MEDIA SCHOLARS AND POLITICAL ACTIVISM

Many scholars are afraid to look biased, especially after the embarrassing incident at The Glasgow University Media Group, a collection of media researchers in Glasgow, Scotland.[23] Their content analyses, interviews and covert participant observation in the 1970s claimed that British television news was biased in favor of powerful elites and against less powerful groups, such as organized working class groups.[24] However, in *TV News, Whose Bias?*, Martin Harrison pointed out that the researchers, who politically lean to the left, selectively identified much of the bias they found. For instance, they interpreted the word "idle," when used in news reports to describe striking workers, as pejorative, even though strikers

---

[22]In Europe, television has a lot more explicit sexual content. Making love is considered to be a good thing. But Europe frowns more on violent content. In the United States, it's the opposite. Making love is taboo, and violence is OK. The irony of this always elicits a chuckle among mass communication scholars.

[23]M. Hammersley and R. Gomm, "Bias in Social Research" *Sociological Research Online, 2* (1997), <http://www.socresonline.org.uk/socresonline/2/1/2.html>.

[24]Glasgow University Media Group and Peter Beharrell, *Bad News* (London: Routledge, 1980).

often used the word themselves.[25]

Although many researchers in the field of mass communication are afraid to look biased, some are not. They actively seek to change public policy. They point out, very convincingly, that the mainstream social scientist's decision not to get involved in the political arena is itself a biased decision, because it can significantly reduce the chances of fixing problems and, thus, results in a bias that supports the status quo and existing power groups. Among those media scholars who are active in the political process, the most prominent are the neo-Marxists and Noam Chomsky.

Noam Chomsky: America's Dissident

Noam Chomsky is often called the father of modern linguistics. During the 1950s, he argued that the linguistics scholars should focus more on describing a "universal grammar" — a model that underpins all human language — than on formulating specific grammars for different languages. People, he argued, are "born knowing" and that allows children to acquire the language to which they are exposed. In other words, he was arguing that the basic structure of language comes from nature, not nurture. Experts say his theory of generative grammar is a milestone.[26]

But during the Vietnam War, Chomsky earned the distinction of being America's best known dissident after his essay "The Responsibility of Intellectuals" was published Feb. 23, 1967, as a special supplement in *The New York Review of Books*. Chomsky criticized social scientists and technocrats who he believed were providing pseudo-scientific justification for U.S. involvement in the Vietnam War.[27] His first political book, *American Power and the New Mandarins*, was published in 1969 and further cemented his reputation as America's foremost critic and protestor. The book criticized intellectual liberals who supported the Vietnam conflict

---

[25]Martin Harrison, *TV News, Whose Bias?* (Hermitage, UK: Policy Journals, 1985).

[26]Noam Chomsky, *Syntactic Structures* (The Hague/Paris: Mouton, 1957).

[27]Noam Chomsky, "The Responsibility of Intellectuals," *The New York Review of Books*, 8 (1967).

or who opposed it not because it was morally wrong but because of the high level of U.S. casualties.[28]

Since the Vietnam War, one of Chomsky's passions has been analyzing the role and function of mass media. In 1989, he and University of Pennsylvania economist Edward S. Herman completed the final draft of their book, *Manufacturing Consent: The Political Economy of the Mass Media.*[29] In it, they wrote that "the mass media of the United States are effective and powerful ideological institutions that carry out a system-supportive propaganda function by reliance on market forces, internalized assumptions, and self-censorship, and without significant overt coercion."[30] In other words, the mass media are tools of propaganda for powerful politicians and corporate America.

Although *Manufacturing Consent*, which was published in 1988, contains no citations to the works of Karl Marx and only a few citations of works associated with the Critical Theory genre,[31] it shares a great deal of common ground with these works. In fact, one could reasonably conclude that the Herman and Chomsky book plows no new theoretical ground. But the book does make three significant contributions to the field. First, it provides real-world anecdotes and case studies in support of Critical Theory. Second, the book's early discussion of "filters" provides a useful metaphor for explaining to media bias. Third, the writing is accessible to an educated general audience, unlike most scholarly work in the field.

> In contrast to the standard conception of the media as cantankerous, obstinate, and ubiquitous in their search for truth and their independence of authority, we have spelled out and applied a propaganda model that

---

[28]Noam Chomsky, *American Power and the New Mandarins* (Harmondsworth, England: Penguin, 1969).

[29]Edward S. Herman and Noam Chomsky, *Manufacturing Consent: The Political Economy of the Mass Media* (New York: Pantheon, 1989).

[30]*Ibid.*, p. 306.

[31]The absence of such citations is perplexing, because the theory shares so much common ground with the neo-Marxist literature. One possible explanation is that Herman and Chomsky feared critics would classify them as Marxists, which in turn can marginalize a scholar and his work very quickly in mainstream politics. Chomsky has stated many times that he is not a Marxist.

indeed sees the media as serving a "societal purpose," but not that of enabling the public to assert meaningful control over the political process by providing them with the information needed for the intelligent discharge of political responsibilities. On the contrary, a propaganda model suggests that the "societal purpose" of the media is to inculcate and defend the economic, social, and political agenda of privileged groups that dominate the domestic society and the state.[32]

"Profit orientation" is one of the major reasons (or "filters," as Herman and Chomsky called them) why media produce content that supports the status quo. Herman and Chomsky are particularly critical of the so-called "large media corporations," which they define in terms of the amount of revenue they generate.

> In sum, the dominant media firms are quite large businesses; they are controlled by very wealthy people or by managers who are subject to sharp constraints by owners and other market-profit-oriented forces; and they are interlocked, and have important common interests, with other major corporations, banks, and government.[33]

Other filters include advertising, reliance on powerful governmental and corporate elites for news, "flak" from powerful people or organizations that criticize mass media performance, and the "ideology of anti-communist." These filters place constraints on mainstream mass media, ensuring that the content doesn't stray too far from dominant values and the interests of powerful elites.

In a separate unpublished paper,[34] Chomsky also made the intriguing argument that the propaganda system in the United States is far more insidious than propaganda systems in communist countries, because most people in the United States think their news media are free and independent and, thus, are more likely to believe what they read and hear. In contrast,

---

[32]Herman and Chomsky, *Manufacturing Consent*, p. 298.

[33]*Ibid.*, p. 14.

[34]Noam Chomsky, "The Manufacture of Consent" (Minneapolis: Silha Center, University of Minnesota, 1986).

most people in communist countries know their news media are biased and so are often skeptical of official news reports.

To support their propaganda theory, Herman and Chomsky provide numerous examples of "biased" media coverage of international events where U.S. government interests are at stake. They include coverage of wars or events in El Salvador, Guatemala, Nicaragua, Vietnam, Laos and Cambodia, as well as the KGB-Bulgarian plot to kill the pope. The central theme is that U.S. government elites, including past presidents, are able to easily control U.S. news media coverage. Other empirical research, both neo-Marxist and mainstream, also provides a great deal of support for Herman and Chomsky's main thesis. Mass media, like other social institutions (schools, police, churches), produce content that generally supports dominant societal values and institutions, often to the detriment of groups that represent the interests of the poor, minorities, laborers, women, environmentalists, homosexuals, antiwar, antiglobalization and other groups.[35]

---

[35]See, e.g., Karen E. Altman, "Consuming Ideology: The Better Homes in America Campaign," *Critical Studies in Mass Communication, 7*:286-307 (1990); J. Herbert Altschull, *Agents of Power* (New York: Longman, 1984); W. Lance Bennett, *News: The Politics of Illusion,* 2nd ed. (New York: Longman, 1988); Stanley Cohen and Jock Young (eds.), *The Manufacture of News* (London: Constable, 1981); David Pearce Demers, The *Menace of the Corporate Newspaper: Fact or Fiction?* (Ames: Iowa State University Press, 1996); Edward Jay Epstein, *News From Nowhere* (New York: Random House, 1973); Stuart Ewin, *Captains of Consciousness: Advertising and the Social Roots of the Consumer Culture* (New York: McGraw Hill, 1976); Mark Fishman, *Manufacturing the News* (Austin: University of Texas Press, 1980); Doris A. Graber, *Mass Media and American Politics,* 3rd ed. (Washington, DC: Congressional Quarterly Press, 1989); Herbert J. Gans, *Deciding What's News* (New York: Vintage, 1979); Todd Gitlin, *The Whole World Is Watching: Mass Media in the Making and Unmaking of the Left* (Berkeley: University of California Press, 1980); Harvey Molotch and Marilyn Lester, "Accidental News: The Great Oil Spill as Local Occurrence and National Event," *American Journal of Sociology, 81*:235-260 (1975); David L. Paletz and Robert M. Entman, *Media Power Politics* (New York: The Free Press, 1981); David L. Paletz, Peggy Reichert and Barbara McIntyre, "How the Media Support Local Government Authority," *Public Opinion Quarterly, 35*:80-92 (1971); Fred Powledge, *The Engineering of Restraint* (Washington, DC: Public Affairs Press, 1971); Leon Sigal, *Reporters and Officials* (Lexington, MA: Heath, 1973); and Phillip J. Tichenor, George A. Donohue and Clarice N. Olien, *Community Conflict and the Press* (Beverly Hills, CA: Sage, 1980).

One weakness of the propaganda model, though, is that it fails to account for social change. Herman and Chomsky concede that the propaganda machine in the United States "is not all-powerful." A good example was public opposition to the Vietnam War after 1968. Their theory of propaganda does not provide an extended explanation about how opposition ideas or groups form, nor does it address many of the social changes that occurred during the 20th century in which elites were forced to give up some rights and privileges. These include expansion of union worker rights, civil rights, women's rights, and increased protection of the environment.

But the shortcomings of his propaganda model have not detracted from his popularity. In 1992, a film ("Manufacturing Consent") was made based on the book, and it was shown on many college campuses around the world and broadcast on Public Broadcast System in the United States. Chomsky has lectured extensively in the United States, Europe and Third World countries, often criticizing governments and Western media for failing to show the shortcomings of modern democracies. Wherever Chomsky goes, he draws large crowds, especially on college campuses. He also is popular among antiglobalization and antiwar activists. In 2006, Venezuelan President Hugo Chávez held up a copy of Chomsky's book, *Hegemony or Survival*,[36] when he spoke to the United Nations General Assembly.

Unlike most scholars, Chomsky is actively seeking to change the world. But how much impact has he had?

Scholars largely agree that his impact on college students and professors has been profound. He is widely admired in the academy, and professors jockey with each other to have a chance to meet him when he comes to campus. Lecture halls are frequently jammed beyond capacity.

However, in terms of affecting ordinary Americans, mainstream journalists and politicians, his impact has been far less effective. A search of *The New York Times* archives in early 2011 retrieved nearly 400 stories

---

[36]Noam Chomsky, *Hegemony or Survival: America's Quest for Global Dominance* (New York: Henry Holt & Company LLC, 2003).

that have cited Chomsky since 1981. About a dozen or so of them refer to Chomsky as a "leftist" scholar or professor. But, interestingly, the newspaper never refers to mainstream researchers as "mainstream" or "middle of the road." Chomsky supporters point out that he gets even less recognition from broadcast media, who rarely seek his opinion on matters of public policy. Instead, mainstream media rely heavily on mainstream sources. They avoid radicals at both ends of the political spectrum, scholarly research shows, even though their press ideology allegedly welcomes voices from all sides of a controversy. Chomsky's impact on policymaking probably has been greater outside of America, where he often gets more media coverage, including appearances on television and radio stations operated by British Broadcasting Corporation (BBC).

The Politics of Critical Theory

Noam Chomsky is not the only scholar actively seeking to change the world. Some current and former scholars who research shares affinities with Critical Theory (or political economy of the media) also have been active.

One of those is media scholar Robert W. McChesney. He has written that "the political economy of communication — like political economy in general — has a prescriptive mission. The purpose of its critique is to assist the process of social change, both in terms of specific media policies within the context of a capitalist political economy and in terms of assisting broader social change toward a postcapitalist and more democratic society."[37] Although McChesney has been called a scholar working in the Marxist tradition,[38] his reformist-oriented platform does not call for the elimination of market-based economic systems. Rather, he urges others to create alternative "democratic" media with either private or public funds.

---

[37]Robert W. McChesney, "The Political Economy of Global Communication," pp. 1-26 in Robert W. McChesney, E. M. Wood, and J. B. Foster (eds.), *Capitalism and the Information Age: The Political Economy of the Global Communication Revolution* (New York: Monthly Review Press, 1988), p. 8.

[38]Denis McQuail, *McQuail's Mass Communication Theory* (Thousand Oaks, CA: Sage, 2003).

He co-founded and is president of the Free Press, a nonprofit media group that is actively trying to influence public policy at the legislative (Congress and Senate) and administrative (Federal Communications Commission) levels. Free Press is the largest media reform organization in the United States, serving more than a half-million members. It has 30 full-time staff members. The organization is often given partial credit for helping prevent the Federal Communications Commission from allowing cross-media television/newspaper ownership in the early 2000s.

Some critics, like McChesney, have softened their criticism of capitalism in recent years. Early critical theorists like Herbert Marcuse and Walter Benjamin hoped for the demise of capitalism as an economic institution. But during the late 1970s and 1980s that mission may have been sidetracked when Critical Theory was criticized for failing to take into account oppositional resistance (such as protest groups) and the media's potential to give some favorable coverage to them.[39] Media have both a regressive and progressive potential, the critics argued. "It is ... mistaken to define television as a monolithic tool of a unified ruling class," critical media scholar Douglas Kellner wrote in 1981. "Instead, television reflects divisions and conflicts within the ruling class and the entire society about the direction of public policy."[40]

Todd Gitlin is another critical scholar who, through his lifetime, has moved from the extreme left on the political spectrum toward the middle. But even his popular 1980 book on the media coverage of the anti-Vietnam War student movement, *The Whole World Is Watching,* did not advocate revolutionary change. He maintained that social movements can produce

---

[39]Nicholas Abercrombie, Stephen Hill and Brian S. Turner, *The Dominant Ideology Thesis* (London: Allen & Unwin, 1980); Peter Bruck, "Strategies for Peace, Strategies for News Research," *Journal of Communication, 39*(1): 108-129 (1989); Celeste M. Condit, "Hegemony Is a Mass-mediated Society: Concordance about Reproductive Technologies," *Critical Studies in Mass Communication, 11*: 205-230 (1994); Jonathon Fiske, *Television Culture* (New York: Methuen, 1987); William A. Gamson, *Talking Politics* (New York: Cambridge University Press, 1992); and David J. Sholle, "Critical Studies: From the Theory of Ideology to Power/Knowledge," *Critical Studies in Mass Communication, 5*: 16-41 (1988).

[40]Douglas Kellner, "Network Television and America Society: Introduction to a Critical Theory of Television," *Theory and Society, 10*: 31-55 (1981), p. 45.

and should work for meaningful change.[41] Similarly, critical scholar Korinna Patelis, in her 2000 critique of the Internet, did not argue that the commercialized aspect of that medium should be abolished. Instead, she advocated a "public service Net" to "reverse the current commercialization trends."[42]

Although these critical scholars and the organizations they support have had some impact on public policy or on influencing the ideas of scholars and the public, they are the exception rather than the rule. Like most mainstream social science, most critical scholars prefer the comfort of the ivory armchair to the protest sidewalk.

ANOTHER PLENARY

In 2000, a plenary session was organized as a follow-up on the 1997 plenary session conducted in Chicago — the one where Jesse Jackson upstaged the professors[43] (see Chapter 1). The session was titled "Does Journalism and Mass Communication Research Matter?" and was conducted during the annual meeting of the Association for Education in Journalism and Mass Communication in Phoenix.

Robert F. Rich, who was cited earlier in this book, was one of the panelists. He was joined by three mass communication scholars on the panel:[44] Theodore Glasser, a professor of communication at Stanford University; Kasisomayajula Viswanath, an associate professor of mass communication at The Ohio State University who had just accepted a new job as a researcher at the National Cancer Institute (and is now a research professor at Harvard University); and Joanne Cantor, a professor of communication arts at the University of Wisconsin-Madison (now retired). About three hundred professors attended — far fewer than the thousand

---

[41]Todd Gitlin, *The Whole World Is Watching: Mass Media in the Making and Unmaking of the Left* (Berkeley: University of California Press, 1980), pp. 291-292.

[42]Korinna Patelis, "The Political Economy of the Internet," pp 84-106 in James Curran, (ed.), *Media Organizations in Society* (London: Arnold, 2000), p. 99.

[43]See Chapter 1.

[44]The plenary was conducted August 10, 2000, at the Hyatt Regency in Phoenix.

who came to see Jesse Jackson three years earlier. But that was still impressive, given that of the panelists was a national celebrity.

The moderator[45] began the session with a brief discussion about what happened in Chicago in 1997 and then added:

> It would be inaccurate to say that communication research in particular and social science research in general has no impact on public policy. Social scientists often help define or redefine social problems. And empirical research produced within governmental organizations often influences public policy.
>
> However, it would be a mistake to overestimate the influence of the social sciences themselves. Public policy studies show that social science research plays a relatively limited role in public policy decision making ... There are many reasons for the relative political impotence of social science research, including the fact that the academy offers little incentive to scholars who attempt to influence public policy. But herein lies the dilemma: If social science research has relatively little impact on public policy, then what can be its expected impact on solving social problems like poverty, malnutrition, poor health care, child abuse, crime, drug abuse, and discrimination? ...
>
> Does social science research in general and journalism and mass communication research in particular matter? Can they influence public policy and solve social problems? Can they influence public policy or professional practice? If so, under what conditions can scholars have the most impact? Or, alternatively, is social science research mostly ritual, whose main functions are to regulate scholars' entry into the Ivory Tower, build egos and create social cohesion?

Viswanath: Indirect Impacts

In contrast to 1997, the panelists at this plenary provided at least two examples of the impact of social science research. Viswanath said research in the social sciences played a key role from the 1950s onward in raising

---

[45]I organized and moderated the session, largely in response to the 1997 plenary, which deeply concerned me. Part of my interest stemmed from the fact that I was a former newspaper reporter and had a fair amount of experience watching policymaking in action.

awareness about the hazards of smoking cigarettes and the causes of cardiovascular disease. He pointed out that increased public awareness saved lives in both areas.

> Based on research in epidemiology, sociology, psychology and communication, among other fields, activists have efficaciously promoted several restrictions on smoking, including vending machine sales, tobacco promotions and advertising, and regulating cigarette sales ... Activists have successfully worked with scholars in promoting the media and public agenda for tobacco control.[46]

The only challenge to this statement came from a member of the audience after the session, who said that doctors and medical scientists played a more central role in influencing the public agenda than did social scientists, because mass media give far more coverage to medical scholars and physicians than to social scientists. But Viswanath pointed out that the process through which social science influences public policy is often complex, involving an interplay between medical researchers, social scientists, public policymakers and social activists. He added:

> We might suggest ... that communication research couldn't be expected to demonstrate its potency by itself. My plea is that an expectation that the *direct* impact of communication research must be demonstrated to evaluate its efficacy is unreasonable, unrealistic and simplistic. My argument is that communication research does have an impact, albeit one that is conditional and over the long term and in confluence with other institutions.[47] [italics in original]

---

[46]This comment is taken from a short essay that Viswanath contributed to *Journalism Studies* shortly after the conference. See K. Viswanath, "The Impact of Communication Research," *Journalism Studies* 2(4): 617-620 (2001), p. 618. All four members of the panel also contributed essays. I quote from them because they provide a more accurate and complete picture of their thinking at that time.

[47]*Ibid.*, p. 620.

As a research professor at Harvard, Viswanath is in a position to influence public policy more than most social scientists. U.S. Department of Health and Human Services Secretary Michael Levitt appointed him chair of the Board of Scientific Counselors for the National Center for Health Marketing at the Centers for Disease Control and Prevention. Viswanath conducts research in three areas: access to health information and implications of unequal access; the sociology of medical and health journalism; and effects of the mass media on health knowledge, attitudes and behaviors. According to his website, "The findings from this body of work are useful in designing: (a) strategies to not only enhance access to health information among the underserved, but to make this information understandable to low-literacy populations; and (b) effective messages and communication systems to reduce cancer risk and promote prevention."[48]

Cantor: Lack of Academic Rewards

Cantor, an expert on television and its impact on children, said her research in the 1990s contributed to the development of a content-based rating system for television programs and the V-chip. The television industry wanted an age-based system that would notify viewers, prior to a television show, of the ages for which a program was suitable. But her survey research showed that parents want information about the content of the programming, such as acts of violence, sex, coarse language, etc. The television industry eventually capitulated and the content-based guidelines were approved in 1997. The V-chip also became standard equipment in televisions two years later, a year before the plenary session. Although the impact of these two changes was not as profound as she and other researchers had expected, she remained optimistic about the utility of social science.

So in this case, it may be argued that communication research had an impact on public policy. "But did it really matter?" some might ask ...

---

[48]See <http://www.hsph.harvard.edu/faculty/kasisomayajula-viswanath>.

It may still be early to notice an effect, but the fact is that surprisingly few parents even know about the V-chip, and understanding of the rating system has actually declined over the years.[49] So it is difficult to argue that in supporting the legislation that ... communication research has made a difference in children's lives or in society in general. But it is my opinion that communication research can matter even if it does not affect legislation. Communication research matters if it is used to educate the general public in ways that can be helpful to society.[50]

Cantor pointed out that during the 1990s she spent more time writing materials that reached out to other audiences, including doctors and the general public. For example, she published a book called *Mommy, I'm Scared*[51] and wrote articles for *Family Circle* and *Our Children* magazines.

Of course, I am not the only communication researcher doing these things. Many of my communication colleagues are using their research findings and expertise to promote similar goals. And that's a good thing. And it matters.[52]

However, Cantor conceded that "academia does not usually weigh these forms of public service very heavily in merit and tenure decisions." She pointed out that even though her university rewarded her for publishing a book that reached a broad audience, "there are subtle ways in which our field looks down on the popularization of one's work." She concluded that "communication research does matter, but it could and should matter a lot more. Increasing our efforts to communicate with the outside world could help society confront some of its most pressing problems."[53]

---

[49]These problems are discussed in Dale Kunkel, "The Road to the V-Chip: Television Violence and Public Policy," pp. 227-245 in Douglas A. Gentile (ed.), *Media Violence and Children: A Complete Guide for Parents and Professionals* (Westport, CT: Praeger, 2003).

[50]Joanne Cantor, "Notes from the Trenches of the Media Violence Wars," *Journalism Studies, 2*(4): 620-623 (2001), p. 621.

[51]Joanne Cantor, *"Mommy, I'm Scared": How TV and Movies Frighten Children and How We Can Protect Them* (San Diego, CA: Harvest Books, 1998).

[52]Cantor, "Notes from the Trenches," p. 622.

[53]*Ibid.*, p. 623.

After the plenary session, one scholar told me that even though communication scholars may have influenced legislation on the television ratings system, they have been relatively powerless to do anything about the amount of sex and violence on television. "Communication researchers have had a difficult time changing the content of the programming," the researcher pointed out.

Glasser: Asking the Wrong Questions

Unlike Viswanath and Cantor, Glasser did not provide examples of research affecting public policy. Years later he told me via e-mail that

> I like to think that my work in and beyond the classroom makes a difference in the practice of journalism. But who knows? It's a difficult thing to monitor. Does inspiring one journalist count as evidence of influence? Does changing one editor's mind matter?[54]

His comments during the plenary mostly were directed at a critique of motives or reasons that many mainstream social scientists employ to study the world. He said many researchers do not understand or appreciate the motives that propel them to collect and analyze data.

> [S]cholarship as a form of knowledge needs to be understood with reference to researchers' interests and the interests of the type of research being practiced ... [R]esearchers cannot "know" a good research problem without their own sense of what "good" means ... in the final analysis the quality of scholarship rests not on explanations alone but also on the justification for them, a justification that makes explicit the motives of the scholar and the interests being advanced by the research. *To put it bluntly and probably contentiously, any good study of journalism, whatever the topic, requires a theory of good journalism; any theory of good journalism requires answers to a series of successively larger questions about what "good" means.*

---

[54]E-mail from Theodore Glasser (November 10, 2008).

Glasser did not define what he means by "good." But his research program suggests that "good" should be determined at least in part through a deliberative, democratic process — a process that involves not just journalists or researchers but people in the community as well.[55]

Glasser's approach shares some affinities with critical/neo-Marxist scholarship, which sees mainstream social science — especially grant-generated research — not as a tool for emancipation but as a tool of repression, as a way for powerful political and economic institutions to gain greater control over working and middle class people. Building on the criticism of America sociologists Robert Lynd, Bent Flyvbjerg, a Danish professor of planning, attacked mainstream social science research head on in 2002:

> If we want to re-enchant and empower social science ... then we need to do three things. First, we must drop the fruitless efforts to emulate natural science's success in producing cumulative and predictive theory; this approach simply does not work in social science. Second, we must take up problems that matter to the local, national, and global communities in which we live ... we must focus on issues of values and power like the great social scientists have advocated from Aristotle and Machiavelli to Max Weber and Pierre Bourdieu. Finally, we must effectively communicate the results of our research to fellow citizens. If we do this, we may successfully transform social science from what is fast becoming a sterile academic activity, which is undertaken mostly for its own sake and in increasing isolation from a society on which it has little effect and from which it gets little appreciation.[56]

In short, critical scholars contend that traditional social scientific research is failing to solve social problems because it is asking the wrong questions, making incorrect assumptions about the nature of human

---

[55]See, e.g., Theodore L. Glasser and Peggy J. Bowers, "Justifying Change and Control: An Application of Discourse Ethics to the Role of Mass Media, pp. 399-424 in David Demers and K. Viswanath (eds.), *Mass Media, Social Control, and Social Change: A Macrosocial Perspective* (Ames: Iowa State University Press, 1999).

[56]Bent Flyvbjerg, *Making Social Science Matter: Why Social Inquiry Fails and How It Can Succeed Again* (Cambridge, United Kingdom: University Press, 2001), p. 166.

behavior, and using the wrong methodology. The real solution to the alleged problems, these scholars argue, is to nurture a social science that is patterned more after the humanities than the natural sciences and embraces participatory democratic principles.

Rich: Ideology and Self-Interest

Robert Rich, the nonmedia professor on the panel, pointed out that government and science, including social science, historically worked under the assumption that science would produce knowledge and policymakers would use that knowledge to address particular problems or issues. But government began to question the utility of this "social contract"[57] in the 1960s, after the presidential administration of Lyndon B. Johnson launched the Great Society programs with the help of scores of social scientists (see Chapter 2 for more details). According to Rich, the government was asking:

> What is the return on our investment? What is the utility of the research that is being financed out of public funds? There seemed to be a growing feeling that funded research should ... have utility and that researchers applying for government funding should address the question: how is this information going to be used? Consequently, some real tension developed between the scientific community and its professional associations and some policymakers and other governmental officials.

Although the U.S. government has spent billions of dollars on social scientific research, Rich pointed out that governmental and scientific "cultures" have a "deep distrust for each other." One consequence is that policymakers often ignore that research. They tend to elevate ideology (the party's platform) over facts. Research also shows, Rich pointed out, that the source of the information (e.g., a trusted aide versus an unknown social

---

[57]The term "social contract" generally implies that people give up some rights to a government and other authority in order to preserve social order.

scientist) is far more important than the quality of information itself. Social science research is most likely to have an impact on public policy when policymakers themselves specifically request the research or when it fits into the ideological needs of the policymakers (i.e., supports their policies and values). This proposition was the main conclusion of his 1981 book, *Social Science Information and Public Policy Making*, which was reprinted shortly after the Phoenix panel session. The back cover and the forward of his book provide good summaries:

> A survey of federal officials reveals the belief that government should make the fullest possible use of social science information — and yet most of the information developed by social scientists winds up in specialized libraries or data banks, where it remains unused. Why don't public officials make greater use of the information social scientists develop?[58]

> [T]he probability of information being used is less a consequence of the appropriateness of the information to the substantive policy than it is of the utility of the information to bureaucratic interests. There is, then, a politics of information that exists prior to the use of the information for selecting among policy options.[59]

In other words, Rich concluded that if the research information promoted the ideological interests of the policymakers or could advance the career of a staffer within the policymaking organization, then its probability of influencing the policymaking process was enhanced. These and findings from other research have helped debunk the "classic" or "rational" model of knowledge effects, or the idea that policymakers will make decisions based upon knowledge that social scientists create (see Chapter 1).[60]

---

[58]Robert F. Rich, *Social Science Information and Public Policy Making* (New Brunswick, NJ: Transaction Publishers, 2002), from the back cover.

[59]Kenneth Prewitt, "Foreword," pp. xxxvii-xli in Robert F. Rich, *Social Science Information and Public Policy Making* (New Brunswick, NJ: Transaction Publishers, 2002), p. xxxix.

[60]A good example was President George W. Bush's refusal to recognize research on effects of pollution on global warming and sign the Kyoto Protocol.

RESEARCH VS. SOCIAL MOVEMENTS

The plenary clarified the debate over the impact of scholarship on public policy, and it showed that social science has impacts on public policy. However, the plenary failed to put to rest concerns that social science research's impact is far less than what it could or should be. The feedback after the plenary reinforced this conclusion. Many scholars conceded that social scientists can play a key role in identifying or legitimating social problems. Some mentioned, for example, the progress that has been made in reducing racial discrimination.

But other scholars pointed out that most of the credit for ameliorating social problems (e.g., race, sex, age discrimination) goes not to the social scientists who study them but to social activists like Jesse Jackson and to social movements like the National Association for the Advancement of Colored People — people and organizations that play an active role in the policymaking process.[61] Although social movements can and do draw upon social science research to support their arguments, none of the plenary scholars could identify a clear example of social science research playing the lead role in the political process or in resolving a social problem. In fact, years later, when four media historians on a panel that was examining media coverage of racism from the 1930s to the 1950s were asked whether they had found any evidence of professors playing a significant role in the civil rights struggles at that time — none had.[62]

The best defense of social science mustered came from mass communication scholar Steven Chaffee, who was a member of the first plenary in 1997 and was now, in 2000, distinguished professor of communication at the University of California, Santa Barbara. After briefly tracing the history of violence in mass media in an e-mail, he wrote:

---

[61]See, e.g., Marco Giugni, Doug McAdam and Charles Tilly (eds.), *How Social Movements Matter* (Minneapolis: University of Minnesota Press, 1999) and T. K. Oommen, *Protest and Change: Studies in Social Movements* (New Delhi: Sage, 1990).

[62]One sociologist who clearly did have some impact, however, was W. E. B. Du Bois. However, he became disillusioned with the pace of change in the United States and moved to Africa, where he died a short time later. See Chapter 8 for details.

[A]t least the research findings on effects of media violence are not being dismissed as the work of a small claque of goody-goodies. They are given wide credence in our society. I notice that a lot of high school kids believe that TV violence is bad for them and for their peers and siblings. If norms must underlie policy shifts, as a lot of social scientists argue, this is an area of success to me. I could go into this at much greater length. But my point is that ... we tend to underestimate the influence of our research because we look for dramatic and controversial policy pronouncements from on high. If we look at how people conduct their life and work, we can often see the results of the research in action.[63]

Chaffee's point was echoed earlier by criminologist Joan Petersilia and Viswanath. Some impacts are conceptual, indirect. In fact, the field of policy studies has created two concepts to refer to the idea that the impact of social science research is either long-term or indirect. The first is called the "serendipity rationale," which is the idea that "at the time the research is done, the researchers have no idea how it might be used, but some day somebody finds something that can be applied somewhere." The second is the "enlightenment argument," or the idea that social science research does not lead directly to policy decisions but broadens the understanding of policymakers and therefore makes some positive contribution. Although the enlightenment argument is comforting to defenders of social science, Cornell University professor William Foote Whyte points out that "some works of fiction also offer enlightenment."[64] In fact, it might be argued that fiction books like *The Grapes of Wrath, Atlas Shrugged, Ulysses* and *Fahrenheit 451* have had more impact on society than most scholarly books.

---

[63]Personal e-mail from Steven Chaffee, October 13, 1999. Chaffee died in 2001.

[64]William Foote Whyte, "On the Uses of Social Science Research," *American Sociological Review, 51*: 555-563 (Augustin 1986), p. 555. I often tell my students that some of the greatest works in sociology are fiction, such as John Steinbeck's *The Grapes of Wrath* and Charles Dickens' *David Copperfield.* Both books resulted in legislative changes to protect laborers.

Naturally, it would be foolhardy not to argue that social scientific research has subtle impacts on public policy. As political scientist Erik Albæk notes:

> Scientifically generated knowledge constitutes an important, but on the whole unquantifiable part of the enormous store of knowledge which participants in the politico-administrative decision-making process apply to their practical tasks ... This makes the contribution of science to policy making both less tangible *and potentially more influential than is usually assumed.*[65] [emphasis added]

A good example of impact is University of Michigan professor Catharine MacKinnon's 1979 book *Sexual Harassment of Working Women.*[66] MacKinnon didn't discover the problem of sexual harassment, nor did she coin the term. But her book helped legitimize the problem and mobilize the women's movement to pressure government to develop rules and laws banning unwanted sexual advances in the workplace.[67] Many more examples of the impact of social scientific research also could be cited.[68]

As Glasser also pointed out, social scientists can impact the world through their teaching. Almost everyone who attends college can tell a story about a professor who played a positive role in their lives. Some scholars might argue that the social sciences can justify themselves solely upon this basis. The social sciences do not need to show, they could argue,

---

[65]Erick Albæk, "Between Knowledge and Power: Utilization of Social Science in Public Policy Making," *Policy Sciences, 28*: 79-100 (1995), p. 79.

[66]Catharine MacKinnon, *Sexual Harassment of Working Women* (New Haven, CT: Yale University Press, 1979).

[67]John Markert, *The Social Impact of Sexual Harassment: A Resource Manual for Organizations and Scholars* (Spokane, WA: Marquette Books, 2010).

[68]In 1966, James S. Coleman and several other scholars conducted a study of 150,000 K-12 students and found that school funding has little effect on student achievement. A student's (parental) socioeconomic status is much more important. The study suggested that teachers and educational philosophies have a limited capacity to improve student performance. James S. Coleman, *Equality of Educational Opportunity (Coleman) Study* (Ann Arbor, MI: Inter-university Consortium for Political and Social Research, 1966).

that the knowledge they produce is used to change the world in a way that people can easily see.

But would this argument appease taxpayers and policymakers? Would society be satisfied if a social science discipline argued that its research has serendipitous, enlightening or subtle impacts? These arguments might work for the humanities, which can justify themselves solely on the idea that a work of art or literature can bring pleasure or be inspirational. As British philosopher Craig Smith writes,

> Research in the humanities is highly useful in terms of promoting cultural richness and exploration of new ideas. It has independent academic and artistic merit. It is not necessary for academics in these fields to be overly depressed by the fact that they are not consulted by a government committee.[69]

However, the social sciences were specifically founded on the idea of solving real-world problems. Besides, if people can see how money, power and ideology play a direct role in policymaking, then why are they unable to see social scientific knowledge doing the same?

STAGE FRIGHT AND BETA BLOCKERS

Some critics of social science say the answer to that question is simple: Social scientists have isolated themselves too much from the real world. According to former history professor Carl Brauer,

> the vast majority of academics in traditional arts and science disciplines rarely venture forth to confront, enlighten, or change the world. Some academics are so used to talking only to each other that they do not know how to communicate with anyone else ... Scholars in the social

---

[69]However, Smith argues that the humanities should still become more involved with policymakers at least in part to get more research money for their fields. Craig Smith, "A Review of the British Academy Report, Punching Our Weight: The Humanities and Social Sciences in Public Policy Making," *Economic Affairs* (Institute for Economic Affairs, September 2009), pp. 95-97.

sciences and the humanities who stick to pure research can work without ... the distractions and interruptions that applying their efforts in the real world might entail. But monasticism does have its shortcomings. It contributes to excessively narrow specialization; it impedes teaching by making it too removed from the world most students hope to occupy; it denies the practical world the benefit of academic knowledge and thought; and it denies professors the benefit of having their work tested in the world of practice.[70]

A good example of ivory-tower isolation occurred in fall 2000, when the scholarly journal *Communication Education* published a special issue containing an extended debate between communication scholars representing opposing positions on the so-called "nature/nurture debate." On one side were communications scholars who contend that biology and genetics play a powerful role in explaining communication behaviors. On the other were scholars who favor cultural or social structural explanations. The latter group, by the way, represents the vast majority of scholars in the social sciences, and it has vigorously criticized those in the nature camp.[71]

Professor Joe Ayres, the editor of the journal, was himself an expert on communication apprehension (more commonly called stage fright) and was a cognitive or "social learning" theorist, meaning he was closer to the nurture camp. The goal of many communication apprehension scholars is to find ways to help people overcome or control their fears about communicating with others. They usually do this through training and "social learning" exercises. They focus on changing beliefs and emotions.

Ayres asked communication scholars James C. McCroskey and Michael J. Beatty to argue the communibiological position. He then gave that paper to Celeste M. Condit, who represented the cultural perspective. McCroskey and Beatty then responded, and so forth. The two positions produced a total of five essays. A third group of respondents wrote an essay about the impact of various treatment approaches.

---

[70]Carl Brauer, "More Scholars Should Venture Forth to Confront, Enlighten or Change the World," *The Chronicle of Higher Education* (March 14, 1990).

[71]Jan Sapp, *Genesis: The Evolution of Biology* (New York: Oxford University Press, 2003), p. 260.

In their first article, McCroskey and Beatty pointed out that social learning or cognitive approaches haven't worked well in terms of explaining communication behavior or in ameliorating such ailments as communication apprehension.

> When we advanced [in the late 1990s] what has come to be called the "communibiological paradigm," it was our intent to suggest an alternative perspective for communication theorists and researchers ... We raised serious questions concerning the usefulness of the social learning paradigm which has dominated thought in the communication literature for most of the 20th century. *We noted that theories advanced under this paradigm were supported by research which in most instances indicated that theories accounted for very little variance in human communication behavior.* As a result, we argued that an alternative perspective should be considered and that the one we advanced had a much higher probability of generating research accounting for substantially more variance, thus establishing more parsimonious and valid theories of human communication behavior.[72]
> [bracketed material and emphasis added]

McCroskey and Beatty maintained that "inborn, neurobiological structures are responsible for communication behavior and associated processes. As such, the influence of cultural, situational, or environmental stimuli are (sic) comparatively trivial."

Not true, responded Celeste M. Condit, the cultural theorist whom Ayres selected as the respondent:

> There is certainly room for the study of ... individual differences in communication, and there is room in that study for a consideration of biological inputs, but neither individual difference nor biological components provide a broad enough basis for a paradigm for the discipline of communication. A robust paradigm for communication study can not seek to reduce all variables to one type of variable, but

---

[72]James C. McCroskey and Michael J. Beatty, "The Communibiological Perspective: Implications for Communication in Instruction," *Communication Education, 49*(10): 1-6 (January 2000), p. 2.

rather must devise ways of incorporating variables that operate in radically different ways.[73]

She added: "I am not particularly sanguine about our efforts to achieve that goal, given the complexity of the task, the scarcity of our resources, and our tendency to see scholarship as a threat to good teaching."

In the third article, McCroskey and Beatty charged that some of Condit's remarks were "seriously flawed." She then responded, in a fourth article, that "it is distressing ... to see genetics introduced to the communication discipline with precisely such a combination of narrow determinism and pernicious social policy." In a fifth article, McCroskey and Beatty countered that Condit "further misrepresents our position and our claims."[74]

A sixth article, written by two other scholars in the field, examined, among other things, possible treatment options for ailments like communication apprehension.[75] They included systemic desensitization, cognitive therapies, and skills training. The authors conclude that "all of the major treatment approaches may have some utility in alleviating communication anxiety, even if the communibiological theory is adopted."[76]

The final article didn't question the value of various treatment programs. Oddly, though, none of the scholars involved in the debated mentioned one of the most effective treatments ever discovered for intermittent bouts of communication apprehension: beta blockers, a class of drugs that are commonly used to treat high blood pressure. Medical research shows that beta blockers are very effective in reducing anxiety

---

[73]Celeste Michelle Condit, "Culture and Biology in Human Communication: Toward a Multi-causal Model," *Communication Education, 49*(1): 7-24 (January 2000), p. 23.

[74]By the way, debates like this are also common in the natural sciences, but the level of discord is much greater in the social sciences because the subject matter (human behavior) is far more complex and more difficult to explain or predict.

[75]Lynne Kelly and James A. Keaten, "Treating Communication Anxiety," *Communication Education, 49*(1): 45-57 (January 2000).

[76]*Ibid.*, p. 52.

(butterflies in the stomach) in many people.[77] A search on the World Wide Web also reveals that musicians have been using beta blockers for decades to relieve anxiety before a public performance. Beta blockers sometimes are even referred to as the "musician's underground drug."[78]

One interesting aspect of beta blockers is that they work whether the cause of anxiety is psychological, biological, social or cultural. Beta blockers slow the flow of nerve impulses to the heart. They do that by restricting the flow of adrenaline. Research on beta blockers seemed to be powerful ammunition for the communibiological approach, but a more important issue for the debate on the impact of social science is how a prominent group of scholars could wage an extended debate about the nature-versus-nurture and fail to mention beta blockers as an effective treatment, or possibly the most effective treatment short of total personality change.

Critics might argue that cognitive researchers refuse to acknowledge beta blockers because they diminish the importance of cognitive research. But another explanation, some would argue, is that the entire field has become too disconnected from the real world. With increasing specialization in an academic discipline, the potential universe of explanations for a phenomenon shrinks. "People only see what they are

---

[77]By 2005, only a handful of scholars had studied the use of beta blockers, and most of them were focused on the question of whether musical or singing performance was enhanced. The findings generally showed that performance was enhanced under some conditions and those taking the medication reported less anxiety. See Klaus A. Neftel, Rolf H. Adler, Louis Kappeli, Mario Rossi, Martin Dolder, Hans E. Kaser, Heinz H. Bruggesser, and Helmut Vorkauf, "Stage Fright in Musicians: A Model Illustrating the Use of Beta Blockers." *Psychosomatic Medicine, 44*(5): 461-469 (1982); C. O. Brantigan, T. A. Brantigan and N. Joseph, "Effect of Beta Blockade and Beta Stimulation on Stage Fright," *American Journal of Medicine, 72*(1): 88-94 (January 1982); and G. A. Gates, J. Saegert, N. Wilson, L. Johnson, A. Shepherd , and E. M. Hearne 3rd, "Effect of Beta Blockade on Singing Performance," *Ann Otol Rhinol Laryngol, 94*(6): 570-574 (November/December 1985). Beta blockers also have been effective in reducing text-taking anxiety and boosting test scores. See H. C. Faigel, "The Effect of Beta Blockade on Stress-Induced Cognitive Dysfunction in Adolescents," *Clinical Pediatrician, 30*(7): 441-445 (July 1991).

[78]See <www.ethanwiner.com/BetaBlox.html>. The Federal Drug Administration has approved the use of beta blockers for treatment for heart attacks, heart failure, high blood pressure, and other ailments, but it has never approved the usage of beta blockers for stage fright or communication apprehension.

prepared to see," as Ralph Waldo Emerson once said.

Beyond the finding that beta blockers are an effective treatment, it is worth noting that some of the most potent or effective results to emerge in research have occurred at the intersection of biology and the medical and social sciences. Antidepressant medication is the quintessential example. It has been very effective in helping people who suffer from depression and anxiety. Although culture and social structure may be the source or cause of much depression, the ailment itself may be successfully treated, at least in part, with various medications. This doesn't mean culture or social structure should be ignored when addressing the social causes of depression, but an overemphasis on these factors to the exclusion of others can clearly inhibit progress in the social sciences.

FAILURES AND EXPLANATIONS

This book maintains that critical humanist and mainstream mass communication research both have generated a great deal of knowledge useful to the policymaking process. Research has shown, among other things, that violent content on television can lead to increased aggression among some children; news media produce content that generally promotes the interests and values of government and private business elites and their institutions, often to the detriment of minority or disadvantaged groups or the general public; advertising images of thin models can contribute to inaccurate self-perceptions among young women and to adverse health consequences[79]; and mass media can, on occasion, produce content critical

---

[79]R. F. Fox, *Harvesting Minds: How TV Commercials Control Kids* (Westport, CT: Praeger Publishing, 1996); L. Dittrick, "About-Face facts on BODY IMAGE," About-Face website, available online at <http://about-face.org/r/facts/bi.shtml>; "Magazine Models Impact Girls' Desire to Lose Weight," American Academy of Pediatrics (1999); P. Hamburg, "The Media and Eating Disorders: Who Is Most Vulnerable?" (Public Forum: Culture, Media and Eating Disorders, Harvard Medical School, 1998); and C. Maynard, "Body Image," *Current Health, 2* (1998).

of the powerful elites and institutions, which can lead to social change that benefits disadvantaged groups.[80]

But the weight of the anecdotal and secondary research clearly shows that many of these findings and others are not being given due consideration in the policymaking process. As noted earlier, part of the blame can be attributed to the structure of America's political system. The First Amendment restricts government from banning many forms of content that some parent and religious groups deem offensive, including most forms of pornography and violence. Some blame also can be passed on to policymakers themselves, who often ignore scholarly research and follow the ideological dictates of their political parties and business interests.[81] Only when research benefits the interests of the policymaker or bureaucrat is it likely to receive attention in the policymaking process. And part of the blame can be assigned to university administrators, who create reward systems that discourage faculty involvement in policymaking decisions.[82]

But mass communication scholars also must shoulder a fair amount of responsibility for the political impotency of their research. Many have refused to get involved in policymaking because it is too much extra work or because they believe it will adversely affect the objectivity of research. Some believe they have no moral obligation to make sure that knowledge is used for good purposes. Policymakers are supposed to play that role. But what many fail to understand is that a decision not to get involved IS a political decision, and it has a built-in bias, one that lends support to the status quo. Failing to get involved often means that partisan politics rather than knowledge becomes the basis for public policy.

---

[80]David Demers, "Corporate News Structure, Social Control and Social Change," pp. 375-398 in David Demers and K. Viswanath (eds.), *Mass Media, Social Control, and Social Change: A Macrosocial Perspective* (Ames: Iowa State University Press, 1999).

[81]The decisions of the Federal Communications Commission, for example, are often split along party lines (the sitting president and/or his political party can select three of the five members; the other two go to the other party).

[82]One mass communication scholar at a research university was punished in annual reviews because he redirected his program of research to include a desire to influence citizens, undergraduate students and policymakers.

Mainstream and critical scholars, too, are guilty of failing to do enough. This is particularly disturbing with respect to the latter group, whose philosophical mantra allegedly includes the idea that ordinary people should be part of the process of reforming (or overthrowing) capitalism and its penchant for exploitation. In their defense, critical scholars sometimes argue that mass media and political and economic elites have subverted their attempts to make people aware of the problems of capitalism. Certainly the media and political and economic elites are not very receptive to ideas that draw on neo-Marxist theories. But there are other possible explanations for the failure of critical scholarship to secure a widespread acceptance among the public.

One simply may be that capitalism has succeeded in making people happy. Although the "robber barons" of the late 19th century clearly exploited the workers, capitalism eventually accommodated labor unions, created a middle class whose material needs were well met, and supported other social institutions (churches, schools, volunteer organizations, neighborhood groups) that met people's spiritual and emotional needs. In other words, the adaptive capacity of modern capitalism — not ideology — may better explain why critical theorists have failed to convince people that they are being manipulated or exploited.

But there may be another, even more pragmatic reason for the inability of critical scholars to mobilize the citizenry behind their cause: poor communication. The vast majority of critical scholars, with the notable exceptions of Noam Chomsky and Robert McChesney, are not actively seeking support for their cause. Most of their scholarship is written for scholars, not for ordinary people. In this respect, they share a lot of common ground with mainstream social scientists: they publish mostly in academic journals. Their primary concern is getting tenure, promotion and raises, not solving social problems.

CHAPTER 7

IMPACT OF OTHER
SOCIAL SCIENCE DISCIPLINES

"**M**en have more physical strength than women, but women have more stamina, because they bear the children and perpetuate the species."

That comment by Margaret Mead in November 1977 drew cheers and applause from the 300 students and faculty at Oakland University in Rochester, Michigan. They were there to hear the world's most famous anthropologist and social scientist talk about culture and society and about the roles that women and men play in different societies.

At the time, Mead was one of the few social scientists known to the general public. She was a "woman's libber," as people used to say back then. The foundation of her reputation was her 1928 book, *Coming of Age in Samoa*.[1] The book presented the results of a research project in which she attempted to determine whether adolescents in a traditional culture also have a difficult time making the adjustment from childhood to adulthood, as was the case for many youths in America and other Western nations. As Mead put it: "I have tried to answer the question which sent me to Samoa: Are the disturbances which vex our adolescents due to the nature of adolescence itself or to the civilization? Under different conditions does adolescence present a different picture?"[2]

---

[1]Margaret Mead, *Coming of Age in Samoa: A Psychological Study of Primitive Youth for Western Civilisation* (New York: W. Murrow and Company, 1928).

[2]*Ibid.*, p. 11.

Margaret Mead, circa 1940 *(Photograph by Edward Lynch, New York World-Telegram.*
Photo in the public domain. Source: Library of Congress Prints and Photographs Division,
New York World-Telegram and the Sun Newspaper Photograph Collection.)

To answer this question, she interviewed (through an interpreter) 68
young girls and women between the ages of 9 and 20 who lived in a village
of 600 people on the island of Ta'u. She concluded that the transition from
childhood to adulthood in Ta'u was smooth and not marked by emotional
or psychological distress, anxiety, or confusion as was the case in the
United States. The book stirred a controversy, however, when she reported
that Samoan women engaged in casual sex before marriage. Mead
advocated that women in America should also have the freedom to choose
casual sex, a position that made her a central figure in the women's
movement of the 1960s, even though she didn't like the label "feminist."

Mead died several months after her appearance at Oakland University.
Five years later, in 1983, another anthropologist, Derek Freeman,
challenged the findings in Mead's book. Freeman spent four years of field

experience in Samoa, during which time he also interviewed some of Mead's surviving informants. In *The Making and Unmaking of an Anthropological Myth*, Freeman asserted that the women lied to Mead, and they told him that they did not have casual sex as young women.[3] Freeman said virginity was highly valued in Samoan culture, even though it was only required of women of high social rank. Freeman's book touched off a firestorm of controversy in the field, and to this day anthropologists still are unable to determine whose research is more accurate.

As noted throughout this book, disputes like this are very common in the social sciences. According to some critical scholars, they are evidence that the social sciences are incapable of generating knowledge and truth. However, even if Mead's study was flawed, anthropologists widely agree that Mead helped expand rights for women and knowledge to the field of anthropology. Her greatest legacy to the field was showing that human behavior is driven more by culture than biology. She had an impact.

But is she an anomaly in the field of anthropology, or in the social sciences in general? Are some social science disciplines more successful than others when it comes to the impact of their research? If so, what accounts for that?

THE McCALL-WEBER PROJECT

Answering these questions is not easy. One big problem is how to define a social problem itself. Poverty, for example, can be defined as a social, political or economic problem, or any combination thereof. Researchers from many different disciplines are studying the problem from different perspectives. However, even though problems are often interdisciplinary, policymaking processes are often segmented. When unemployment is raised as an issue, for example, the economists are often called in to testify before state and national governmental committees, while other social

---

[3]Derek Freeman, *Margaret Mead and Samoa: The Making and Unmaking of an Anthropological Myth* (Cambridge, MA: Harvard University Press, 1983).

scientists who study the impact of unemployment on divorce and crime rates (e.g., sociologists) are left on the sidelines.

In an ideal world, every social science discipline would devote a fair amount of resources to investigate how much impact it is having on public policy and on solving social problems. Self-evaluation should be institutionalized, some scholars would maintain. But this doesn't exist, now or in the past. Sociologists George J. McCall and George H. Weber were well aware of the lack of self-evaluation when in 1982 they undertook a study of the impact of social science. To get around that problem, they asked top scholars from six social sciences — anthropology, history, psychology, sociology, economics and political science — to evaluate the relationship between research and problem solving in their respective fields. The articles were prepared for a symposium conducted at the University of Missouri-St. Louis and published in a book.[4] Although somewhat dated, most of the issues and empirical data presented in the book are still relevant today.[5] In the Preface, the editors open with a statement that buttresses the findings of many other policy studies:

> We learned, first of all, how commonly and how deeply it is felt that the social science disciplines have the most to offer to policy studies [policymaking] but, for a variety of reasons, have actually contributed relatively little.[6] [bracketed material added for clarification]

---

[4]George J. McCall and George H. Weber, *Social Science and Public Policy: The Roles of Academic Disciplines in Policy Analysis* (Port Washington, NY: Associated Faculty Press, 1984).

[5]To the best of my knowledge, the McCall and Weber book is the only literature in the market that has attempted to assess the impact of the social sciences across a wide range of disciplines.

[6]The editors cited these works to back up their statement: Yehezkel Dror, *Design for Policy Sciences* (New York: Elsevier, 1971); Carol H. Weiss (ed.), *Using Social Research in Public Policy Making* (Lexington, MA: Lexington Books, 1977); Laurence E. Lynn (ed.), *Knowledge and Policy: The Uncertain Connection* (Washington, D.C.: National Academy of Science, 1978); Charles E. Lindblom and David K. Cohen, *Usable Knowledge: Social Science and Social Problem Solving* (New Haven: Yale University Press, 1979); Robert A. Scott and Arnold R. Shore, *Why Sociology Does not Apply: A Study of the Use of Sociology in the Public Policy* (New York: Elsevier, 1979); and Martin Bulmer, *The Uses of Social Research: Social Investigation in Public Policy-Making* (London: Allen & Unwin, 1982).

In the first chapter, McCall elaborated on the gap between what social science has to offer and what it is actually contributing. He pointed out that the "social science movement, and the social forces which underlay its emergence, have profoundly affected modern conceptions of the social world." For one, the movement's core concern with social welfare created a social institution that people now routinely refer to as "welfare state," or the idea that government is at least partly responsible for the well-being of its citizens. This movement has also given rise to the field of policy studies, which focuses on "the scientific improvement of public policymaking."[7] The logic is that scientific knowledge is a more reliable guide for public policy than the "vagaries and corruptions of practical politics." However, he adds:

> Viewed from such a policy-sciences perspective, social science research has so far had precious little effect on public policy making, particularly at the national level ... Policy-sciences spokesmen find that a very large proportion of applied social science studies fail to derive any policy action implications whatsoever. Furthermore, these spokesmen find the few purported cases of national policy input to have been more illusory than real.[8]

There are three major reasons for this, according to McCall. First, policy recommendations from social scientists, such as presidential commissions, are rarely enacted into policy. Second, policymakers usually reject the recommendations as impractical or politically infeasible. And third, even when social science research is said to influence public policy, the research usually supported decisions arrived at on other grounds.

Nevertheless, McCall pointed out that social science can influence public policy in a number of more subtle ways, including what he calls "social reporting" (or what others would call "enlightenment" or "conceptual" use of information). This is the notion that social science

---

[7]George J. McCall, "Social Science and Social Problem Solving: An Analytic Introduction," pp. 3-18 in George J. McCall and George H. Weber, *Social Science and Public Policy: The Roles of Academic Disciplines in Policy Analysis* (Port Washington, NY: Associated Faculty Press, 1984), p. 5.

[8]*Ibid.*, p. 6.

HOW RESEARCH CAN AFFECT POLICY

Policy studies researchers have identified three different ways that social science can be used in policymaking.

The first is called the "direct problem solving model," which, as the label suggests, means that empirical research findings have a direct bearing upon specific policy issues. An example would be a decision by policymakers — after hearing the research evidence about violent programming — to pass a law that restricts violent programming to hours after 9 p.m. This is called an "instrumental use" of research, and, as pointed out in Chapter 1, this is the classic model of how social science is supposed to work. Policy researchers often point out that it is difficult to find examples of immediate and direct effects.

The "symbolic model" involves using empirical results, sometimes out of context, to support a pre-determined position held by a policymaker or to justify other decisions that have been made for other reasons. An example here would be an action that attributes increasing crime rates to increased levels of violence on television, even though the research only documented the crime went up, not the causes of it. Interestingly, social scientists who are knowledgeable in a particular area of research often recognize the symbolic model when they hear or read about politicians who quote research out of context or select only those findings that support their ideological position. This is a great source of irritation to social scientists, but even those who proactively protest such incidents (e.g., letters to the editor) are rarely able to change the practice or affect the outcome of a policy debate.

The "enlightenment" or "conceptual" model holds that social science research doesn't necessarily have a direct impact on policymaking, but, rather, that it influences the way policymakers think about problems. An example here is when media researchers recommend that good parenting and good communication are necessary to help minimize the impact of television violence on children. The enlightenment model often means that effects cannot be readily measured or seen. It can take decades or longer for such effects to be perceived.

provides precise (or more precise) information or facts about a particular problem, and policymakers can then use that information in the decision-making process. British political scientist Patrick Dunleavy also argues that regardless of whether social research has a direct and immediate influence on policy, all social science research contributes to what he calls a "dynamic knowledge inventory," which sparks healthy debates about social problems.[9] Of course, even though social science might add precision to the understanding of problems, other social scientists point out that this doesn't guarantee good decision-making, especially because ideology often trumps knowledge.

Other contributors to the McCall and Weber book reached similar conclusions. All of them pointed out that research in their fields has had some impact on public policy, but the amount of impact was often negligible and much less than it could or should be. The articles, which are described briefly below along with citations to more recent research, also showed that each of the disciplines has unique ways of defining the problems as well as solutions.

Anthropology

In the field of anthropology, Joe R. Harding and J. Michael Livesay point out that several scholars during the 19th century compiled histories of Native American tribes with the hope that policymakers in Washington, D.C., would develop a more objective national policy toward Native Americans.[10] The scholars included Henry Schoolcraft, who published a six-volume history of American Indians between 1852 and 1857; James Mooney, who wrote about the "The Ghost Dance Religion and the Sioux

---

[9]His comments were made at the April 23-24, 2009, conference at the London School of Economics and Political Science, which was titled, "Informing Public Policy: New Agendas for Social Research.," retrieved December 3, 2010, from <http://www.promarta.co.uk/ipp>.

[10]Joe R. Harding and J. Michael Livesay, "Anthropology and Public Policy," pp. 51-90 in George J. McCall and George H. Weber, *Social Science and Public Policy: The Roles of Academic Disciplines in Policy Analysis* (Port Washington, NY: Associated Faculty Press, 1984), p. 52-53.

Outbreak of 1890" and mostly blamed the military and Indian service for confrontations between Indians and the military; John Wesley Powell, who created The Bureau of American Ethnology (BAE) in 1879 to help the government develop policies to deal with Indian-white conflict; and Franz Boas, who in the early 1900s attacked genetic superiority beliefs and with his students attempted to reconstruct American Indian lifestyles prior to Westward expansion. However, Harding and Livesay maintain that policymakers ignored most of this research because it wasn't concerned with assimilating and acculturating Native Americans, which was, at the time, the dominant political paradigm of Washington bureaucrats. Harding and Livesay also point out that most of the work of Boas and the other early anthropologists was devoted to abstract anthropology rather than to applied science.

President Franklin D. Roosevelt's New Deal brought many anthropologists into the employ of the federal government during the 1930s. One major success of this period was the development of self-governance organizations for certain Native American tribes. However, although special purpose policy research units conducted 75 studies related to the welfare of Native Americans from 1936 to 1946, the units "had little impact on policy for a variety of scheduling, administrative, and personal ideological reasons."[11]

While the period before World War II "saw a dramatic expansion into new topical areas, the role of the applied anthropologist remains quite limited in scope," writes John van Willigen, who compiled a bibliography of the development of applied anthropology.[12] "The typical applied anthropologist of this period works as a research or training consultant in government on private sector development activities. They rarely activated a central role in decision making."

Harding and Livesay point out that the government hired many anthropologists during World War II and the studies they produced "were partially responsible for the success of postwar policies in Japan. However,

---

[11]*Ibid.*, p. 56.

[12]John van Willigen, *Anthropology in Use: A Bibliographic Chronology of the Development of Applied Anthropology* (New York: Redgrave Publishing Co., 1980), p.5.

after the war, public policy activities dramatically declined in the 1950s and 1960s as anthropologists flocked to the universities, which offered research grants and tenure jobs. Anthropologists also became disenchanted because their skills were being used to implement government policy as opposed to protecting "native" people from abuse at the hands of various governments, including the United States (e.g., Southeast Asia and Vietnam). By 1973, only 55 anthropologists were employed by the U.S. government.

Anthropologists during the 1960s and 1970s were conducting a great deal of research. Some of it found its way into programs that sought to ameliorate social problems. These included the Peace Corp, VISTA, Job Corps, Headstart and the Fox Project (action program for American Indian community). However, most of the research was influenced by academic, not real-world, concerns. "Much of the research could have been utilized by policymakers, but little of it reached appropriate destinations," Harding and Livesay conclude.

A decade after the McCall and Weber book was published, Merrill Eisenberg, a consultant in program planning and evaluation, pointed out that good research, and presenting it in a comprehensible way, is not enough to influence the policymaking process. Anthropologists must also understand the political context and policy culture surrounding a project. Merrill argues that anthropologists must use their skills and knowledge to change the behavior of not only the intended beneficiaries of policies, but also the policymakers themselves.[13]

Most contemporary anthropologists now recognize, like other social scientists, that the classic model of policymaking (see Chapter 1) does not reflect the real-world policymaking process. Today there also is a greater focus on examining the role of power in the policy arena. Anthropologist Janine R. Wedel and her colleagues encourage others to focus more on how policies "actively create new categories of individuals to be governed."[14]

---

[13]Merrill Eisenberg, "Translating Research into Policy: What More Does It Take?" *Practicing Anthropology, 16*(4): 35-38 (1994).

[14]Janine R. Wedel, Cris Shore, Gregory Feldman, and Stacy Lathrop, "Toward an Anthropology of Public Policy," *The Annals of the American Academy of Political and Social Science, 600:* 30-51 (July 2005), p. 30.

Sociology

Sociologist Albert J. Reiss offered a mixed view of the impact of sociology on public policy.[15] He pointed out that "few sociologists in the United States have served in major advisory or administrative positions to government leaders in the United States; even fewer have occupied major positions of governmental power."[16] But he added that sociologists have played some administrative or research roles in some government agencies and a fair number have served on presidential commissions and various government task forces.[17] The contributions of these sociologists tend to be limited to two major areas — crime and population problems — because these fields are more strongly linked to policy and practice.

For example, he noted that in the 1940s criminologists E. W. Burgess and Clark Tibbitts created a scale of items for estimating the probability of recidivism for parolees.[18] That predictive device helped parole boards in Illinois select inmates for parole. The Illinois Parole Board even created the post of Sociologist-Actuary within the parole system. The "predictive tables" idea later was extended to juvenile delinquency studies, but criminologists were never able to come up with highly accurate measures. Instead, as pointed out in Chapter 5, policymakers in many states

---

[15]Albert J. Reiss, Jr., "Sociology and Public Policy," pp 19-50 in George J. McCall and George H. Weber, *Social Science and Public Policy: The Roles of Academic Disciplines in Policy Analysis* (Port Washington, NY: Associated Faculty Press, 1984).

[16]*Ibid.*, p. 27.

[17]They include: Commission on Obscenity and Pornography, National Commission on the Causes and Prevention of Violence, Commission on Population Growth and the American Future, Commission on the Accident at Three-Mile Island, Task Force on Assessment of the Nature and Scope of Crime for the President's Commission on Law Enforcement and Administration of Justice, National Institute of Mental Health, National Institute of Education, National Institutes of Child Health and Development, National Advisory Committee on Juvenile Justice and Delinquency Prevention, Bureau of Justice Statistics, National Institute of Justice of the U.S. Department of Justice, and the National Bureau of Prisons.

[18]E. W. Burgess, "Factors Determining Success or Failure on Parole," pp. 205-249 in Andrew A. Bruce et al., (eds.), *The Workings of Indeterminate Sentencing Law and the Parole System in Illinois* (Springfield, IL: Parole Board of Illinois, 1928) and Clark Tibbitts, "Success and Failure on Parole Can Be Predicted," *Journal of Criminal Law and Criminology, 20*: 405-413 (1923).

circumvented the issue in the 1990s and enacted three-strikes-your-out laws.

Although not mentioned by Reiss, agricultural extension programs during the 20th century were good examples of sociology's impact on policy and on solving social problems. The Morrill Act of 1862 established land-grant universities for the purpose of educating citizens in agriculture, home economics, mechanical arts, and other practical professions.[19] The Smith-Lever Act of 1914 formalized extension programs by establishing a partnership between the agricultural colleges and the U.S. Department of Agriculture. These programs were highly visible in communities (many counties had their own "extension agents"), but as the numbers of people living in agricultural areas declined, so did the programs themselves. At one point in time, the rural sociology unit at the University of Minnesota had more than two dozen agents and scholars working in an applied capacity. That unit was closed in the early 2000s.

Although other examples could be cited to show how sociology and its subfields (e.g., criminology, social work) have been involved in public policy issues,[20] Reiss implies that the field as a whole is not structurally organized to maximize that involvement. He points out that none of the major theories in sociology at the time was policy-oriented, an observation that remains true today. Part of this, he said, may stem from the fact that many sociologists believed a policy orientation could impinge upon the objectivity of social science research. They were worried that political pressures could bias the research. Sociologists do conduct a great deal of research on social problems, but "they do not generally do applied research," Reiss writes. Instead, their efforts in the policy area usually involve evaluating and assessing policy models (evaluation research). "Sociologists are more likely to debunk than to create or inform policies and policy-based research; to seek to expose the vulnerabilities of polices and their practices than to buttress them."[21] This, of course, can be viewed

---

[19]A brief history of extension services is provided at the U.S. Department of Agriculture website <http://www.csrees.usda.gov/qlinks/extension.html>.

[20]See Chapter 3 in this book.

[21]Reiss, "Sociology and Public Policy," p. 24.

as an impact. But critics point out that this "negative impact" — absent concomitant recommendations for ameliorating social problems — is hardly sufficient for legitimizing a field of study.

Reiss also notes that sociological analyses have concluded that bureaucracies resist change and tend to reproduce policies that support the status quo. Bureaucracies often don't want to change because they usually benefit from the existing social order. Reiss concludes that sociology has less to offer in the public policy arena than other social science disciplines, because sociologists themselves have failed to develop explanatory models to help policymakers do their job. Instead, sociologists often criticize the power structure.

> The kind of sociology that has emerged over the decades emphasized the limiting conditions of organized systems, their recalcitrance to change, and the inconsequential effects of short-run changes. These models and their test discourage managers and policymakers whose job it is to develop and implement policies. That is not to say that they are of no utility to them, but their utility lies primarily in excusing failure rather than in shaping a course of change or in adapting to changing conditions.[22]

Reiss' criticism received moral support in 1993, when Sage published a book titled, *Sociology and the Public Agenda* and edited by former American Sociological Association president William Julius Wilson.[23] The volume points out that pushing for social change was a central value of the field but now has become only a minor part of the sociological agenda. Wilson contends that sociology's "ostrich-like stance" threatens the relevancy of the discipline in society and compromises the support given to the field by policymakers, donors or grant-makers, and the public. Wilson urges sociologists to become more attuned to the public agenda and work to influence public policy through both short- and long-range studies.

---

[22]*Ibid.*, p. 43.
[23]William Julius Wilson (ed.), *Sociology and the Public Agenda* (Newbury Park, CA: Sage, 1993).

There is no evidence to suggest that sociology has heeded Wilson's advice. In fact, some sociologists are even predicting the demise of sociology in the near future. Enrollments have dropped substantially since the 1970s; specialization has fragmented the field, according to some scholars; grants for research have dried up; and sociology has no overarching theory and set of concepts to keep it unified.[24]

History

All of the social science disciplines have disagreements within them about the extent to which the discipline itself can be called a science. But history leads the pack in this controversy. History is usually classified more as a humanity than a social science. Nevertheless, whether viewed as one of the humanities or one of the social sciences, historians have often played a role in public policy analysis, albeit one that is somewhat different from its empirical cousins. Peter N. Stearns clarifies:

> History in any rigorous sense — as opposed to bits and pieces, even chunks, of historical data that are used in policy analysis derived from a different disciplinary base — most commonly services to set a background to policy analysis. It provides the framework, helps define the ingredients of the problem, but does not really enter into policy research directly.[25]

The most obvious and numerous examples are histories of individuals and institutions associated with policymaking at a national, state or local level. At the national level, almost every major federal agency has one or more histories of itself. These are used to influence public opinion, orient an employee, or legitimize the institution itself. A second example is the historian who is employed by government. Perhaps the most famous

---

[24]Nazrul Islam, "Sociology in the 21st Century: Facing a Dead End," *Bangladesh e-Journal of Sociology, 1*(2): 1-8 (July 2004).

[25]Peter N. Stearns, "History and Public Policy," pp. 91-128 in George J. McCall and George H. Weber, *Social Science and Public Policy: The Roles of Academic Disciplines in Policy Analysis* (Port Washington, NY: Associated Faculty Press, 1984), p. 100.

example is Arthur Meier Schlesinger Jr., a
Pulitzer Prize recipient and "court historian"
to President John F. Kennedy from 1961 to
1963. Schlesinger wrote a detailed history of
the Kennedy administration as well as a
biography of Sen. Robert Kennedy. These
and other books he wrote influenced many
people in and out of government. A third
example is the history that is written to trace
the evolution of a policy decision, which in
turn is designed to provide guidance for
future policy decisions. Presidential
Commissions often draw upon such
historians for making their recommendations.

Arthur M. Schlesinger Jr.,
President Kennedy's historian
*(Public domain photo taken in
early 1960s by the U.S.
Information Service)*

A fourth category might be added here,
one that would include histories which become even more important that
the content or substance within them. Case in point: the infamous "History
of the U.S. Decision-Making Process on Viet Nam Policy," better known
as a "Pentagon Papers" — a government-funded research report which
revealed that the U.S. government frequently lied to the American people
about its role in Vietnam and that the U.S. government deliberately
provoked the North Vietnamese to attack a U.S. ship in order to justify
more U.S. military involvement. *The New York Times* published the first
installment in June 1971. The Nixon Administration responded with a
lawsuit that culminated in a U.S. Supreme Court decision establishing the
principle that the government has the burden of proof when trying to
prohibit publication of so-called "secret intelligence." This example
illustrates that historical research, or all research for that matter, can have
unintended consequences, and that assessing the impact of research can be
far more complex than either direct or conceptual effects.

Stearns argues that although history rarely plays a direct role in policy
making, there is one important exception: military policy.

The basic approach involves use of analogies from the past, on the basic
assumption that history is a relevant laboratory for discovering and,

though historical evaluation, testing strategies that may usefully guide policy decisions in the future. The approach is applied particularly to battle strategy itself, but has extended to weapons evaluation, the miliary role in diplomacy and polices of military governance.[26]

Despite this exception, Stearns points out that "few policy institutions routinely employ historians as part of research teams — or, if they do, they typically limit the historical contribution by expectations of memorialist or background efforts ... Clearly, a lack of a track record, outside the military policy area, limits the assessment of applied history for all parties concerned." He adds that historians are often seen as generalists, as lacking expertise, and that even though they claim to be experts in social change, policy analysis has focused more on rational action or demographic changes than on complex theoretical models. Paradoxically, though, the production of "more elaborate models of change may continue to bedevil policy efforts." Policymakers have an aversion to complex theories and research. Moreover, applied historians tend to see policymakers as irrational at times, which sets up tension between the two groups.

Stearns points out that historical research has played a role in understanding real-world problems, like mental illness and stress caused by home or work-related environments.[27] Historians have a role to play in educating policymakers and the public, in providing background and context for policy issues, and for categorizing social change. "But it is obvious," he adds, "that these traditional features have not led history to a central policy role in recent years."[28]

Applied historians, in sum, have a job of selling to do, even while building on the important existing contracts between history and policy ... Their success will depend not only on their own efforts, but also on the willingness of policymakers to add to the existing disciplinary mix.[29]

---

[26]*Ibid.* p. 103.
[27]*Ibid.*, pp. 112-121.
[28]*Ibid.*, p. 121.
[29]*Ibid.*, p. 122.

Social Psychology

Some scholars argue that the field of psychology is not a social science, because it emphasizes the individual and often ignores social or historical factors in its theories and explanations and in treatment programs. They often accuse psychology of focusing so much on person-centered characteristics that it ends up "blaming the victim" for all of his or her problems.[30] When someone who has lost her job slips into clinical depression, the therapist often focuses on personality flaws or coping skills of the individual rather than social structure (e.g., a recession or a mean-spirited boss) as the source or cause of the problem. Some fields of study, like cognitive psychology, which examines the neurological or biological bases of human activity (e.g., measuring how human senses perceive external stimuli), completely ignore social or cultural influences. Psychologists N. Dickon Reppucci and Robert Harry Kirk argue that the "ahistorical, asocial individual focus has probably been a major factor in psychology's relatively minor role in public policy formation."[31] After all, they point out, to apply the principles of psychology to the real world, practitioners normally do not need the assistance of policymakers and do not need to change a policy or law; rather, they simply work directly with the individuals who are in need (e.g., therapy sessions).[32]

Nevertheless, criticism of psychology is muted by the fact that most psychologists would not deny that many individual problems have their

---

[30]A distinction is made here between psychology and psychiatry. The former is based largely on positivistically oriented research, while the latter stems from the work of Sigmund Freud and is much more humanists and impressionist in orientation. The discussion here applies only to the discipline of psychology.

[31]N. Dickon Reppucci and Robert Harry Kirk, "Psychology and Public Policy," pp. 129-158 in George J. McCall and George H. Weber, *Social Science and Public Policy: The Roles of Academic Disciplines in Policy Analysis* (Port Washington, NY: Associated Faculty Press, 1984), p. 131.

[32]For example, studies have reported that the psychological effects of spanking far outweigh its advantages as a means of correcting the behavior of children. Many parents who keep up with the news are aware of this and have made a conscious decision not to use corporal punishment as a method of discipline. A public policy was not needed to make such a change, even though many states now define physical punishment of children as a crime or improper behavior.

roots in social or environmental conditions. Reppucci and Kirk point out that psychologists, from time to time, have been involved in public policy issues, especially clinical, community, organizational and social psychologists. Instead, Reppucci and Kirk criticize the field for not doing more to influence public policy.

> [P]sychologists, as a group and as part of their training, have spent little, if any, time understanding, researching, and/or participating in the process of policy formation, implementation, and evaluation. Although there have been several calls for psychologists to do this, few have accepted the challenge.[33]

In 1969, American Psychological Association President George Miller called upon his colleagues to disseminate the knowledge they've created directly to the public. Six years later another president was again emphasizing that theme, implying, of course, that not enough had been done and that the discipline needed to do that partly for the continued viability of the discipline. However, one of the big problems, according to Reppucci and Kirk, was deciding what to disseminate and to whom. APA at the time had 42 different divisions, which alone "is often perplexing to policymakers at all levels who hope for answers rather than perspectives."

The first major contact between psychology and public policy occurred during World War I, when intelligence tests were used to classify recruits for various jobs. Psychologists later suggested applying these tests to immigration policy and the result was more restrictive practices toward Southeastern Europeans. Early psychologists failed to appreciate the role of social and cultural variables in terms of their effects on the tests. The government also called upon psychologists for assistance during World War II. Yale psychologist Carl Hovland conducted a number of studies in an attempt to understand the effects of military films designed to inform

---

[33] *Ibid.*

soldiers and motivate them to fight.[34] Clinical psychology also grew rapidly during the after the war.

However, psychologists did little to influence or change public policy in the years after the war. Reppucci and Kirk argue that this lack of concern stemmed from the fact that psychology had adopted the medical model, which focused mainly on "curing" the individual, not society. "What is missing from the strictly medical perspective of individual treatment of deficit," they write, "is consideration of the entire range of social variables and group interaction effects that constitute the domain of public health perspective, and indeed of public policy in general." Without this concern, policymakers easily accepted the "blaming the victim" approach and saw the solution as fixing the individual rather than as changing public policy.

Another factor contributing to psychology's lack of impact on public policy is the view among practitioners themselves that much of the research in the academy doesn't have any value to what they do. Reppucci and his colleague, Seymour B. Sarason, found many psychologists employed by human service institutions "largely avoiding research and action" from the academy, primarily because they operate under the "blaming the victim" medical model.[35] Moreover, some psychologists argue that psychological research isn't capable yet of even providing enough guidance to policymakers or to practitioners. Citing Charles A. Kiesler, Reppucci and Kirk write that "we lack 'techniques and methods of interacting that allow sciences to easily assert a consensual view of particular human problems and possible solutions.'"[36] Confounding the problem even more is the fact that some psychologists believe social problems are essentially intractable and cannot really be solved. As such, they believe it is erroneous to argue, for example, that the social sciences lost the "War on Poverty." Such problems cannot be solved "once and for all." Furthermore, although policymakers "expect direct policy guidance from social research ...

---

[34]Carl I. Hovland, Arthur A. Lumsdaine and Fred D. Sheffield, *Experiments on Mass Communication* (Princeton: Princeton University Press, 1949).

[35]Reppucci and Sarason, "Public Policy and Human Service Institutions."

[36]Charles A. Kiesler, "Psychology and Public Policy," in Leonard Bickman (ed.), *Applied Social Psychology Annual, Vol. 1* (Beverly Hills, CA: Sage, 1980), p. 57.

[which] ought to be convergent,"[37] social scientists research rarely is presented in a manner.

But amidst all of this confusion two things do seem to be clear. The first is that "psychologists have spent minimal effort in the exploration of the policy process," according to Reppucci and Kirk.[38] They add that psychologists do not understand that policymakers often have to balance many different concerns when making decisions that could be influenced by research, including interests of their constituents, social values and resources. And the second is that psychological research can provide significant insights for enhancing the understanding of social problems.

Marshall H. Segall argues that psychologists have three major roles to play in public policy: expert witness, policy evaluator, and social engineer.[39] The first role involves testifying or providing facts and knowledge to policymakers and others. Reppucci and Kirk point out that psychologists have been practicing this role for many years, but "it has been relatively rare until recently that psychologists have testified before legislative committees, and in courts, as other than an expert on a particular individual."[40] Segall's second role involves trying to help policymakers determine the effectiveness of various social programs. This is known in the business as "evaluation research." The third role, social engineer, involves the controlling the behavior of social actors. Reppucci points out that social engineering has been used in small scale projects but has not in a large-scale public program. Needless to say, this role is the most controversial, because it raises issues about authoritarian control over people.

University of Michigan psychology professor James S. Jackson suggests a fourth role: the psychologist as activist/collaborator. He argues

---

[37]For this quote, Reppucci and Kirk cite David K. Cohen and Janet A. Weiss, "Social Scientists and Decision Makers Look at the Usefulness of Mental Health Research," in Carol H. Weiss (ed.), *Using Social Research in Public Policy Making* (Lexington, MA: Heath, 1977), p. 68.

[38]Reppucci and Kirk, "Psychology and Public Policy," p. 140.

[39]Marshall H. Segall, *Human Behavior and Public Policy: A Political Psychology* (New York: Pergamon, 1976).

[40]*Ibid.*, p. 144.

that if psychologists believe they have "something to offer in terms of redressing societal ills and thus contributing to the positive mental health of the nation, then we should be willing to advocate solutions which are appropriate ... [and] ... be willing to utilize legal methods and procedures for influencing legislation affecting psychology and human welfare."[41] However, policymakers would be the ones to make the decisions.

Reppucci and Kirk report that the American Psychological Association also has become more involved in public policy issues since the 1960s. For example, they approved measures that condemned the Vietnam War, refused to hold conventions in states that did not adopt the Equal Rights Amendment, submitted *amicus curiae* (friend of the court) briefs in a lawsuit involving the commitment of juveniles to a training school, and promoted the right of clinical psychologists to have their own insurance reimbursement. "However," Reppucci and Kirk write, "even with the increased activity by APA and the very active role the AAP [Association for the Advancement of Psychology] has begun to play in its lobbying capacity, few psychologists have actually begun to engage in the activist/collaborator role or pursued a career as a policy administrator or legislative staff officer."[42] Citing Patrick H. DeLeon and his colleagues, they write: "Psychology has a long scientific history, but a short political one."[43]

Not much has changed since the 1980s. According to psychologists John F. Dovidio and Victoria M. Esses,

> [d]espite the substantial potential of psychology for enhancing the public's understanding of social issues, for addressing social problems, and for guiding public policy, *it is a promise that has not yet been significantly fulfilled.* Some of the barriers to communicating beyond

---

[41]James S. Jackson, "Promoting Human Welfare Through Legislative Advocacy: A Proper Role for the Science of Psychology," pp. xxx in Richard A. Kasschau and Frank S. Kessel (eds.), *Psychology and Society: In Search of Symbiosis* (New York: Holt, Rinehart & Winston, 1980).

[42]Reppucci and Kirk, "Psychology and Public Policy," p. 149.

[43]Patrick H. DeLeon, Anne Marie O'Keefe, Gary R. VandenBos, and Alan G. Kraut, "How to Influence Public Policy: A Blueprint for Activism," *American Psychologist, 27*: 476-485 (1982), p. 476.

the discipline that psychology faces are fundamental to the science itself, such as the use of the scientific method and inferential statistics, and are unlikely to change. Thus, psychologists need to find ways of strengthening their communications to nonscientists within these parameters to increase the influence of research findings on the public and public policy.[44]

Economics

When it comes to assessing the impact of social sciences on public policy, the field of economics has more visibility than its disciplinary cousins. Economists have more direct contact with policymakers and the world of policymaking than any other social science discipline. Governments, banks, corporations and private groups employ economists to address or solve a wide variety of economic problems and issues, and they also often monitor research and knowledge coming out of the academy. Yet, despite this impact, many scholars, policymakers and lay people often question the usefulness of economics as a discipline for solving or preventing economic problems, especially those that affect the nation as a whole. Critics point out that for every period of economic prosperity in the history of United States there is a concomitant period of economic decline, which in turn suggests either economists and their theories failed to predict the impending crisis or that economists failed to convince policymakers on the right course of action to avert the crisis. In either case, economists are blamed.

This criticism is not entirely fair. Economist Ryan C. Amacher points out that "economics cannot predict the future, but only can explain the consequences of certain occurrences." In other words, it allows statements like "if A, then B," but one cannot predict with any certainty the occurrence of A. "Unfortunately, much of the public views economic science in terms of forecasts made by economists. This leads to much suspicion on the part

---

[44]John F. Dovidio and Victoria M. Esses, "Psychological Research and Public Policy: Bridging the Gap," *Social Issues and Policy Review,* *1*(1): 5-14 (December 2007), p. 9.

of the public that economics and economists are 'fortune tellers.'"[45] Economists also cannot be expected to take full responsible for economic problems because they do not have the power or authority to demand that policymakers follow their advice. However, the fact that economists play a bigger role in the policymaking arena than other social scientists does mean that they have fewer excuses. In fact, economics appears to be the only discipline in which policymakers routinely accept their advice.

> [E]conomics does have a long history of applied research to policy problems in many of its subdisciplines. Industrial organization, Agricultural Economics, Economic Development, Public Finance, and International Trade, to name only a few, are areas where there is a long history of policy-oriented research. Thus, though there is a heightened interest in public policy research today, it is by no means a new thing for economists to be interested in policy. For example, the classical English economists who were concerned with mercantilism and international trade had a huge impact on policy and economic theory.[46]

So, Amacher is suggesting that the biggest problem facing economics isn't the fact that it doesn't have the capacity to influence the policymaking process; rather, it's the fact that economists themselves are divided over what is the best policy to pursue.

> There are, of course, differences among economists over the relative importance of various aspects of the economic approach. Indeed, the public at large thinks that economists never agree. This, of course, is not true. Economists agree on a large body of economic science; it is economic policy that produces the disagreement.[47]

Amacher points out that the purpose of "economic science" is to identify the costs and benefits of various actions or governmental policies

---

[45]Ryan C. Amacher, "Economics and Public Policy," pp. 159-179 in George J. McCall and George H. Weber, *Social Science and Public Policy: The Roles of Academic Disciplines in Policy Analysis* (Port Washington, NY: Associated Faculty Press, 1984), p. 162.

[46]*Ibid.*, p. 165.

[47]*Ibid.*, p. 169.

and how a change in policy will affect incentives and, thus, behavior. Because many government policies are zero-sum (e.g., someone loses when someone wins and *vice versa*), a politician who runs for political office will find it difficult to put together a coalition of voters (50 percent plus 1 vote) if every group that is harmed by decisions knows the cost of that damage. Consequently, politicians and policymakers can have an interest in obfuscating or misdirecting economic research. Amacher cited one economist who associates this distortion with international policymaking.

> [J. Michael Finger] argues that economic analysis is ignored, misused, or banished by a decision process that is intended to diffuse potential participants. In this way, the marginal losers do not participate as their potential losses are less than the cost of participation. In these cases, *good policy research that clearly identifies the losers and the gainers is at minimum embarrassing to policymakers and will be an unwelcome input. The economist and the economic approach will likely be ignored or misused in these policy debates.*[48] [emphasis added]

Amacher provides a specific example of where economic policy has failed: disaster assistance. Since the 1960s, federal policy has been to provide massive federal aid to disaster victims (e.g., mud slides in California, hurricanes on coastal areas, flooding along major rivers). Although this is a popular political policy, economic analyses show that "public policy is creating uneconomic use of land and, in fact, contributing to disaster by subsidizing economic activity in potential disaster areas."[49]

In contrast to the tempered view of Amacher, policy researcher William T. Gormley seeks to make a strong case for the idea that economics has played a major role in the policymaking process.[50] In 2007, he pointed out that President Richard Nixon's administration embraced economists' recommendations to provide revenue sharing and block grants

---

[48]*Ibid.*, p. 172. Also see J. Michael Finger, "Policy Research," *Journal of Political Economy, 89*(6) :1270-71 (December 1981).

[49]*Ibid.*, p. 174.

[50]William T. Gormley, Jr., "Public Policy Analysis: Ideas and Impacts," *Annual Review of Political Science, 10*: 297-313 (June 2007).

for local governments and to employ cost-benefit analysis for regulating environmental impacts. The Clean Air Act of 1990 eventually codified the latter into law. During the 1970s and 1980s, economists also played a key role in promoting the concept of Health Maintenance Organizations (HMO). An economist in New Jersey provided economic research evidence that a judge used to force the state to provide early childhood education programs in poorer school districts. And the Federal Trade Commission relied upon an economic report when making its decision to reject the merger between Staples and Office Depot because it violated antitrust laws.

However, for every case Gormley cites except the last one, some governmental agency at some point rejected economists' recommendations. President Lyndon B. Johnson refused to consider a proposal for revenue sharing and block grants. The recommendation was implemented only after a Republican administration, which embraces federalism (decentralization of decision-making to the states), came to power. The same was true for benefit-cost analysis for the environment. The Clean Air Act of 1970 and the Clean Water Act of 1972 actually failed to include benefit-cost analysis, even though economists had strongly urged its adoption. Economists did help promote the idea of HMOs, but Congress refused in 1994 to pass legislation that would have made it a cental part of a nationwide health care plan. And education officials in New Jersey, before the court ruling, refused to fund early childhood education in poorer school districts even though economists had shown that the programs were very effective in enhancing learning.

Gormley also acknowledged that, in terms of 1960s Great Society programs, the connection between public policy evaluation and public was not strong. Nevertheless, he concluded:

> I am more optimistic about the capacity of public policy analysis to shape public policy outputs. Both economists and political scientists have made important contributions to a wide variety of decisions, involving public utility regulation, environmental policy, transportation policy, health policy, early childhood education policy, criminal justice policy, welfare policy, federalism, and the nature of lawmaking itself. Public policy analysts have shaped the debate through their ideas ("the

enlightenment function of social science"), their empirical research, or both.[51]

Political Science

Political scientist Stuart S. Nagel points out that research in political science often has an impact on public policy.[52] One of the best examples occurred during the 1960s, when researchers found that literacy tests and the poll tax — as opposed to lynchings or other violent acts — were the key factors in low black voter registration and turnout across the South. Nagel says the findings from these studies help facilitate the passage of the Voting Rights Act of 1965, which prohibited literacy tests, and the 24th Amendment to the Constitution, which prohibited poll taxes.

Political Scientist Henry Kissinger played a major policy-making role in the Nixon Administration. *(U.S. News & World Report photograph released to the public domain)*

On the other hand, Nagel also points out that some research has led to policy decisions that have failed. During the Nixon administration, for example, many social scientists encouraged the government to create programs that would help poor people purchase their own homes. The theory was that home ownership would positively affect people's self-image as well as help them develop a more favorable attitude toward society. This, in turn, would create more responsible citizens. Relying on that analysis, the Nixon administration created a government-backed mortgage program that offered low-income families low monthly payments, one similar to a program for middle-class people. But the

---

[51] *Ibid.*, p. 309.

[52] Stuart S. Nagel, "Political Science and Public Policy," pp. 180-200 in George J. McCall and George H. Weber, *Social Science and Public Policy: The Roles of Academic Disciplines in Policy Analysis* (Port Washington, NY: Associated Faculty Press, 1984).

program for the poor was a "dismal failure." Homes were sold at inflated values to increase government guarantees to the sellers, and the buyers often took possession of homes that needed a lot of repairs. Because the buyers didn't have the money to make the repairs, many of the homes went into foreclosure.[53] Around this time, political scientists also encouraged Congress to approve legislation that would give all Americans a guaranteed annual income, but Congress declined.[54] Two decades later, Congress also rejected policy scholar Irving Garfinkel's call for universal child support assurance.[55]

Nagel points out that not all policy-oriented research leads to change. For example, attempts to regulate the oil industry before the 1970s often failed because research showed that the industry gave a lot of campaign contributions to members of Congress and the Senate. The research also identified four other historical factors contributing to this power block. Not until the worldwide oil shortage of the 1970s was regulation of the oil industry effective. Nevertheless, a reasonable person could argue that the research provided useful background information that helped understand why change was so difficult.

Although research in political science can influence the policymaking process, Nagel notes:

> Most political science research does not have much value to policymakers because it tends to describe the policy process, and policymakers, as insiders, feel they know the policy process for their purposes much better than political scientists do. Political scientists are likely to be called upon to testify or to be given agency contracts when they do research that deals with the effects of alternative policies. The policies that political scientists tend to be interested in, however, are often on too high a level to be within an agency's jurisdiction and even

---

[53]Nagel suggested that the program might have succeeded if the seller was the government rather than a private entity.

[54]Daniel P. Moynihan, *The Politics of a Guaranteed Annual Income: The Nixon Administration and the Family Assistance Plan* (New York: Random House, 1973).

[55]J. Crowley, *The Politics of Child Support in America.* (Cambridge, UK: Cambridge University Press, 2003).

higher than the legislature's jurisdiction if they are constitutional issues.[56]

Political scientist William T. Gormley Jr. says that political scientists have less impact on public policy than economists and political scientists have had some failures. He noted that many political scientists

> have advocated school vouchers, but Congress has chosen a different set of policies. Many policy proposals have foundered at the state level as well. Authentic voucher systems have been embraced by only a handful of states and school districts. Legislation to combat global warming has often failed at the state level, despite strong scientific evidence that global warming poses a serious threat.[57] In a recent California debate over Proposition 82, several academics, including myself, argued in favor of a ballot initiative establishing a universal pre-kindergarten program, but the voters rejected that idea by a margin of 60%–40%.[58]

Gormley also pointed out that even though Theodore J. Lowi's 1969 book, *The End of Liberalism*,[59] had a major impact on political scientists and others, it didn't impress the U.S. Supreme Court. The book argued that Congress had delegated too much power to the federal bureaucracy and that capitalism is one of its victims. Lowi asserted that delegating power to the federal bureaucracy was unconstitutional, a violation of the nondelegation doctrine.[60] But the Supreme Court ruled that as long as Congress lays "down by legislative act an intelligible principle to which the person or body authorized to (exercise the delegated authority) is directed to conform,

---

[56]*Ibid.,* p.197.

[57]Gormley cites B. Rabe, *Statehouse and Greenhouse: The Emerging Politics of American Climate Change Policy* (Washington, DC: Brookings Institution, 2004).

[58]Gormley, "Public Policy Analysis: Ideas and Impacts."

[59]Theodore J. Lowi, *The End of Liberalism* (New York: W. W. Norton & Company, 1969).

[60]The nondelegation doctrine is the principle that Congress, being vested with "all legislative powers" of Article One, Section 1 of the U.S. Constitution, cannot delegate that power to anyone else.

such legislative action is not a forbidden delegation of legislative power."[61]

On the other hand, Gormley points out that political scientists have played a key role in redistricting, or redrawing legislative voting boundaries. One political scientist, who advocated that people who receive government assistance should work for that entitlement,[62] was able to get Wisconsin to adopt this provision into law, and it became a model for other states. The political scientist also testified several times before Congress; however, the federal government has never enacted the provision. Another example of impact that Gormley cites is the requirement that federal agencies must prepare an "environmental impact statement" when their proposed rules or actions may harm the environment. L. Keith Caldwell, a political scientist and expert on the environment, recommended that change.

Despite the mixed bag of results for political science, Gromley is optimistic.

> Political scientists have sometimes applied their understanding of how political institutions work to institutional choices made by government officials (e.g., work on legislative redistricting). On other occasions, political scientists have influenced raging policy debates ... [e.g., crime and welfare reform] by speaking with a distinctive voice but not necessarily one that reflected well-established political science principles. Both economists and political scientists have influenced debates on the design of public policies and the design of political institutions.[63]

David T. Ellwood, dean of the Harvard Kennedy School and political scientist, also is an optimist. He says political and social scientists have had impact on public policy in two major areas. The first is what is calls "big ideas." This basically refers to the idea that social scientists often identify

---

[61]*Mistretta v. United States*, 488 U.S. 361 (1989), citing *J. W. Hampton, Jr., & Co. v. United States*, 276 U.S. 394, 406, 48 S.Ct. 348, 351 (1928).
[62]Lawrence M. Mead, *Beyond Entitlement: The Social Obligations of Citizenship* (New York: Free Press, 1986).
[63]*Ibid.*, p. 309.

public problems and frame and reframe debates about public problems. The second way social scientists have impact is through evaluations of public policies and education programs. Political scientists, in particular, have impact in this area because program evaluation is one of their specialties.

However, when it comes to public policy development and design (the "detailed policies themselves"), social scientists rarely play a key role. "So the obvious question," Ellwood adds, "is why do so few people from academia actually come and participate, join a team, or at least play a really central role from the outside?"

> Compare the worlds of governance and scholarship. Public policy is about politics, because democracy is about politics ... political values, constituencies, advocacy, courting of moneyed interests ... building alliances, supporting your friends, challenging your enemies. And politics calls for raising money — sometimes from quite self-interested sources. And what do we political and social scientists cherish above all? We are supposed to believe in objective truth. At best, we will talk about politics as a constraint on getting to the truth. We are especially nervous about powerful interests who feel strongly that public policy should go in a certain way. We almost by nature resist any temptation to appease key constituents because we are going to be tainted by their special interests.[64]

Ellwood bolsters his argument by telling a story about an experience he had when he worked for the Clinton administration in its early years.

> I was one of three people ... who were supposedly kind of overseeing welfare reform. And at one point, fairly far along, the chief political officer for the Department of Health and Human Services came to me ... and he said, "You know, David, when the final deal is cut on welfare reform, you won't be in the room." And I said, "I am one of those in charge. We are making these decisions, we are figuring it out, and no

---

[64]David Ellwood, "We Have to Find a Way to Reward Ideas That Have Had an Impact on the World," remarks from acceptance speech delivered at the Newseum on May 7, 2009, upon receiving the 2009 Daniel Patrick Moynihan Prize.

one knows more." And he said, "David, you care more about the impacts on poor people than you do about the political futures of those making the final decisions. You won't be in the room."

Ellwood adds that scholars seek objective truth whereas policymakers are trying to get something done. "[W]hy on earth should or would politicians want to have to deal with scholars ...? ... And why should we scholars enter a process that inevitably forces us to compromise our core values? Does it really matter, anyway?" Yes, he says. "I believe we must have scholars to be involved because democracy needs some voices on the inside who focus on facts before politics."

However, many studies show that even when policymakers enact changes, those changes usually have a strong bias toward the status quo.[65] New ideas are rarely valued.

IMPERFECT KNOWLEDGE BETTER THAN NONE

At the end of their book, McCall and Weber asked political scientist Thomas J. Anton to review and comment on the articles submitted to the symposium. He concluded:

> It is a fair conclusion, I think, that the policy sciences have not matured as rapidly as many practitioners had hoped. Even under very broad definitions of activities that might appropriately be included in the domain of policy sciences, there is little evidence of any distinctive impact of such activities on public policy in the United States or elsewhere.[66]

[65] Aaron Wildavsky, *The Politics of the Budgetary Process*, 4th ed. (Boston: Little, Brown, 1984).

[66] Thomas J. Anton, "Policy Sciences and Social Sciences: Reflections from an Editor's Chair," pp. 201-214 in George J. McCall and George H. Weber, *Social Science and Public Policy: The Roles of Academic Disciplines in Policy Analysis* (Port Washington, NY: Associated Faculty Press, 1984), p. 202.

Anton added:

> If we have learned nothing else during these past few decades of
> expanding social research, it is that society itself is infinitely
> complicated and not nearly as yielding to our questions as we may have
> expected. Theories that can account for social complexity remain
> primitive, in my judgment, leaving us with literally thousands of studies
> that excite interest without advancing knowledge. I must also add, at the
> risk of being overly contentious, that very few of us possess the
> combination of insight and skill necessary to produce a really first-rate
> piece of social research ... All this is a way of suggesting that the social
> science disciplines themselves are not well enough developed to offer
> dramatic contributions to public policy.[67]

Few social scientists would disagree with the conclusion that research
falls far short of achieving the desired goals. However, Anton's statement
implies that social scientists will have no significant impact until they are
able to produce the "first-rate" research that can make "dramatic
contributions" to public policy. Many scholars would disagree with this
comment. The question, for them, is not whether social science research
provides all of the answers or makes "dramatic contributions," but whether
the research, even with its flaws, is capable of creating a body of
knowledge that enables policymakers to make better decisions than they
would without the benefit of such research.

On this point, George H. Weber, who wrote the final essay in the
McCall and Weber book, is an optimist. He said social scientists have a
great deal to contribute. However, they have less impact that they could
simply because they are not as directly involved in day-to-day policy
formulation and reformulation as are other groups, such as special interest
groups and social movements. These groups actively lobby government
policymakers and, thus, are intimately involved in the political process.
Social scientists are too removed from the process and are usually relegated
to playing a tangential role. He concluded: "Social science and social

---

[67]*Ibid.*, pp. 202-203.

policy have an unfulfilled potential for a rich interchange. The potential, however, requires greater opportunities for the two to work out their role in relation to the other."[68]

Although a number of organizations and scholars are trying to improve that relationship, policy scholars often point out that most social scientists continue to operate on the periphery of the policymaking process. Unlike Margaret Mead, many are not willing to take their research to the public arena and push for social change.

---

[68]George H. Weber, "Social Science and Social Policy," pp. 215-232 in George J. McCall and George H. Weber, *Social Science and Public Policy: The Roles of Academic Disciplines in Policy Analysis* (Port Washington, NY: Associated Faculty Press, 1984), p. 230.

CHAPTER 8

DU BOIS AND FINDINGS
FROM POLICY STUDIES RESEARCH

Wiilliam Edward Burghardt Du
Bois was angry.[1] Although many
African Americans had served in the
U.S. Armed Forces during World War
I and some had lost their lives, those
returning were treated like second-
class citizens at home. They were
denied jobs because they were black.
Some were lynched by white mobs for
taking jobs in the north. And those
who remained in the military were
denied promotions.

D uBois in 1907

"By the God of Heaven, we are
cowards and jackasses if now that the
war is over we do not marshal every ounce of our brain and brawn to fight
the forces of hell in our own land," Du Bois wrote in a famous editorial
titled, "Returning Soldier," which was published in *Crisis*, a magazine he
edited. "We return. We return from fighting. We return fighting! Make way

---

[1]Sources for this biography on Du Bois include Gerald C. Hynes, "A Biographical
Sketch of W. E. B. Du Bois," available at <www. duboislc.org>; Manning Marable, *W. E.
B. Du Bois, Black Radical Democrat* (Boston: Twayne, 1986); David L. Lewis, *W. E. B. Du
Bois: Biography of a Race, 1868-1919* (New York: H. Holt, 1993).

for Democracy! We saved it in France, and by the great Jehovah, we will save it in the United States of America, or know the reason why."

Congress responded. It passed legislation that inaugurated black officer training schools, established legal action against lynchers and set up a federal work program for returning veterans.

Du Bois was the first black man to earn a Ph.D. at Harvard.[2] He wrote more than 4,000 papers and books, including *The Souls of Black Folks,* which criticized Booker T. Washington's conservative approach to securing equal rights. Du Bois founded and for 25 years edited *Crisis* magazine, which was published by the National Association for the Advancement of Colored People (NAACP), a group he helped create in 1909. He was a superb writer. His mission was to make people aware of the problems that faced African Americans. He wanted racial equality and he fought all his life to achieve that goal.

Toward the end of his life, Du Bois became disillusioned. The changes he sought — equality, jobs, dignity — were not coming fast enough. He renounced his U.S. citizenship and in 1961 moved to Ghana. Two years later he died at the age of 95.

One can reasonably assume that Du Bois didn't feel he had much impact on public policy. Ironically, though, historians today widely agree that he is the most important black protest leader in the first half of the 20th century. He influenced many later civil rights leaders and writers, including Alex Haley, who wrote *Autobiography of Malcolm X* (1965), which chronicles the life of an African-American man who draws upon Islamic religion to solve problems facing Black Americans (but is assassinated). Haley also wrote *Roots* (1976), which chronicles a slave family before and after emancipation. Both of these books helped mobilize the civil rights movement during the 1960s and 1970s.[3]

---

[2]His dissertation, *The Suppression of the African Slave Trade in America,* remains the authoritative work on that subject.

[3]*Roots* was turned into a popular and award-winning television mini-series. Polls at the time showed that the series also had a tremendous affect on sensitizing white Americans to the historical struggles of African Americans.

Du Bois' impact on society is a good example of "enlightenment model" — it was more indirect than direct, and it took a good deal of time for people to recognize it. Like Margaret Mead and many of the early sociologists, Du Bois was part social scientist and part activist. He wasn't satisfied with just doing research. To him, the scientist/activist roles were one of the same. Neither, alone, was sufficient to achieve the goal of bettering society.

However, empirical research from the 1970s to the present that focuses specifically on measuring the impact of the social sciences on public policy reveals that the activist role is in decline and examples of enlightenment effects are not always easy to identify. In fact, the research overwhelmingly shows that none of the social sciences, even economics, are major players in the public policy stage.

RESEARCH ON THE IMPACT OF SOCIAL SCIENCE

Formal research on the impact of social science goes back to the 1960s. By the 1970s, questions were already being raised about its value in the policymaking process. By the early 1990s, most political scientists and other scholars working in this discipline had pretty much concluded that social science research is a small-time player on the political stage.

This proposition is supported by policy researcher Carol H. Weiss' 1992 edited book *Organizations for Policy Analysis*, which contained articles from fifteen scholars and policy analysts who represent a wide range of nonprofit, university and governmental organizations (or "specialized analytic agencies") and "whose primary task was to provide policy information and advice." These "analytic units" were expected to mobilize intellectual resources in the service of social problem-solving and, in effect, help government think. Weiss conceded that these organizations have influenced the policymaking process. However, at the conclusion of her Introduction, she candidly points out:

> In this volume, and wherever social scientists and policy analysts write, their common lament is that political actors rarely pay enough attention to the knowledge they [social scientists] have so laboriously acquired.

Rather than running the world, they [social scientists] are sitting in their offices, struggling to devise better means of getting their message across and waiting for word that somebody has heard what they have been saying.[4] [bracketed text added]

This complaint is not isolated. Research in policy studies has replicated it over and over again since the 1970s. Below we provide a sample of the findings from these studies. The text is verbatim except where noted (italics added for emphasis):

- Social scientists have conducted hundreds of empirical studies related to various aspect of welfare policies in the thirty-five years since the War on Poverty was declared. *Major findings of this research and their policy implications were virtually ignored, however, in the welfare reform debates leading up to President Clinton's signing of the Personal Responsibility and Work Opportunity Reconciliation Act of 1996 ...* [which] ended the entitlement to cash assistance and dramatically changed the nature of the social safety net.[5]

- The Kennedy, Johnson, and Nixon presidencies were associated with *social reforms in many sectors of the social welfare system.* By and large, these *proved to be disappointing in their effects.*[6]

- [T]he direct and overall impact of the behavioral and social sciences on federal decision making and program implementation usually has been quite modest or even negligible ... *policymakers and the public*

---

[4]Carol H. Weiss (ed.), *Organizations for Policy Analysis: Helping Government Think* (Newbury Park, CA: Sage Publications, 1992), p. 17.

[5]Sheldon Danziger, "Welfare Reform Policy from Nixon to Clinton: What Role for Social Science?" pp. 137-164 in David L. Featherman and Maris A. Vinovskis (eds.), *Social Science and Policy-Making: A Search for Relevance in the Twentieth Century* (Ann Arbor, MI: University of Michigan Press, 2001), p. 137. Also see David T. Ellwood, *Poor Support: Poverty in the American Family* (New York: Basic Books, 1989).

[6]Thomas D. Cook, "Postpositivist Critical Multiplism," pp. 21-62 in R. Lance Shotland and Melvin M. Mark (eds.), *Social Science and Social Policy* (Beverly Hills, CA: Sage Publications, 1985), p. 29.

have been left with considerable disillusionment about the usefulness and objectivity of the behavioral and social sciences.[7]

- The alliance between social science and public policy is an uneasy one for many reasons. The systematic use of social science in policy determination is ... typically mediated and often distorted by funding agencies, the mass media, and other institutions. *Policymakers use only a limited range of the potential contributions of the social sciences. Many governmental agencies,* especially at the state and local levels, *do not use social science at all.*[8]

- Have we learned anything from social science research? Most researchers would say we have. *However, studies of many education and social services settings show little impact of research findings.* The limited impact of social science is, perhaps, most obvious when we contrast the success of physical science and the resulting potential for global nuclear disaster with the limits of our understanding of how to prevent war or crime in our own neighborhoods. From *the practitioners' perspective, most social science research is seen as irrelevant because it does not relate to what they do, or, at best, it provides contradictory guidance on what should be done.*[9]

- With the recent growth in the numbers of Congressional staff, Congress should be better equipped to do policy analysis and to make use of the policy research and analysis done by others ... *Yet despite the growth in committee staffs ... the amount of formal*

---

[7]David L. Featherman and Maris A. Vinovskis, "Growth and Use of Social and Behavioral Science in the Federal Government Since World War II," pp. 40-82 in David L. Featherman and Maris A. Vinovskis (eds.), *Social Science and Policy-Making: A Search for Relevance in the Twentieth Century* (Ann Arbor, MI: University of Michigan Press, 2001), pp. 69-70.

[8]Thomas F. Pettigrew, "Can Social Scientists be Effective Actors in the Policy Arena?" pp. 121-134 in R. Lance Shotland and Melvin M. Mark (eds.), *Social Science and Social Policy* (Beverly Hills, CA: Sage Publications, 1985), pp. 126-127.

[9]Content of promotional material for Spencer A. Ward and Linda J. Reed (eds.), *Knowledge, Structure, and Use Implications for Synthesis and Interpretation* (Philadelphia: Temple University Press, 1983), retrieved December 5, 2010, from <http://www.temple.edu/tempress/titles/335_reg_print.html>.

analysis done in committees is generally low. Even committee staff's use of analytic studies done elsewhere — by Congressional support agencies, the executive branch, or by independent scholars in think tanks or universities — tends to be sporadic ... *This paper examineswhy Congressional committee staffs have not proved to be major consumers of policy research and analysis.*[10]

- [T]he findings and recommendations of Presidential Commissions are not respected at the top levels of government; too frequently, the fate of scholars who devote part of their professional lives to such efforts is to see their findings and recommendations ignored or rejected. "The loss, in my judgment [says Princeton University's Charles F. Westoff, who served on the Commission on Population Growth and the American Future from 1970 to 1972], was not the failure to adopt a particular set of recommendations, or even the harsh criticism of the research procedures and findings. *It was, rather, the failure ... to penetrate the policy realm with the principle that empirical research is relevant.*" ... The probability is high of a disappointing response or no response from the White House to social science findings and recommendations.[11] [emphasis added]

- Despite the tremendous increase in attention to the importance of information in the decision-making process, *recent research indicates that governmental policymakers make little use of information;*[12] at best, social science research findings alter policy-

---

[10]Carol H. Weiss, "Congressional Committee Staffs (Do, Do Not) Use Analysis," pp. 94-112 in Martin Bulmer (ed.), *Social Science Research and Government: Comparative Essays on Britain and the United States* (Cambridge: Cambridge University Press, 1987).

[11]Raymond W. Mack, "Four for the Seesaw: Reflections on the Reports of Four Colleagues Concerning Their Experiences as Presidential Commissioners," pp. in Mirra Komarovsky (ed.), *Sociology and Public Policy: The Case of Presidential Commissions* (New York: Elsevier, 1975), pp.145, 147.

[12]Cheol H. Oh, *Linking Social Science Information to Policy-Making* (Greeenwich, CT: JAI Press, 1996), pp. 9-10. Oh cites these scholars to back up this statement: C. E. Nelson, J. Roberts, C. Maederer, B. Wertheimer, and B. Johnson, "The Utilization of Social Science Information by Policymakers," *American Behavioral Scientist, 30*: 569-577 (1987); W. E. Pollard, "Decision Making and the Use of Evaluation Research," *American Behavioral Scientist, 30*: 661-676 (1987); and A. L. Schneider, "The Evaluation of a Policy Orientation for Evaluation Research," *Public Administration Review, 46:* 356-363 (July/August 1986).

makers' understandings and/or definitions of policy problems over a long period of time (the "conceptual use").[13]

- *In 1985, the Congressional Research Service concluded that the social sciences have contributed little to the planning of government policies or actions.* The social science research was marginalized in part because it often provided critical feedback about government that had been endorsed by policymakers.[14]

- President Barack Obama appointed a number of "distinguished" academic economists and lawyers to his administration, *but few high-ranking political scientists have been named.* In fact, the editors of a recent poll of more than 2,700 international relations experts declared that "the walls surrounding the ivory tower have never seemed so high."[15]

- A Harvard University professor in 2009 reported that scholars *"are paying less attention to questions about how their work relates to the policy world, and in many departments a focus on policy can hurt one's career. Advancement comes faster for those who develop mathematical models, new methodologies or theories expressed in jargon that is unintelligible to policymakers."* A survey of articles published over the lifetime of the *American Political Science Review* found that about one in five dealt with policy prescription or criticism in the first half of the century, while only a handful did so after 1967. Editor Lee Sigelman observed in the journal's centennial issue that *"if 'speaking truth to power' and contributing directly to public dialogue about the merits and demerits of various courses of*

---

[13]Robert F. Rich and N. Caplan, "What Do We Know about Knowledge Utilization as a Field/Discipline — The State of the Art," paper presented at the Research Utilization Conference, University of Pittsburgh (September 1978); Carol Weiss, "Introduction," pp. 1-20 in *Utilizing Social Research in Public Policy Making*, edited by Carol Weiss (Lexington, MA: D.C. Heath, 1977); and Carol Weiss, "Knowledge Creep and Decision Accretion," *Knowledge, 1*: 384-404 (1980).

[14]William Foote Whyte, "On the Uses of Social Science Research," *American Sociological Review, 51*: 555-563 (Augustin 1986), p. 555. The bullet point is summarized from the article.

[15]Joseph S. Nye Jr., "Scholars on the Sidelines," *The Washington Post* (April 13, 2009), p. A15.

action were still numbered among the functions of the profession, one would not have known it from leafing through its leading journal."[16]

- *[I]t is fair to say that the impact of social science research on government in Britain has been patchy at best, non-existent at worst.* Whilst individual academics, and some disciplines, have developed good links with policymakers, there is a growing awareness we often do not do enough to disseminate research findings outside of the academic world ... there is also an awareness within government that sometimes they also don't do enough to reach out to the external research community, and that it's not easy for advice to reach the ears of those who need to hear it. *The result has been a worrying separation of social science research and policy advice.*[17]

- For all the fine rhetoric about "evidence-based" policymaking ... the reality of policymaking in a representative democracy with a developed bureaucracy is likely to be that *research that reinforces desired policies will be supported and publicized, while research that questions existing policy or which suggests alternatives based on empirical research will either not be funded or, if it slips through the net, will be quietly buried.*[18]

- *[S]cientifically based (i.e., justified) public policy,* a dream that has grown ever larger since the Enlightenment and that, perhaps, has reached its apogee toward the close of our own century, *is a myth, a theoretical illusion.* It exists in our minds, our analyses and our

---

[16]*Ibid.*

[17]Liz Campbell, "President's Column," *The Psychologist, 21*(9): 782-785 (September 2008), p. 782.

[18]Craig Smith, "A Review of the British Academy Report, Punching Our Weight: The Humanities and Social Sciences in Public Policy Making," *Economic Affairs* (Institute for Economic Affairs, September 2009), p. 96.

methods only because we seek to find it and, typically, we tend to find that which we seek.[19]

Many scholars, including the one writing this book, would challenge the last assertion — that scientifically based public policy is a myth. As Weiss points out, the policy studies literature does not conclude that social science research has no impact. To the contrary, one can find many examples of that impact even in studies that generally conclude the overall impact is weak. Take the Great Society plan's war on poverty, for instance. Although it didn't eradicate poverty, it did cut poverty rates in half (see Chapter 1). Who could fail to see that cup half full?

The key question isn't whether social scientific research has an impact on public policy, but whether its impact is proportional to the benefits that it can offer in terms of solving social problems, and if that impact isn't proportional then why?

WHY IS SOCIAL SCIENCE POLITICALLY IMPOTENT?

Many of the answers to this question have already been provided in this book. This section organizes them in one place. The key factors inhibiting the impact of social science research include devaluation of the activist role, difficulty in generating knowledge, ideology and self-interest of policymakers, ineffective public relations, and corporatization of higher education.

Devaluation of the Activist Role

Although few university administrators will admit it, the academy places a much higher value on theoretical than applied social science research — or that research undertaken specifically to fix social problems

[19]Robert Formaini, *The Myth of Scientific Public Policy* (New York: Transaction Publishers, 1990), p. 1. See also P. DeLeon, "Democracy and the Policy Sciences," *Policy Studies Journal*, 22: 200-212 (1994) and Carol Weiss, *Organizations for Policy Analysis* (Newbury Park, CA: Sage, 1992).

or influence public policy. Some universities give a small amount of credit at annual review time to faculty who testify before government committees or who write up articles for nonscholarly, popular magazines or newspapers. However, few universities provide significant rewards for such activity. Esoteric peer-reviewed journal articles rule.[20] In fact, tenure and promotion rules and annual reviews always reward faculty for scholarly publications, but they usually say nothing about solving social problems. There is, of course, nothing wrong with rewarding faculty for generating theoretical knowledge and for publishing that knowledge in good journals. However, the failure to reward faculty who seek to influence public policy clearly is an impediment to the goal of trying to solve social problems as well as to the perceived legitimacy of the social sciences as a whole.

Part of this problem can be attributed to regional or national accrediting organizations that evaluate universities and their programs in terms of their quality. Peer-reviewed scholarly publications are often the most important criteria for evaluating the quality of an institution. And to distinguish the quality of one article to another, accrediting agencies and administrators often look at the prestige of the journal, which boils down to the proportion of articles that it accepts from the number that are submitted. Other factors include the number of years a journal has been publishing and prestige of a journal's editorial board. At the end of the year, administrators collect data on faculty publications and then multiply the number of refereed publications by an "impact factor" of the journal. The higher the impact score evaluative agencies give to a journal, the more rigorous the journal, presumably. The rewards are doled out accordingly.

There are many flaws in this system. If one of the major goals of social science is to solve social problems, this method of evaluation misses the mark. The dependent variable should be solving problems, not prestige of a journal. Another problem with the bean-counter approach is that it fails to measure the full impact of scholarly books. The vast majority of scholars who have achieved national or international recognition in the academy do

---

[20]The hard sciences are a different story, whose research is often incorporated into technology or used to improve the quality of products and goods.

so not through journal articles but through books. It is rare, indeed, to find a scholar of fame who has not published a book. But the "bean-counting system," as critics call it, does not have a good means of measuring the impact of books, because the review process varies from publisher to publisher and also is influenced by market factors (e.g., Can the book generate profits?).[21]

Many administrators who require faculty to publish only or mainly in peer-reviewed journals also want (or sometimes require) faculty to bring in research grant money. One factor that really encourages this practice is that grant money is a reward not just the faculty member, but also for the university. Most citizens are unaware that universities skim off anywhere from 25 to 50 percent of the grant money for "overhead costs." The actual overhead costs are almost always much less than the value of the pocketed money, which means the excess can be spent on other things, such as new programs, instruction, administrative salary increases,[22] or administrators' pet projects. In this respect, universities operate like privately held corporations, in that they sell knowledge in exchange for compensation. State funding cuts in recent decades have pushed many universities to find other sources of revenue, and at some universities faculty who do not raise grant money are punished at annual review time (i.e., are denied raises and promotions).

From a philosophical standpoint, the grant-getting model is acceptable to scholars who tend to be reform-oriented. Governments and private foundations generally fund only research that helps them achieve their political goals. But the grant-funding model devalues scholarship that criticizes the status quo or contends that evolutionary reforms cannot solve social problems. For scholars who question the legitimacy and role of mainstream institutions, there is little, if any, grant money available. But even if it were available, many of them would reject it, because grant-

---

[21]One national consulting firm gives a weight of five to books, meaning that books equal five published journal articles. But few universities actually give that much weight to books.

[22]Salaries of university administrators have skyrocketed since the 1980s. Salaries of faculty have only kept pace with inflation.

funded research, to them, cannot offer real solutions to real problems, such as the huge disparities in power and wealth that exist in capitalist systems. Other reject grant-funded research because they do not want government (or what they might call "big brother") or outside groups controlling any aspect of their research programs.

The grant-funding system also contains a built-in bias in favor of quantitative research. Many policymakers perceive research based on numbers as more scientific and valid than qualitative research. This means qualitative researchers often find it more difficult to get funding.

University administrators are not the only ones who devalue research intended for use in public policymaking. Many policymakers are guilty. Some think of academics as eggheads who have lost touch with the real world. Some have, to be honest. But most social scientists genuinely care about making the world a better place. This egghead stereotype persists in part because many politicians lack a college education or formal training or course work in the science of social science. In Washington state, for example, fewer than half of the state legislators have a college degree. To the extent that college provides people with an appreciation for social scientific research, one can reasonably expect that lawmakers without a college degree will, of course, have less appreciation for that research.

Finally, social scientists themselves must take some responsibility for devaluing research seeking to influence public policy. Many believe that if social scientists get too involved in the political process, policymakers and the public will perceive their research as biased or subjective. However, humanist scholars are quick to point out — accurately so — that not getting involved in policymaking is, itself, a bias. Lack of involvement means laws and policies will be more likely to be enacted without the benefit of scientific knowledge, and this, in turn, means more support for the status quo and ideologies that support the powerful rather than ordinary citizens.

In other words, a decision to not get involved in the political process is a moral decision, and it has consequences for the distribution of power in a society. Humanists also point out that if a social scientist believes that a particular policy may harm people or the public, then he or she has a moral obligation to fight against that harm. And although mainstream researchers fear that too much involvement in the political arena may delegitimize the social sciences, too little involvement (i.e., failure to fight against a known harm) could have the same outcome.

The Knowledge Problem

Chapters 3 and 4 of this book addressed the question of whether social scientific research is capable of producing knowledge. There is no need to go over that ground again in any depth. Humanist critics often have argued that positivism and quantitative methods are unable to produce knowledge because they make incorrect assumptions about the nature of social reality and how people come to know it. The most important aspect of this debate is whether human behavior can be attributed to free will or determinism and whether true knowledge can be derived solely from sensory experience and the methods of the natural sciences.

Because these attacks involve metaphysical claims, which are beyond the realm of science or any means of independent verification, this debate cannot be resolved. However, the once contentious debates over this issue in the social sciences have subsided substantially, especially in sociology. A compromise deal, so to speak, was struck: neither agency nor structure is sufficient to explain human activity. Instead, most sociologists and many other mainstream social scientists subscribe to the doctrine of probabilistic social action (even if they don't call it that), which holds that humans can make choices between socially structured alternatives.

But in terms of generating knowledge and influencing public policy, the social sciences still face another daunting problem: lack of intersubjectivity. Although mass communication research shows over-whelmingly that television violence increases aggressive behavior in children, this kind of confidence in social science is rare. Most areas of research across all of the social sciences contain mixed findings. Complicating matters further is that even when intersubjectivity is high, the amount of explained variance is low. Quantitative research, especially survey research, receives the bulk of this criticism. Most studies can explain only about 20 to 30 percent of the variance even after incorporating many different variables into the models. The inability to explain more variance and lack of intersubjectivity certainly has hindered the development of generalizations that could be useful to the policymaking process. Policymakers want facts, usually "now," but the rigor of social science often means that it takes years or even decades to understand a phenomena, and sometimes even that isn't enough.

One way around this problem is to reject the idea that social science is worthless unless it has consistent findings. Waiting for consistent findings is unrealistic. Rather, the goal of social science research is to provide policymakers with more information, even if there is no consensus among those studies. Mixed findings are not worthless; they are useful when it comes to making decisions. Mixed findings can suggest that a social problem is more complex than previously thought, that multiple factors or processes may be at work, or that the findings depend upon the type of methods, statistics or measures used. The assumption this book makes is that the more information available to policymakers, the better the chances a good decision will be made.

Ideology and Self-Interest of Policymakers

Legal scholar and policy researcher Robert F. Rich convincingly has shown that social science research has more effect when its findings support the ideological position of policymakers or their party affiliation, or when the findings advance the self-interest of the policymakers and their staffs. These propositions are not very comforting to social scientists who believe truth and knowledge, not self-interest, should guide decision-making. But the problems of ideology and self-interest are structurally embedded in the concept of democracy itself and, thus, cannot be eradicated without suspending individual rights.

The American political system is based on the idea that the best form of government is one in which different political, social and economic groups and people vie or compete with each other for resources or power. Some of these social actors believe truth and knowledge should play a pivotal role in policymaking. Others disagree. Instead, their mission is to gain advantage for their organizations and themselves, sometimes at any cost. This includes citizens seeking elected office. Without the support of powerful special interest groups, they normally will have a difficult time winning an election. The American political system is not structured to maximize the use of truth and knowledge in decision-making. Instead, as critical scholars have shown quite convincingly, it's structured largely to meet, first, the needs of powerful institutions and elites, and then, second, to serve (sometimes) the interests of other, usually less powerful, groups or individuals.

This does not mean America's political system is wholly hegemonic or repressive. One of the enduring themes of U.S. history is that its political and economic institutions have often changed to accommodate the needs of nonelite or nonmainstream groups and organizations (e.g., labor unions, environmentalists, civil rights movements). This explains in large part the great staying power of capitalism and representative democratic government and, concomitantly, the relative absence of major indigenous revolutionary groups.[23] The United States and other Western countries give their citizens a relatively high degree of freedom to speak, criticize, and move around. Nevertheless, it is difficult to ignore the fact that ideology and self-interest often, if not most of the time, trump knowledge in the public policy arena. And many policymakers will defend this philosophy on moral grounds; after all, that's how a democracy works.

Ineffective Public Relations

Social scientists, according to the research reported in this book, have done a very poor job of marketing themselves and their research to the public and policymakers. One consequence is that the news media often get it wrong. Social psychologist Thomas F. Pettigrew points out that during the 1960s and onward, mass media kept projecting false information about race and education. He says research showed that court-ordered busing

---

[23]David Demers, *History and Future of Mass Media: An Integrated Perspective* (Cresskill, NJ: Hampton Press, 2007) and David Pearce Demers, *The Menace of the Corporate Newspaper: Fact or Fiction?* (Ames: Iowa State University Press, 1996).

actually produced modest achievement in test scores and extensive career gains for black children, and that massive white flight never occurred and differences in social status are responsible for differences between public- and private-school performance, not desegregation.

> Why are these more differentiated, policy-relevant results of social research not better communicated? Clearly, there is a dangerous lack of fit between the mass media and social science. On the media side, social science has yet to be elevated to the status of a specialized "beat." Television networks and a few newspapers and magazines now have economics reporters; but a "science writer" still describes the specialist in physical science or medicine. Only a few work the general social science beat ... On the academic side, few social scientists have experience in dealing with the media ... Social scientists ... should develop a more professional dialogue with specialized reporters.[24]

The importance of strategic communication or, better yet, good public relations (as a good communicator would say), has been emphasized by a number of scholars cited in this book. Many scholars hope the American social sciences will not follow in the footsteps of the British humanities and social sciences (HSS), which were forced to launch a public relations campaign to promote themselves after, rather than before, the British government cut state funding to them (see Chapter 1).

A frequent complaint citizens and policymakers level at social scientists is that they write to impress rather to express. For those not formally trained in social sciences, the scholarly literature is impossible to understand. Sociologist C. Wright Mills once commented that all studies, no matter how complex, can be summarized into a few simple statements or paragraphs with a modicum of effort. There is no reason why social scientists cannot take this advice.

Policymakers also complain that even when they understand the findings in a research study, often it is not clear how the findings can help

---

[24]Thomas F. Pettigrew, "Can Social Scientists be Effective Actors in the Policy Arena?" pp. 121-134 in R. Lance Shotland and Melvin M. Mark (eds.), *Social Science and Social Policy* (Beverly Hills, CA: Sage Publications, 1985), pp. 126-127.

them make better decisions. If social scientists wish to have an impact on public policy, they need to make their research more meaningful for public policy analysis. And policymakers need to be better listeners.

Correcting turgid prose and showing how research can help the policymaking process are relatively easy problems to fix. Universities can sponsor workshops on writing, and they can reward faculty who translate their research for broad audiences. Although making research more people-friendly is an absolute necessary condition for more impact, it will not solve the other three problems discussed above (devaluing of activist role, the knowledge problem, ideology). More systemic changes are necessary, as the next chapter will show.

Corporatization of Higher Education

Some scholars have argued that higher education's increased emphasis on securing state, federal and private research grants, donations and contract work to cover losses in state general fund allocations are adversely affecting the goal of trying to solve social problems. Corporatization of higher education, or the idea of turning public universities into profit-making enterprises, clearly devalues scholarship that takes a critical stance of the status quo, because established grant-giving institutions are unlikely to fund projects that criticize them. Some universities even require social science faculty to obtain grants to get tenure, even though only about 1 percent of all federal research grant money is allocated to the social sciences.[25]

The corporatization thesis has merit to the extent that critical scholarship can devise solutions to social problems and mainstream research cannot. However, if mainstream research is capable of generating good solutions, then corporatization may be characterized as enhancing the

---

[25]The rest of the money goes mainly to the natural, biological and medical sciences. The low level of grant funding for the social sciences raises an interesting question: Do policymakers believe that the social sciences have little to offer in terms of solving social problems or do they see the social sciences as a political threat to their power and the status quo? It's no secret that most social scientists are liberal on the political spectrum.

impact of social science in the policymaking realm. As with so many other
debates in the social sciences, the corporatization controversy is not likely
to be resolved anytime soon.

SOLVING THE IMPACT PROBLEM

Imagine a world without physics, chemistry, mathematics and biology. Technology, as we know it, would cease to progress or even exist. No electricity, running water, sewage treatment, gasoline, roads, modern farming techniques. No businesses or industries, because they depend heavily on universities to train natural scientists and technicians. Some people would like a world without big corporations. But the economy would collapse and most people would suffer.

Imagine a world without the medical sciences. No new doctors, nurses, drugs, treatments. People would be directly and immediately affected. The medical sciences, which overlap considerably with the natural sciences, include research and training in basic sciences (human anatomy, human physiology, biochemistry, pathology, microbiology and pharmacology) and the clinical sciences (pediatrics, surgery, psychiatry, internal medicine, obstetrics, gynecology and family practice). It's not difficult to see that the end of the medical sciences would have an immediate and disastrous effect on people around the world.

Imagine a world in which literature, art, theater, dance, music, linguistics, humanist history, jurisprudence, philosophy, and archaeology are no longer taught or critiqued in an institution of higher learning. Although the humanities may have a difficult time showing how they have a direct impact on solving social problems or on public policy, they have never had to justify themselves in those terms. They can justify themselves as a "secular religion," one that provides inspiration, hope and meaning to creator and end user alike. Who hasn't felt inspired or moved by a good piece of literature or art? That, in and of itself, is enough to justify an entire discipline, many critics would argue.

But now imagine a world without the social sciences — a world without sociology, political science, communication research, social psychology, economics, social history, or anthropology as formal disciplines in the university. How much would that impact people and society? Could the world survive without the social sciences?

"A haunting question for social scientists, no doubt," says Peter Demerath, associate professor of Educational Policy and Administration at the University of Minnesota. "Yeah, I don't think I would disagree there are very large and haunting questions for knowledge transmission and ... utilization, and probably all of this was slowed in the big picture by the postmodernist critique of knowledge and the extent to which knowledge is possible ... You have hit upon something that is quite important."[1]

For the last decade, I've asked many scholars what the world would be like without the social sciences — could it still function? Most have difficulty coming up with a good argument to defend the social sciences. To be fair, they didn't have much time to think about it. Most had never thought of asking the question. They have always assumed that what they do as social scientists is important to society. That was the same thinking among professors in the humanities and social sciences in Britain, just before Parliament cut off funding to them in 2010 (see Chapter 1).

SIXTEEN RECOMMENDATIONS

Scholars have presented a number of different recommendations to enhance the impact of social science research in the policymaking process. Presented below are sixteen of those suggestions, organized into three areas: recommendations from various scholars in the field; recommendations from Joan Petersilia, and recommendations from this author.

---

[1]Telephone interview with Peter Demerath, October 22, 2008.

1. Reward Applied Research

There is widespread agreement among policy scholars that universities should do more to reward faculty who publish materials or conduct research that focuses mainly on solving social problems or influencing public policy. They also agree that the rewards should be equal to those given to scholars who conduct theoretical research, which usually addresses bigger, more complex problems, and consequently has more status than administrative, grant-funded research.[2] However, under the current system, scholars are rewarded for sheer scholarly output, not for answering questions that are urgent to policymakers and school teachers, according to Ellen Condliffe Lagemann, a history of American education professor at Harvard University and former dean of Harvard's Graduate School of Education.[3] "Usable knowledge generated from research is not likely to be tenurable research," she said. "So there are many disincentives to doing such work. Overcoming those incentives will require fundamental reform of the university."

Lagemann's colleague at Harvard, political science professor Joseph S. Nye Jr., adds that the "solutions must come via a reappraisal within the academy itself."

> Departments should give greater weight to real-world relevance and impact in hiring and promoting young scholars. Journals could place greater weight on relevance in evaluating submissions. Studies of specific regions deserve more attention. Universities could facilitate interest in the world by giving junior faculty members greater incentives to participate in it. That should include greater toleration of unpopular policy positions. One could multiply such useful suggestions, but young people should not hold their breath waiting for them to be implemented.

---

[2]This generalization may only apply to the social sciences, not to the natural, biological or medical sciences.

[3]David Glenn, "Education Researchers and Policymakers Not in Sync, Scholars Say Article tools," *The Chronicle of Higher Education* (June 1, 2007), p. A11.

If anything, the trends in academic life seem to be headed in the opposite direction.[4]

Nye's conclusion is supported by the job-hunting experiences of David T. Ellwood, director of the Harvard Kennedy School.

> I remember when I was in the job market long ago and I went to various universities and I would occasionally dare to say, "I am kind of interested in doing public policy work." And some places would implicitly say, "Why didn't you tell us this earlier? We could have saved your plane fare." The more open-minded suggested, "You know, policy work is fine. Some people play basketball with their free time, you can do policy, as long as it does not interfere with your work." We really do have to decide, if we believe this, that we are actually going to reward it so that young people do it. I believe our democracy and our scholarship urgently need a more supportive atmosphere.[5]

Some scholars believe that providing rewards to professors for becoming involved in the public policymaking process is one of the easiest and simplest ways to enhance the impact of social science research. But it may not be that easy. Giving more money or resources to one group of scholars almost always means other groups have to give something up. The result can be a protracted power struggle, because universities are fond of passing new ideas through many committees and bureaucratic heads. A final decision can often take years, even decades. One possible solution to the zero-sum resource problem is for state or federal governments or universities to provide funds, like block grants, outside of the university budgeting system.

---

[4] Joseph S. Nye Jr., "Scholars on the Sidelines," *The Washington Post* (April 13, 2009), p. A15. Nye is a University Distinguished Service Professor and former dean of the Harvard Kennedy School.

[5] David Ellwood, "We Have to Find a Way to Reward Ideas That Have Had an Impact on the World," remarks from acceptance speech delivered at the Newseum on May 7, 2009, upon receiving the 2009 Daniel Patrick Moynihan Prize.

2. More Grants or the Alumni-Giving Model

Many social scientists believe the impact of their research could be enhanced if government and industry would provide more grants for research. As it stands now, social scientists receive a very small slice of the federal grant pie (about 1 percent). The vast majority of research funds go to the medical, life, and natural sciences. As such, universities have been encouraging faculty to create partnerships with industry and business. Some scholars are eager to help. But not all.

The problem, critics of a mainstream research point out, is that government/industry-backed research can compromise the search for knowledge and truth. Industry generally funds research that will help them make more money. Some critics see this administrative research as possessing repressive qualities. Such research takes the existing power structure for granted and rarely raises serious questions about the morality of capitalism and institutional power. Philosophy professor Steven Fuller of the University of Warwick in Coventry, England, urges universities to wean themselves off military-industrial government grants and funding, because government-financed knowledge production will lead to knowledge that is bent to the will of the government.[6] Citing philosopher Thomas Kuhn, Fuller argues that science "is basically an authoritarian community."

> So there's a paradigm. And you've got the keeper of the paradigm, the department heads and so on. So what happens to you as a scientist? You become acculturated, and you apprentice with these guys, and you become certified to do science. And that's what you do, in a protected space, for the rest of your life. Filling out the world picture behind the paradigm. There's nothing democratic about the process at all. It's rather a process of unconditional commitment.

---

[6]Steve Fuller, *Governance of Science: Ideology and the Future of the Open Society* (Buckingham: Open University Press, 1999).

"Mr. Fuller's views," reporter Jeff Sharlet writes *The Chronicle of Higher Education*, "exhibit an unusual blend of utilitarian thinking and Foucaultian philosophy. Information locked in an ivory tower isn't really knowledge for its own sake, he argues, because it has the practical effect of increasing the power of its guardians."[7] Fuller argues that instead of relying on government grants, universities should pursue the alumni-giving model. The university would then become a balance to the power of the market.

Fuller's ideas about using alumni donations to fund research are compelling. But many social scientists would have a difficult time accepting Fuller's recommendation to reject government funding outright. Although scholars often agree that governments and businesses have their faults and often serve their own interests, they point out that established institutions are not always the "oppressors." They have identified social problems that affect ordinary people or disenfranchised groups, and they have provided some solutions and assistance, however meager critics may claim. Moreover, if social scientists reject government assistance altogether, then other critics would have even more ammunition to criticize the social sciences, because they would be seen as cloistering themselves in the ivory tower even more.

3. Interdisciplinary Problem-Focused Teams

Another compelling, creative and controversial plan for enhancing the impact of social science research calls for replacing contemporary fields of study (e.g., sociology, political sciences, economics, etc.) with interdisciplinary teams of scholars that instead would identify and work together to solve specific social problems. According to Mark C. Taylor, chairman of the religion department at Columbia University,

> Graduate education is the Detroit of higher learning. Most graduate
> programs in American universities produce a product for which there is

---

[7]Jeff Sharlet, "A Philosopher's Call to End All Paradigms," *The Chronicle of Higher Education* (September 15, 2000), p. A19.

no market (candidates for teaching positions that do not exist) and develop skills for which there is diminishing demand (research in subfields within subfields and publication in journals read by no one than a few like-minded colleagues), all at a rapidly rising cost (sometimes well over $100,000 in student loans).[8]

Taylor argues that universities must be radically restructured if they are to thrive in the 21st century. He proposes that universities "abolish permanent departments, even for undergraduate education, and create problem-focused programs. "These constantly evolving programs would have sunset clauses, and every seven years each one should be evaluated and either abolished, continued or significantly changed. It is possible to imagine a broad range of topics around which such zones of inquiry could be organized: Mind, Body, Law, Information, Networks, Language, Space, Time, Media, Money, Life and Water." He also recommends that universities impose mandatory retirement and abolish tenure.

> Initially intended to protect academic freedom, tenure has resulted in institutions with little turnover and professors impervious to change. After all, once tenure has been granted, there is no leverage to encourage a professor to continue to develop professionally or to require him or her to assume responsibilities like administration and student advising.

Many scholars would challenge Taylor's recommendations to abolish tenure and forced mandatory retirement. They would argue that these changes would have the opposite effect, reducing the influence of the social sciences in the real world. In particular, abolishing tenure could have an adverse impact on the number of new ideas for solving social problems. Scholars would be less likely to present ideas that are controversial, for fear of reprisal from colleagues or administrators.

---

[8]Mark C. Taylor, "End of the University as We Know It," *The New York Times* (April 27, 2009), retrieved April 28, 2009, from <www.nytimes.com/2009/04/027/opinion/27taylor.html?_r=3&pagewanted=print>.

However, the idea of creating "zones of inquiry" is certainly interesting and worth exploring, although it's not completely new. Universities have been urging scholars to engage in more interdisciplinary research for many decades. In the social sciences, the "zones of inquiry" could be organized more closely around various social problems, such as crime, poverty, discrimination, lacks of health care, etc. Past efforts to address problems in this manner have not always been very successful. The problem is that interdisciplinary teams often have difficulty coming to agreement, because the participants each have specialized knowledge and along with that comes different methods, theories and proposed solutions.

However, if scholars could organize as teams at universities and then connect with other teams at other universities, they could substantially enhance their power as change agents, and politicians would have a more difficult time ignoring them, according to Canadian parliament member and historian John Godfrey.[9] He and Canadian physician Fraser Mustard point out that numbers do matter, and scholars who unite can have more impact. "Politicians never lead parades," Mustard adds. "They only lead when a parade has been created."[10]

Canada's Social Sciences and Humanities Research Council also has encouraged social scientists to draw more public attention to their work. "We have traditionally said 'publish or perish,'" Marc Renaud, president of SSHRC told *Times Higher Education*. "Now it is 'go public or perish.'"[11] SSHRC has pushed the Canadian government to provide more funding for research that can be used in the policymaking process.

"I think we have to get more involved in making the public aware of what we do," Ratna Ghosh, dean of the McGill College of Education, told the student newspaper on his campus.[12] "If we don't fund research in the social sciences and humanities in Canada, we'll end up taking our solutions

---

[9]Philip Fine, "Go Public or Perish," *Times Higher Education* (October 12, 2001), retrieved May 20, 2009, from <www.timeshighereducation.co.uk/story.asp?storyCode=165255&sectioncode=26>.

[10]*Ibid.*

[11]*Ibid.*

[12]Philip Fine, "Go Public or Perish," *McGill Reporter* (November 19, 1998), retrieved April 10, 2009, from <http://reporter-archive.mcgill.ca/Rep/r3106/sshrc.html>.

for social problems from other countries — especially from one particular country south of the border. We don't want American solutions to Canadian problems."

4. Work More Closely with Mass Media and Stakeholders

Psychology professor Thomas Pettigrew argued in Chapter 8 that social scientists also must learn to work more closely with the mass media to get their message to the public and policymakers (see Chapter 8). He warns that "unless such alterations are made in both the media and academia ... inadequate reporting of policy-relevant social science work will continue ... and [will promote] *ad hominem* attacks that social scientists have nothing to contribute to policy debates save their own politicized opinions."[13]

Another factor affecting whether social scientists can impact public policy, according to the former president of the American Psychological Association, is the degree to which those who are directly affected by the policy (stakeholders) are given a role in the decision-making process. This was a concern raised in Chapter 4 by philosophy professor Michael Root. Patrick H. DeLeon, who is a clinical/forensic psychologist and executive assistant to U.S. Senator Daniel K. Inouye of Hawaii, says giving stakeholders a voice in the process increases the changes of policy change. He followed this advice when he helped support legislation that gave prescription privileges to psychologists in Hawaii, the first state to enact such a measure.

> [I]t has always seemed to me that if one wants to foster meaningful change, it is critical that those who might be directly impacted by the proposed modifications be given a real opportunity to substantively dialogue about both the substance of the proposed change and also the process involved ... It has also been my observation that such dialogue

---

[13]Thomas F. Pettigrew, "Can Social Scientists be Effective Actors in the Policy Arena?" pp. 121-134 in R. Lance Shotland and Melvin M. Mark (eds.), *Social Science and Social Policy* (Beverly Hills, CA: Sage Publications, 1985), pp. 126-127.

is always more productive if one first takes the time to meet with and get to personally know all of the parties potentially involved. To skip this fundamental step is to significantly reduce the likelihood of one's ultimate success, no matter how meritorious one's proposal might seem.[14]

RECOMMENDATIONS FROM PETERSILIA

Although many scholars have offered solutions for increasing the impact of social science, one of the most impressive and comprehensive lists of recommendations comes from Joan Petersilia, the criminologist whose ideas were discussed in Chapter 5. She was director of RAND Corporation's Criminal Justice Program and was a research professor of criminology for many years at the University of California, Irvine. She currently is a distinguished professor at Stanford University.

In 2007, the Academy of Experimental Criminology conferred upon her the Joan McCord Award. In her acceptance lecture, Petersilia provided seven lessons for "increasing the relevance of criminology in public policy"[15] — lessons that can be applied to other disciplines in the social sciences.

5. Policy Relevance and No Jargon

Research matters, but the topic must have immediate and understandable policy relevance, and the results must be delivered without jargon, Petersilia says. "Facts do not speak for themselves," and "most academics publish in journals that policymakers do not read." She says, "We must help the policymaker answer why they should care about our conclusions, and, if they do care, what they should do about them."

---

[14]Patrick H. DeLeon, "Reflections Upon a Very Rewarding Journey: Almost a Decade Later," *Rehabilitation Psychology,* 55(4): 530-535 (November 2008).

[15]Joan Petersilia, "Influencing Public Policy: An Embedded Criminologist Reflects on California Prison Reform: The Academy of Experimental Criminology 2007 Joan McCord Prize Lecture," *Journal of Experimental Criminology* , 4(4):335-356 (December 2008).

6. Understand Your Audience

Know your audiences and pay keen attention to their legal, political, institutional, and resource constraints. In other words, try to "walk a mile in their shoes." This recommendation reinforces the comment made earlier by Merrill Eisenberg, a consultant in program planning and evaluation, who urged anthropologists to understand the political context and policy culture surrounding a project.

7. Timing Is Crucial

Timing is everything. Petersilia says scholars need to keep up with political events and only introduce certain reforms when the timing is right.

8. Program Implementation Is Crucial, Too

The current literature on "what works" in offender rehabilitation programs is insufficient to guide policy without corresponding literature on program implementation. Petersilia argues here that the best designed program will not succeed if one lacks the knowledge and resources to implement it.

9. Rigorous Research Does Matter

Rigorous research, especially randomized experiments, really does matter. Petersilia criticizes much of the research in her field because it is methodologically weak. Not all fields of study in the social sciences can employ randomized experiments, nor should they. But she pointed out that policymakers do care about the quality of research that is produced and educating them on the best approaches is crucial.

10. Roll Up Your Sleeves and Accept Responsibility

Public criminology [or social science] is incredibly demanding, both personally and professionally. The price is higher than many academics are willing to pay. But impact doesn't come without some sweat. Petersilia writes:

> Academics are now urging a more public criminology, where scholars roll up their sleeves to help the real world. After all, the argument goes, society's problems are so huge and our knowledge so relevant. This clarion call for relevance is not unique to criminology but is permeating all of the social sciences ... We continue to bemoan the fact that our universities reward peer-reviewed academic journal articles far more than public service and suggest that, if the rewards were different, many of us would be more engaged in public policy. I have written about these disincentives and still believe they are real and detrimental to influencing practice. However, my recent experiences convince me that our university reward structures are not the main culprit, but, rather, the hard and overwhelming nature of the work, the inflexibility of unrealistic time frames, and the public scrutiny and sometimes mean-spirited attacks that presumed power and visibility bring.

11. Keep Your Expectations Reasonable

The science of criminology and its role in public policy is necessary but ultimately insufficient to alter fundamentally our nation's justice system, according to Petersilia. Science is not the only factor influencing policy and social scientists should not set unrealistic goals.

"In the final analysis, I learned that scientific knowledge does not drive crime policy and probably never will. There are other powerful, legitimate, players at the table — for example, staff, legislators, the public, and offenders themselves — and scientific knowledge is just one important consideration. Criminologists have a role to play in this mosaic, but we should not delude ourselves of our centrality."

RECOMMENDATIONS FROM AUTHOR

I do not believe that eliminating the social sciences from the academy would have no serious repercussions for people and organizations around the world. The social sciences have made us aware that human behavior cannot be reduced simply to the psychology or biology of the mind or genetics. Human decisions and behaviors are shaped by the social, political, cultural and economic environments in which they are made. Many college students want to go to Harvard, but the fact that few go there has less to do with psychological conditions or factors (motivation) than it does with access to economic and social resources. Students need money to pay the tuition and they also need the grades, and students who come from higher SES families, research shows, have a major advantage, even though the university has shown a commitment to enrolling more students from disadvantaged backgrounds..

Social scientific political polls also have helped society better understand voters during an election. Economists generate data about economic processes and trends that help government and business understand the marketplace and make better decisions. Criminologists have generated much useful information about the social factors influencing crime (e.g., age, gender, race), even though they are still searching for better solutions. Political scientists have identified many shortcomings in the structure of representative democracy, including and especially the problem of unequal distribution of power and money. And although television contains a lot of violent content, it might contain even more today had mass communication scholars not drawn attention to the problem in the 1970s.

I believe the social sciences are capable of producing knowledge and have played a key role in identifying social problems. But in terms of solving those problems, they clearly are failing to live up to the promises created by the Enlightenment philosophers and early social scientists.

12. Require "Social Impact Studies"

In my opinion, the most important impediment to enhancing the impact of social science research is ideology. In fact, America's political system is structurally organized to maximize the role of ideology, not truth or knowledge. The policymaking process encourages people and organizations to present their ideas (or ideologies) in the competition for limited resources, including money and power. The two major political parties in America (Democrat and Republican) embody, at the most abstract level, many of the ideas, beliefs and values upon which the debate for limited resources takes place. Elected officials of the parties can certainly make decisions or vote in a way that counters the prevailing ideology of their respective political parties and constituents, but this is not the norm, as there are serious consequences for those officials who routinely ignore their party platform, including lack of donations for reelection.

Political scientists could spend a lifetime trying to convince politicians and the public that the current political system is rife with injustice and unfairness. I hope some do. But trying to change the values or opinions held by policymakers or citizens so that they enact legislation or rules that elevate the status of truth and knowledge in decision-making is an extremely difficult thing to do, especially in the short run. So, instead of changing the psychology of the participants, a better, more pragmatic approach is to change the structure of the system.

Specifically, the social sciences should adopt the "environmental-impact-study model" and apply it to their own fields of study. When policymaking involves decisions that would harm or help people, the government or controlling agency should require the parties involved to conduct "social impact studies," which would assess the effects these changes would have on the psychological, social and cultural well-being of those people or groups affected by the change. Social scientists would be called upon to create these studies. Ideally, the "social impact study" would be mandatory for all levels of government, national, state and local. Collaboration among social scientists would be encouraged across disciplines, but agreement about the impact is not necessary. In fact, disagreement among scholars studying a policy often enhances, not detracts from, the process. Even bad ideas or conclusions can often generate new, better ideas.

Social impact studies would not guarantee that social scientists have more impact on public policy, but they would increase the chances of such impact, because policymakers would have access to more information than they would without such impact studies. The studies would make policymakers more accountable to citizens (i.e., Was it appropriate for those policymakers to ignore the research?). They alsoo would help reconnect social scientists to their communities. There are many details and challenges to creating a policy that would require or, at a minimum, encourage social impact statements. Funding, of course, is always an issue. Social scientists also may need training to prepare such reports for public consumption. But spending a little money up front may reduce the number of bad decisions, which can produce big savings down the road.

13. Create Formal Propositions of Knowledge

Some professional associations in various fields have created lists of propositions that attempt to summarize key bodies of knowledge and then actively lobby political organizations and government bodies to incorporate these propositions into public policy. This practice should be encouraged. Although it is rare to find scholars in complete agreement over findings in their fields, the knowledge propositions could be developed mainly through referenda votes of association memberships. They might consider setting a "supermajority" minimum before going public with a policy statement. Or they might simply release the results of the votes and allow policymakers and the public to decide whether and how to use the information in the decision-making process. More effective public relations campaigns and lobbying efforts are also needed for the social sciences to expect more impact in the policymaking arena.

14. Develop Educational Programs

Professional associations, universities and governmental agencies should develop and fund programs specifically geared to give scholars and administrators more training on how to influence public policy and to give policymakers a better understanding of how science can help the decision-making process. Graduate-level courses on how the public policy process works and how research fits into that process should be required in all social science disciplines. As Petersilia pointed out, many Ph.D.s know little about how the policy process works.

15. Create Websites of Knowledge

Social scientists often feel there is little they can do as individuals to influence public policy or public opinion. However, they can make a stronger effort to disseminate their own research to the public via websites and social media. A good example of this can be found at <www2.potsdam.edu/hansondj/index.html>, where a professor is educating the public and policymakers on the effects of alcohol advertising. Universities might also reward faculty who set up such websites.

16. Find or Create an Organization to Lead the Effort

No undertaking as significant as the attempt to increase the influence of social science research can succeed without the sustained support and leadership of a major organization. One of the best suited for the job, in my opinion, is the American Academy of Political and Social Science, one is of the nation's oldest learned societies (founded in 1887). AAPSS is "dedicated to the use of social science to address important social problems" and "to bridging the gap between academic research and the formation of public policy." According to Douglas S. Massey, president of the AAPSS in 2011, "The Academy is devoted to employing the rigor of social science and empirical research to address questions that matter in the real world." Policy Studies Organization, discussed in Chapter 2, also has the potential to play a leadership role. Alternatively, a number of different organizations and professional associations could come together to create a new organization to lead the effort (my preference).

WHAT IS THE LIKELIHOOD OF REAL CHANGE?

Although many social scientists and some policymakers will embrace some or all of the recommendations above, others will point out that the prospects for increasing the impact of the social sciences in the policymaking process are not good. They are probably right. Academic and government bureaucracies resist change.[16] They are often intolerant of individuals and organizations that challenge their authority. Sociologist Max Weber was the one of the first to recognize these problems.

Max Weber's Theory of Bureaucracy

Weber defined a bureaucracy as a corporate organization that was goal-oriented. He pointed out that modern society could not exist without them, partly because they were efficient. However, bureaucracies resist change, for three major reasons.

First, "once it is fully established, bureaucracy is among those social institutions which are hardest to destroy."[17]

> The ruled, for their part, cannot dispense with or replace the bureaucratic apparatus of authority once it exists. For this bureaucracy rests upon expert training, a functional specialization of work, and an attitude set for habitual and virtuoso-like mastery of single yet methodically integrated functions ... More and more the material fate of

---

[16]My personal belief is that no change is likely until the federal government cuts research funding to the social sciences. This is a real possibility if Republicans can regain control of Congress, the Senate and the Presidency, especially if the cuts to humanities and social sciences in the United Kingdom have little impact beyond shifting the burden of cost to students.

[17]H. H. Gerth and C. Wright Mills (eds.), *From Max Weber: Essays in Sociology* (New York: Oxford University Press, 1946), p. 228.

the masses depends upon steady and correct functioning of the increasingly bureaucratic organizations of private capitalism. The idea of eliminating these organizations becomes more and more utopian.[18]

Second, Weber feared that bureaucracies would use their power to trample on individual rights. Much of their power came from the fact that they monopolize information. "Every bureaucracy seeks to increase the superiority of the professionally informed by keeping their knowledge and intentions secret."[19] Bureaucracies, including universities, also resist being accountable for their actions.

And the third problem, according to Weber, is that bureaucracies often act in ways incompatible with democratic principles. A bureaucracy, by its nature, is hierarchically structured, and decision-making usually is top-down. Weber was, in fact, very pessimistic about the long-term consequences that bureaucracies would have for individual freedom and autonomy and democratic decision-making.[20] In this respect, he suggested that a bureaucracy can be an "iron cage."[21]

Iron Law of Oligarchy

Weber's student Robert Michels took this argument a step farther. He developed what he called the "iron law of oligarchy," which contends that bureaucracies are incompatible with democratic processes. Although leaders of new organizations often start with a commitment to democracy, the demands of the organization compel them to hire a bureaucracy of professional staff and to centralize power. To retain their power, leaders often oppose efforts to democratize their organizations through free

---

[18] *Ibid.*, p. 229.

[19] *Ibid.*, p. 233.

[20] *Ibid.*, p. 224-8. Also see Robert Michels, "Oligarchy," pp. 48-67 in Frank Fischer and Carmen Sirianni, *Critical Studies in Organization and Bureaucracy* (Philadelphia: Temple University Press, 1984).

[21] Weber called it *stahlhartes Gehäuse*, which was translated by American sociologist Talcott Parsons to mean "iron cage." Other sociologists dispute this translations, saying "shell as hard as steel" or "steel-hard housing" would be more appropriate.

elections or other means.[22] This produces what he called an "oligarchy," or the idea that a handful of elites in the organization end up with most of the power.

> It is organization which gives birth to the domination of the elected over the electors, of the mandataries over the mandators, of the delegates over the delegators. Who says organization says oligarchy.[23]

Michels' theory challenged Jean-Jacques Rousseau's concept of direct popular democracy. In *The Social Contract,* Rousseau argued that the ideal form of government was a democracy, where the will of the people reigned supreme.[24] In a state of nature, humans are competitive. But humans can preserve their freedom by joining together into civil society through a "social contract." Sovereignty (e.g., the power to make law) should be in the hands of the people and the government is charged with implementing and enforcing the will of the people. Direct democracy is the ideal form of governance. He was opposed to representative democracy.

Michels asserted that Rousseau was wrong, because as organizations grow they inevitably fall victim to the "iron law of oligarchy." In fact, large-scale organization cannot exist without turning over power to a handful of people at the top. To test his theory, Michels examined socialist parties in Germany and elsewhere, which were highly committed to the principles of direct democracy, free speech and equality. Of course, he found ample evidence that the organizations themselves didn't practice what they preached. But the most damning evidence to Rousseau's thesis came from political events in 1914 and 1917. The first was a decision of the German Social Democratic Party, which had opposed German militarism for years, to support the Kaiser's declaration of war. The second was the Russian Revolution, the first successful socialist revolution in the world but

---

[22]Robert Michels, *Political Parties: A Sociological Study of the Oligarchical Tendencies of Modern Democracy,* translated by Eden Paul and Cedar Paul (New York: Free Press, 1962, originally published in 1911).

[23]*Ibid.,* p. 365.

[24]Jean-Jacques Rousseau, *The Social Contract,* trans. Maurice Cranston (Middlesex, England: Penguin Books, 1968).

one which eventually led to brutal suppression of democracy principles and individual rights.

Are Bureaucracies Efficient?

A number of empirical studies also have questioned the extent to which bureaucracies or corporations are rational or efficient. Sociologist Robert K. Merton has argued, for example, that employees of bureaucracies often place more importance on following the rules than on achieving the goals of the organization.[25] "Adherence to the rules, originally conceived as a means, becomes transformed into an end-in-itself; then there occurs the familiar process of *displacement of goals* whereby 'an instrumental value becomes a terminal value.'"[26]

In addition to overconformity to rules and displacement of goals, some scholars have suggested that as bureaucracies grow they become more inefficient, particularly when bureaucratic growth is disproportionate to actual tasks or outputs.[27] Large-scale organizations often have more difficulty adjusting to changes in the environment and are often said to have a low capacity for innovation. Such was the case during the 1970s (and again in 2008) in the U.S. automobile industry when sales slumped but inventories kept piling up. Nepotism and political disputes also can contradict the rule of impersonality and can turn a meritocractic recruitment and promotion system into an oligarchical one.

Sociologist Michael Crozier even contends that bureaucracies are self-destructive and are unable to acknowledge their faults.[28] "A bureaucratic organization is an organization that can not correct its behaviour by learning from its errors."[29] The received wisdom in the legal circles

---

[25]Robert K. Merton, "Bureaucratic Structure and Personality," pp. 195-206 in Robert K. Merton (ed.), *Social Theory and Social Structure* (London: The Free Press, 1957 [1949]).

[26]*Ibid.,* p. 199.

[27]Marshall W. Meyer, William Stevenson and Stephen Webster, *Limits to Bureaucratic Growth* (New York: De Gruyter, 1985).

[28]Michael Crozier, *The Bureaucratic Phenomenon* (Chicago: The University of Chicago Press, 1964).

[29]*Ibid.*, p. 187.

provides strong support for Crozier's assertion that bureaucracies are unable to admit their faults. Lawyers constantly advise aggrieved clients that the offending bureaucracy will never apologize for its mistakes. The bureaucracy would much rather pay a large sums of money than admit guilt. Crozier adds that a bureaucracy is "not only a system that does not correct its behaviour in view of its errors; it is also too rigid to adjust, without crises, to the transformations that the accelerated evolution of the industrial society makes more and more imperative."[30] Numerous other criticisms of Weber's model have been put forth.[31]

Overcoming Bureaucratic Resistance

All of these criticisms do not bode well for making fundamental changes in the university or in government. But the theories of Weber, Michels and Crozier are a bit too rigid. Bureaucracies can and do change, especially when faced with a crisis. If funding to the social sciences in the United States were to be cut off, no doubt social scientists and administrators would be motivated to make changes.

But a major crisis is not the only way to move a bureaucracy. Another option is to identify benefits for social actors near or at the top of the hierarchy. If those who hold power in a bureaucracy can see advantages for themselves ("What's in it for me?"), they would be more likely to favor a proposed change. And they are the ones who have the power to make the change. The key, then, is to find ways to reward top-level university administrators for creating programs to enhance the impact of social science research (even if they don't deserve such rewards).

---

[30]*Ibid.*, p. 198.

[31]For a summary, see Dean J. Champion, *The Sociology of Organizations* (New York: McGraw-Hill, 1975), pp. 36-40.

CONCLUSION

Although I hope universities and governmental agencies adopt many of the recommendations provided in this chapter, I am not overly confident this will happen without some kind of major crisis such as that which occurred in the United Kingdom (i.e., a complete cut in funding; see Chapter 1 for details). However, no change can occur unless people and organizations become aware of the problem, and that has been one of the major goals of this book — to draw more attention to the impact problem and to point out that if the social sciences abandon the activist ideals of the early founders of the field, they very well may follow in the footsteps of the Babylonians.

BIBLIOGRAPHY

Aaron, Henry J., *Politics and Professors: The Great Society in Perspective* (Washington, D.C.: Brookings Institution, 1978).

Abbott, Andrew, "Of Time and Place," *Social Forces, 75*: 1149-1182 (1997).

Abbott, Andrew, "Seven Types of Ambiguity," *Theory and Society, 26*: 357-391 (1978).

Abercrombie, Nicholas, Stephen Hill and Brian S. Turner, *The Dominant Ideology Thesis* (London: Allen & Unwin, 1980).

Adams, Stuart, "Evaluation: A Way Out of Rhetoric," pp. 75-91 in Robert Martinson, Ted Palmer and Stuart Adams (eds.), *Rehabilitation, Recidivism, and Research* (Hackensack, NJ: National Council on Crime and Delinquency, 1976).

Albæk, Erick, "Between Knowledge and Power: Utilization of Social Science in Public Policy Making," *Policy Sciences, 28*: 79-100 (1995).

Albæk, Erick, "Between Knowledge and Power: Utilization of Social Science in Public Policy Making," *Policy Sciences, 28*: 79-100 (1995).

Alexander, Jeffrey C., "The New Theoretical Movement," pp. 77-101 in N. J. Smelser (ed.), *Handbook of Sociology* (Beverly Hills, Calif.: Sage, 1988).

Alexander, Jeffrey C., and Paul Colomy, "Traditions and Competition: Preface to a Postpositivist Approach to Knowledge Cumulation," pp. 27-52 in George Ritzer (ed.), *Metatheorizing* (Newbury Park, CA: Sage Publications, 1992).

Altman, Karen E., "Consuming Ideology: The Better Homes in America Campaign," *Critical Studies in Mass Communication, 7*:286-307 (1990).

Altschull, J. Herbert, *Agents of Power* (New York: Longman, 1984).

Amacher, Ryan C., "Economics and Public Policy," pp. 159-179 in George J. McCall and George H. Weber, *Social Science and Public Policy: The Roles of Academic Disciplines in Policy Analysis* (Port Washington, NY: Associated Faculty Press, 1984).

Aminzade, Ronald, "From the Chair," *Facets* (Minneapolis: College of Liberal Arts and Department of Sociology, 2005).

Andrade, James, "Letter to the Editor," *The Observer* (February 6, 2011), retrieved February 21, 2011, from <http://www.guardian.co.uk/commentisfree/2011/jan/30/nick-cohen-higher-education-cuts>.

Anton, Thomas J., "Policy Sciences and Social Sciences: Reflections from an Editor's Chair," pp. 201-214 in George J. McCall and George H. Weber, *Social Science and*

Public Policy: The Roles of Academic Disciplines in Policy Analysis (Port Washington, NY: Associated Faculty Press, 1984).

Aufderheide, Patricia, _Communications Policy and the Public Interest: The Telecommunications Act of 1996_ (New York: Guilford, 1998).

Babbie, Earl, _The Practice of Social Research_, 2nd ed. (Belmont, CA: Wadsworth, 1979).

Babbie, Earl, _The Practice of Social Research_, 4th ed. (Belmont, CA: Wadsworth, 1986),

Babich, Babette E., "Physics vs. Social Text: Anatomy of a Hoax," _Telos, 107_ (1996).

Bailey, Walter C., "Correctional Outcome: An Evaluation of 100 Reports," _Journal of Criminal Law, Criminology and Police Science, 57_: 153-160 (1966).

Bandura, Albert, _Aggression: A Social Learning Analysis_ (Englewood Cliffs, N.J.: Prentice-Hall, 1973).

Barak-Glantz, I., and C. Ronald Huff (eds.), _The Mad, the Bad, and the Different: Essays in Honor of Simon Dinitz_ (Lexington, MA: D.C. Heath, 1981).

Barber, Bernard, _Science and the Social Order_ (Glencoe, IL: The Free Press, 1952),.

Bartholow, Bruce D., Karen E. Dill, Kathryn B. Anderson and James J. Lindsay, "The Proliferation of Media Violence and Its Economic Underpinnings," pp. 1-18 in Douglas A. Gentile (ed.), _Media Violence and Children: A Complete Guide for Parents and Professionals_ (Westport, CT: Praeger, 2003).

Bechtel, William, _Philosophy of Science: An Overview for Cognitive Science_ (Hillsdale, NJ: Lawrence Erlbaum Associates, 1988).

Ben-David, Joseph, and Awraham Zloczower, "Universities and Academic Systems in Modern Societies," _European Journal of Sociology, 3_: 45-84 (1962).

Bennett, W. Lance, _News: The Politics of Illusion_, 2nd ed. (New York: Longman, 1988).

Berger, Peter L., and Thomas Luckmann, _The Social Construction of Reality: A Treatise in the Sociology of Knowledge_ (Garden City, NY: Doubleday & Company, 1966; Anchor Books edition, 1967).

Berleman, William C., and Thomas W. Steinburn, "The Value and Validity of Delinquency Prevention Experiments," _Crime & Delinquency, 15_: 471-478 (1969).

Bernard Berelson, _Graduate Education in the United States_ (New York: McGraw-Hill, 1960).

Beutel, Frederick K., _Some Potentialities of Experimental Jurisprudence as a New Branch of Social Science_ (Lincoln: University of Nebraska Press, 1957).

Bleyer, Willard Grosvenor, _Main Currents in the History of Journalism_ (New York: Houghton Mifflin, 1927).

Blumstein, Alfred, Jacqueline Cohen and Daniel Nagin (eds.), _Deterrence and Incapacitation: Estimating the Effects of Criminal Sanctions on Crime Rates_ (Washington, D.C.: National Academy of Sciences, 1978).

Boffey, Philip M., "Youth Crime Puzzle Defies a Solution," _The New York Times_ (March 5, 1982), retrieved September 5, 2008, from <http://query.nytimes.com/gst/fullpage.html?res=9F00EFDE153BF936A35750C0A964948260&sec=health&spon=&pagewanted=all>.

Bohman, James, *New Philosophy of Social Science* (Cambridge, MA: The MIT Press, 1993, paperback edition; first published in 1991).

Braman, Sandra, "Introduction," pp. 1-9 in Sandra Braman (ed.), *Communication Researchers and Policy Making* (Cambridge, MA: MIT Press, 2003).

Brantigan, C. O., T. A. Brantigan and N. Joseph, "Effect of Beta Blockade and Beta Stimulation on Stage Fright," *American Journal of Medicine, 72*(1): 88-94 (January 1982).

Brauer, Carl, "More Scholars Should Venture Forth to Confront, Enlighten or Change the World," *The Chronicle of Higher Education* (March 14, 1990).

Brown v. Board of Education of Topeka, 347 U.S. 483 (1954).

Bruck, Peter, "Strategies for Peace, Strategies for News Research," *Journal of Communication, 39*(1): 108-129 (1989).

Bulmer, Martin, *The Uses of Social Research: Social Investigation in Public Policy-Making* (London: Allen & Unwin, 1982).

Burgess, E. W., "Factors Determining Success or Failure on Parole," pp. 205-249 in Andrew A. Bruce et al., (eds.), *The Workings of Indeterminate Sentencing Law and the Parole System in Illinois* (Springfield, IL: Parole Board of Illinois, 1928).

Butler, Judith, "Further Reflections on the Conversations of Our Time," *Diacritics*, 27(1): 13-15 (Spring 1997).

Caldwell, Robert G., "The Deterrent Influence of Corporal Punishment upon Prisoners Who Have Been Whipped," *American Sociological Review 9*: 171-177 (April 1944).

Calhoun, Craig, "Sociology in America: An Introduction," pp. 1-38 (Chapter 1) in Craig Calhoun (ed.), *Sociology in America: A History* (Chicago: University of Chicago Press, 2007).

Calhoun, Craig, *Sociology in America: A History* (Chicago: University of Chicago Press, 2007).

Callon, Michel, "Whose Impostures? Physicists at War with the Third Person," *Social Studies of Science, 29*(2): 261-86 (1999).

Campbell, Liz, "President's Column," *The Psychologist, 21*(9): 782-785 (September 2008).

Cantor, Joanne, *"Mommy, I'm Scared": How TV and Movies Frighten Children and How We Can Protect Them* (San Diego, CA: Harvest Books, 1998).

Cantor, Joanne, "Notes from the Trenches of the Media Violence Wars," *Journalism Studies, 2*(4): 620-623 (2001).

Carey, James W., "Mass communication Research and Cultural Studies: An American View," pp. 407-425 in J. Curran, M. Gurevitch and J. Woollacott (eds.), *Mass Communication and Society* (Beverly Hills, CA: Sage, 1979).

CASRO (Council of American Survey Research Organizations) 2007 Data Trends Survey, retrieved Jan. 19, 2009, from <www.casro.org/pdfs/2007%20CASRO%20Data% 20Trends%20Survey.pdf>.

Castel, John, *The Group in Society* (Thousand Oaks, CA: Sage, 2010).

CBS Television Network, *60 Minutes: It Doesn't Work* (Transcript), 7: 2-9 (August 24, 1975).

Chambliss, William J., "The Deterrent Influence of Publishment," *Crime and Delinquency,* *12*: 70-75 (January 1966).

Champion, Dean J., *The Sociology of Organizations* (New York: McGraw-Hill, 1975).

Chiricos, Theodore G., and Gordon P. Waldo, "Punishment and Crime: An Examination of Some Empirical Evidence," *Social Problems, 18*: 200-217 (Fall 1970).

Chomsky, Noam, "The Manufacture of Consent" (Minneapolis: Silha Center, University of Minnesota, 1986).

Chomsky, Noam, "The Responsibility of Intellectuals," *The New York Review of Books, 8* (1967).

Chomsky, Noam, *American Power and the New Mandarins* (Harmondsworth, England: Penguin, 1969).

Chomsky, Noam, *Hegemony or Survival: America's Quest for Global Dominance* (New York: Henry Holt & Company LLC, 2003).

Chomsky, Noam, *Syntactic Structures* (The Hague/Paris: Mouton, 1957).

Christians, Clifford, and James W. Carey, "The Logic and Aims of Qualitative Research" pp. 342-362 in G. H. Stempel & B. H. Westley (Eds.), *Research Methods in Mass Communication* (Englewood Cliffs, NJ: Prentice-Hall, 1981).

Cohen, David K., and Janet A. Weiss, "Social Scientists and Decision Makers Look at the Usefulness of Mental Health Research," in Carol H. Weiss (ed.), *Using Social Research in Public Policy Making* (Lexington, MA: Heath, 1977).

Cohen, Nick, "Academia Plays into the Hands of the Right: The Cuts in Arts, Humanities and Social Science Courses Can Be Seen as a Self-inflicted Wound," *The Guardian* (January 30, 2011), retrieved February 6, 2011, from <http://www.guardian.co.uk/commentisfree/2011/jan/30/nick-cohen-higher-education-cuts>.

Cohen, Patricia, "Ivory Tower Unswayed by Crashing Economy," *The New York Times* (March 5, 2009)

Cohen, Percy S., "Is Positivism Dead?" *Sociological Review, 28*(1): 141-176 (February 1980).

Cohen, Stanley, and Jock Young (eds.), *The Manufacture of News* (London: Constable, 1981).

Coleman, James S., *Equality of Educational Opportunity (Coleman) Study* (Ann Arbor, MI: Inter-university Consortium for Political and Social Research, 1966).

Comstock, George, and Erica Scharrer, "Meta-Analyzing the Controversy over Television Violence and Aggression," pp. 205-226 in Douglas A. Gentile (ed.), *Media Violence and Children: A Complete Guide for Parents and Professionals* (Westport, CT: Praeger, 2003).

Comstock, George, S. Chaffee, N. Katzman, M. McCombs and D. Roberts, *Television and Human Behavior* (New York: Columbia University Press, 1978).

Comte, Auguste, *The Positive Philosophy of Auguste Comte,* vol. 1, translated and condensed by Harriet Martineau (London: Bell, 1896; reissued by Cambridge University Press, 2009).

Condit, Celeste M., "Hegemony Is a Mass-mediated Society: Concordance about Reproductive Technologies," *Critical Studies in Mass Communication, 11*: 205-230 (1994).

Condit, Celeste Michelle, "Culture and Biology in Human Communication: Toward a Multi-causal Model," *Communication Education, 49*(1): 7-24 (January 2000).

Cook, Philip J., "Punishment and Crime: A Critique of Current Findings Concerning the Preventive Effects of Punishment,"*Law and Contemporary Problems, 41*: 200-208 (Winter 1977).

Cook, Thomas D., "Postpositivist Critical Multiplism," pp. 21-62 in R. Lance Shotland and Melvin M. Mark (eds.), *Social Science and Social Policy* (Beverly Hills, CA: Sage Publications, 1985).

Cornish, D., and R. Clark (eds.), *The Reasoning Criminal* (New York: Springer-Verlag, 1986).

Coser, Lewis, *Masters of Sociological Thought: Ideas in Historical and Social Context* (New York: Harcourt Brace Jovanovich, Inc., 1971).

Crone, James A., *How Can We Solve Our Social Problems?* 2nd ed. (Thousand Oaks, CA: Pine Forge Press, 2011).

Crother, Carol, "Crimes, Penalties and Legislatures," *The Annals of the American Academy of Political and Social Science, 381*: 147-158 (January 1969).

Crowley, J., *The Politics of Child Support in America.* (Cambridge, UK: Cambridge University Press, 2003).

Crozier, Michael, *The Bureaucratic Phenomenon* (Chicago: The University of Chicago Press, 1964).

Cullen, Francis T., "The Twelve People Who Saved Rehabilitation: How the Science of Criminology Made a Difference — The American Society of Criminology 2004 Presidential Address," *Criminology 43*(1):1-42 (2005).

Cullen, Francis T., and Paul Gendreau, "From Nothing Works to What Works: Changing Professional Ideology in the 21ˢᵗ Century," *The Prison Journal, 81*: 323-338 (2001).

Dahl, Robert A., "The Behavioral Approach in Political Science: Epitaph for a Monument to a Successful Protest," *American Political Science Review, 55*(4): 763-772 (December 1961).

Danziger, Sheldon, "Welfare Reform Policy from Nixon to Clinton: What Role for Social Science?" pp. 137-164 in David L. Featherman and Maris A. Vinovskis (eds.), *Social Science and Policy-Making: A Search for Relevance in the Twentieth Century* (Ann Arbor, MI: University of Michigan Press, 2001).

Darwin, Charles Robert, *The Origin of Species,* Vol. XI, The Harvard Classics (New York: P. F. Collier & Son, 1909–14; originally published in 1859).

DeLeon, P., "Democracy and the Policy Sciences," *Policy Studies Journal, 22*: 200-212 (1994).

DeLeon, Patrick H., "Reflections Upon a Very Rewarding Journey: Almost a Decade Later," *Rehabilitation Psychology, 55*(4): 530-535 (November 2008).

DeLeon, Patrick H., Anne Marie O'Keefe, Gary R. VandenBos, and Alan G. Kraut, "How to Influence Public Policy: A Blueprint for Activism," *American Psychologist, 27*: 476-485 (1982).

Demers, David, "Corporate News Structure, Social Control and Social Change," pp. 375-398 in David Demers and K. Viswanath (eds.), *Mass Media, Social Control, and Social Change: A Macrosocial Perspective* (Ames: Iowa State University Press, 1999).

Demers, David, *History and Future of Mass Media: An Integrated Perspective* (Cresskill, NJ: Hampton Press, 2007).

Demers, David Pearce, The *Menace of the Corporate Newspaper: Fact or Fiction?* (Ames: Iowa State University Press, 1996).

Department of Defense Dictionary of Military and Associated Terms, Joint Publication 1-02 (April 12, 2001).

Dewey, John, *Democracy and Education: An Introduction to the Philosophy of Education* (New York, The Macmillan Company, 1916).

Dewey, John, *Experience and Education* (New York, The Macmillan Company, 1938).

Diamond, Larry, *The Spirit of Democracy: The Struggle to Build Free Societies Throughout the World* (New York: Times Books, 2008).

Dinitz, Simon, an oral history, interview conducted by Adrienne Chafetz (November 8, 2005), retrieved September 18, 2008 from <https://kb.osu.edu/dspace/handle/1811/29289>.

Dinitz, Simon, and David K. Demers (1983), "Money: Is It Real or Is It Reprographed?" Proprietary paper prepared for the Battelle Memorial Institute, Columbus, Ohio, under contract to the U.S. Department of Treasury, Columbus, OH.

Dittrick, L., "About-Face facts on BODY IMAGE," About-Face website, available online at <http://about-face.org/r/facts/bi.shtml>.

"Domestic Research Priorities," National Science Foundation (April 1988), cited in Joan Petersilia, "Policy Relevance and the Future of Criminology — The American Society of Criminology 1990 Presidential Address," *Criminology 29*(1): 1-15 (1991).

Donohue III, John J., and Steven D. Levitt, "Impact of Legalized Abortion on Crime," *Quarterly Journal of Economics, 116*(2): 379-420 (May 2001).

Donohue, John J., and Steven D. Levitt, "Measurement Error, Legalized Abortion, and the Decline in Crime: A Response to Foote and Goetz," *Quarterly Journal of Economics, 123*(1): 425-440 (2008).

Douglas, Hernán Cortés, "What Macroeconomists Don't Know," Gold-Eagle.com (January 24, 2002), retrieved May 12, 2009, from <www.gold-eagle.com/editorials_02/cortes012402pv.html>

Dovidio, John F., and Victoria M. Esses, "Psychological Research and Public Policy: Bridging the Gap," *Social Issues and Policy Review, 1*(1): 5-14 (December 2007).

Dror, Yehezkel, *Design for Policy Sciences* (New York: Elsevier, 1971).

Durkheim, Émile, *Suicide* (London, Routledge and Kegan Paul, 1952; originally published in 1897).

Durkheim, Émile, *The Division of Labor in Society* (New York: Macmillan, 1933), p. xxvi (Trans. of *De la Division due Travail Social*, doctoral dissertation, completed in 1893).

Dutton, Denis, "Language Crimes: A Lesson in How Not to Write, Courtesy of the Professoriate," *The Wall Street Journal* (February 5, 1999), retrieved October 21, 2010, from <http://denisdutton.com/language_crimes.htm>.

Dutton, Denis, "The Bad Writing Contest: Press Releases 1996 to 1998," retrieved Oct. 21, 2010, from <http://denisdutton.com/bad_writing.htm>.

Eisenberg, Merrill, "Translating Research into Policy: What More Does It Take?" *Practicing Anthropology, 16*(4): 35-38 (1994).

Ellwood, David, "We Have to Find a Way to Reward Ideas That Have Had an Impact on the World," remarks from acceptance speech delivered at the Newseum on May 7, 2009, upon receiving the 2009 Daniel Patrick Moynihan Prize.

Ellwood, David T., *Poor Support: Poverty in the American Family* (New York: Basic Books, 1989).

Epstein, Edward Jay, *News From Nowhere* (New York: Random House, 1973).

Ewen, Stuart, *PR! A Social History of Spin* (New York: Basic Books, 1996).

Ewin, Stuart, *Captains of Consciousness: Advertising and the Social Roots of the Consumer Culture* (New York: McGraw Hill, 1976).

Faigel, H. C., "The Effect of Beta Blockade on Stress-Induced Cognitive Dysfunction in Adolescents," *Clinical Pediatrician, 30*(7): 441-445 (July 1991).

Feagin, Joe R., "Soul-Searching in Sociology: Is the Discipline in Crisis?" *The Chronicle of Higher Education* (October 15, 1999).

Featherman, David L., and Maris A. Vinovskis, "Growth and Use of Social and Behavioral Science in the Federal Government Since World War II," pp. 40-82 in David L. Featherman and Maris A. Vinovskis (eds.), *Social Science and Policy-Making: A Search for Relevance in the Twentieth Century* (Ann Arbor, MI: University of Michigan Press, 2001).

Fincher, Cameron, "Recalling Robert S. Lynd's: Knowledge for What?" *IHE Perspectives* (Athens: Institute of Higher Education, University of Georgia, October 2001).

Fine, Philip, "Go Public or Perish," *Times Higher Education* (October 12, 2001), retrieved May 20, 2009, from <www.timeshighereducation.co.uk/story.asp?storyCode= 165255&sectioncode=26>.

Fine, Philip, "Go Public or Perish," *McGill Reporter* (November 19, 1998), retrieved April 10, 2009, from <http://reporter-archive.mcgill.ca/Rep/r3106/sshrc.html>.

Finger, J. Michael, "Policy Research," *Journal of Political Economy, 89*(6) :1270-71 (December 1981).

Fischer, Klaus P., *America n White, Black, and Gray: The Stormy 1960s* (London: Continuum International Publishing Group, 2006).

Fishman, Mark, *Manufacturing the News* (Austin: University of Texas Press, 1980).

Fiske, Jonathon, *Television Culture* (New York: Methuen, 1987).

Flyvbjerg, Bent, *Making Social Science Matter: Why Social Inquiry Fails and How It Can Succeed Again* (Cambridge, United Kingdom: University Press, 2001).

Foote, Christopher L., and Christopher F. Goetz, "The Impact of Legalized Abortion on Crime: Comment," *Quarterly Journal of Economics, 123*(1): 407-423 (2008).

Formaini, Robert, *The Myth of Scientific Public Policy* (New York: Transaction Publishers, 1990),

Fox, R. F., *Harvesting Minds: How TV Commercials Control Kids* (Westport, CT: Praeger Publishing, 1996).

Freeman, Derek, *Margaret Mead and Samoa: The Making and Unmaking of an Anthropological Myth* (Cambridge, MA: Harvard University Press, 1983).

Fuller, Steve, *Governance of Science: Ideology and the Future of the Open Society* (Buckingham: Open University Press, 1999).

Galbraith, John Kenneth, *The Affluent Society* (Boston: Houghton Mifflin, 1958).

Gamson, William A., *Talking Politics* (New York: Cambridge University Press, 1992).

Gans, Herbert J., *Deciding What's News* (New York: Vintage, 1979).

Gartrell, C. David, and John W. Gartrell, "Positivism in Sociological Practice: 1967-1990," *The Canadian Review of Sociology and Anthropology* (May 1, 1996).

Gates, G. A., J. Saegert, N. Wilson, L. Johnson, A. Shepherd, and E. M. Hearne 3rd, "Effect of Beta Blockade on Singing Performance," *Ann Otol Rhinol Laryngol, 94*(6): 570-574 (November/December 1985).

Gendreau, Paul, and R. R. Ross, "Revivification of Rehabilitation: Evidence from the 1980s," *Justice Quarterly, 4*(3): 349-407 (1987).

Genovese, Frank C., "In Memoriam: Robert J. Lampman, 1920-1997," *The American Journal of Economics and Sociology* (January 1998), retrieved November 1, 2008, from <http://findarticles.com/p/articles/mi_m0254/is_n1_v57/ai_20538773/pg_2?tag=artBody;col1>.

Gentile, Douglas A. (ed.), *Media Violence and Children: A Complete Guide for Parents and Professionals* (Westport, CT: Praeger, 2003).

Gentile, Douglas A., Muniba Saleem and Craig A. Anderson, "Public Policy and the Effects of Media Violence on Children," *Social Issues and Policy Review, 1*(1): 15-61 (2007).

Gerbner, George, Larry Gross, Michael Morgan, and Nancy Signorielli, "Growing Up With Television: The Cultivation Perspective," pp. 17-42 in J. Bryant and D. Zillmann (eds.), *Media Effects: Advances in Theory and Research* (Hillsdale, NJ: Lawrence Erlbaum Associates, 1994).

Gerth, H. H., and C. Wright Mills (eds.), *From Max Weber: Essays in Sociology* (New York: Oxford University Press, 1946)

Gibbs, Jack P., "Crime, Punishment, and Deterrence," *The Southwestern Social Science Quarterly, 48*: 515-530 (March 1968).

Gibbs, Jack P., *Crime, Punishment, and Deterrence* (New York: Elsevier Scientific Publishing Co., Inc., 1975).

Giddens, Anthony, *Central Problems of Social Theory* (Berkeley: University of California Press, 1979).

Giddens, Anthony, *The Constitution of Society Constitution of Society: Outline of the Theory of Structuration* (Berkeley: University of California Press, 1984).

Gitlin, Todd, "Media Sociology: The Dominant Paradigm," pp. 73-121 in G. Cleveland Wilhoit and Harold de Bock (eds.), *Mass Communication Review Yearbook*, Vol. 2 (Beverly Hills, CA: Sage, 1981). Originally published in *Theory and Society, 6*(2): 205-253 (1978).

Gitlin, Todd, *The Whole World Is Watching: Mass Media in the Making and Unmaking of the Left* (Berkeley: University of California Press, 1980).

Giugni, Marco, Doug McAdam and Charles Tilly (eds.), *How Social Movements Matter* (Minneapolis: University of Minnesota Press, 1999).

Glasgow University Media Group and Peter Beharrell, *Bad News* (London: Routledge, 1980).

Glasser, Theodore L., and Peggy J. Bowers, "Justifying Change and Control: An Application of Discourse Ethics to the Role of Mass Media, pp. 399-424 in David Demers and K. Viswanath (eds.), *Mass Media, Social Control, and Social Change: A Macrosocial Perspective* (Ames: Iowa State University Press, 1999).

Glenn, David, "Education Researchers and Policymakers Not in Sync, Scholars Say Article tools," *The Chronicle of Higher Education* (June 1, 2007), p. A11.

Glueck, Sheldon, and Eleanor Glueck, *Criminal Careers in Retrospect* (New York: The Commonwealth Fund, 1943).

Gormley, Jr., William T., "Public Policy Analysis: Ideas and Impacts," *Annual Review of Political Science, 10*: 297-313 (June 2007).

Graber, Doris A., *Mass Media and American Politics,* 3rd ed. (Washington, DC: Congressional Quarterly Press, 1989).

Gramsci, Antonio, *Prison Notebooks* (New York: International Publishers, 1971).

Grasmick, Harold G., and George J. Bryjak, "The Deterrent Effect of Perceived Severity of Punishment," *Social Forces, 59*: 471-491 (December 1980).

Gray L. N., and D. J. Martin, "Punishment and Deterrence: Another Analysis of Gibbs' Data," *Social Science Quarterly, 50*: 389-395 (1969).

Gross, Paul R., and Norman Levitt's *Higher Superstition: The Academic Left and Its Quarrels With Science* (Baltimore: Johns Hopkins University Press, 1994).

Gunter, Barrie, "The Question of Media Violence," pp. 163-212 in J. Bryant and D. Zillmann (eds.), *Media Effects: Advances in Theory and Research* (Hillsdale, NJ: Lawrence Erlbaum Associates, 1994).

Habermas, Jürgen, "On Systematically Distorted Communication," *Inquiry, 13*: 205-218 (1970).

Habermas, Jürgen, "Towards a Theory of Communicative Competence," *Inquiry, 13*: 360-375 (1970).

Habermas, Jürgen, *Legitimation Crisis*, trans. by T. McCarthy (Boston: Beacon Press, 1975).

Habermas, Jürgen, *The Philosophical Discourse of Modernity: 12 Lectures*, trans. by Frederick Lawrence (Cambridge, MA: MIT Press, 1987).

Habermas, Jürgen, *The Theory of Communicative Action*, Volumes 1 and 2, translated by T. McCarthy (Boston: Beacon Press, 1984 and 1987, respectively).

Hald, Andreas, *History of Mathematical Statistics from 1750 to 1930* (New York: Wiley & Sons, Inc., 1998)

Hall, Evelyn Beatrice (writing under the pseudonym of Stephen G. Tallentyre), *The Friends of Voltaire* (London: Smith, Elder and Co., 1902).

Hamburg, P., "The Media and Eating Disorders: Who Is Most Vulnerable?" (Public Forum: Culture, Media and Eating Disorders, Harvard Medical School, 1998).

Hammersley, M. and R. Gomm, "Bias in Social Research" *Sociological Research Online, 2* (1997), <http://www.socresonline.org.uk/socresonline/2/1/2.html>.

Harding, Joe R., and J. Michael Livesay, "Anthropology and Public Policy," pp. 51-90 in George J. McCall and George H. Weber, *Social Science and Public Policy: The Roles of Academic Disciplines in Policy Analysis* (Port Washington, NY: Associated Faculty Press, 1984).

Harrington, Michael, *The Other America: Poverty in the United States* (New York, Macmillan, 1962)

Harrison, Martin, *TV News, Whose Bias?* (Hermitage, UK: Policy Journals, 1985).

Harvey, David, *The Condition of Postmodernity: An Enquiry into the Origins of Cultural Change* (Cambridge, MA: Blackwell, 1989).

Heath, Timothy B., "The Reconciliation of Humanism and Positivism in the Practice of Consumer Research: A View from the Trenches," *Journal of the Academy of Marketing Science, 20*(2): 107-118 (Spring 1992).

Held, David, *Introduction to Critical Theory* (Berkeley: University of California Press, 1980).

Herman, Edward S., and Noam Chomsky, *Manufacturing Consent: The Political Economy of the Mass Media* (New York: Pantheon, 1989).

Holquist, Michael, and Robert Shulman, "Sokal's Hoax: An Exchange," *The New York Review of Books* (October 3, 1996), p. 54.

Horgan, John, "A Prescription for the Malaise of Social 'Science,'" *The Chronicle of Higher Education* (Feb. 13, 2011), retrieved Feb. 14, 2011, from <http://chronicle.com/article/A-Prescription-for-the-Malaise/126311>

Hovland, Carl I., Arthur A. Lumsdaine and Fred D. Sheffield, *Experiments on Mass Communication* (Princeton: Princeton University Press, 1949).

Hynes, Gerald C., "A Biographical Sketch of W. E. B. Du Bois," available at <www.duboislc.org>.

Irvine, J. M., *Disorders of Desire: Sex and Gender in Modern American Sexology* (Philadelphia: Temple University Press, 1990).

Islam, Nazrul, "Sociology in the 21st Century: Facing a Dead End," *Bangladesh e-Journal of Sociology, 1*(2): 1-8 (July 2004).

Israel, Bill, *A Nation Seized: How Karl Rove and the Political Right Stole Reality, Beginning with the News* (Spokane, WA: Marquette Books, 2011).

Izzo, Phil, "Obama, Geithner Get Low Grades From Economists," *The Wall Street Journal* (March 11, 2009).

J. W. Hampton, Jr., & Co. v. United States, 276 U.S. 394, 406, 48 S.Ct. 348, 351 (1928).

Jackson, James S., "Promoting Human Welfare Through Legislative Advocacy: A Proper Role for the Science of Psychology," pp. xxx in Richard A. Kasschau and Frank S. Kessel (eds.), *Psychology and Society: In Search of Symbiosis* (New York: Holt, Rinehart & Winston, 1980).

Joyce, Theodore J., "A Simple Test of Abortion and Crime," *Review of Economics and Statistics* (2008) available at SSRN: <http://ssrn.com/abstract=1011168 >.

Kahane, Leo, David Paton and Rob Simmons, "The Abortion-Crime Link: Evidence from England and Wales," *Economica, 75*(297): 1-21 (2008).

Kant, Immanuel, "Beantwortung der Frage: Was ist Aufklärung?" ("Answering the Question: What Is Enlightenment?"), *Berlinische Monatsschrift* (*Berlin Monthly*) (December 1784).

Kaplan, Abraham, "Positivism," *International Encyclopedia of the Social Sciences* (Detroit, MI: Gale, 1968). Available online at Encyclopedia.com. <www.encyclopedia.com/doc/1G2-3045000974.html>.

Keat, Russell, *The Politics of Social Theory: Habermas, Freud and the Critique of Positivism* (Chicago: University of Chicago Press, 1981).

Kellner, Douglas, "Network Television and America Society: Introduction to a Critical Theory of Television," *Theory and Society, 10*: 31-55 (1981).

Kelly, Lynne, and James A. Keaten, "Treating Communication Anxiety," *Communication Education, 49*(1): 45-57 (January 2000).

Kiesler, Charles A., "Psychology and Public Policy," in Leonard Bickman (ed.), *Applied Social Psychology Annual, Vol. 1* (Beverly Hills, CA: Sage, 1980).

Kramnick, Isaac, (ed.), *The Portable Enlightenment Reader* (New York: Penguin, 1995).

Kuhn, Thomas S., *The Structure of Scientific Revolutions* (Chicago: University of Chicago Press, 1962).

Kunkel, Dale, "The Road to the V-Chip: Television Violence and Public Policy," pp. 227-245 in Douglas A. Gentile (ed.), *Media Violence and Children: A Complete Guide for Parents and Professionals* (Westport, CT: Praeger, 2003).

Lakatos, Imre, "Falsification and the Methodology of Research Programmes," pp. 91-196 in Imre Lakatos and A. Musgrave (eds.), Criticism and the Growth of Knowledge (Cambridge, England: Cambridge University Press, 1970).

Lazarsfeld, Paul F., "Some Remarks on Administrative and Critical Communications Research," *Studies in Philosophy and Social Science, 9*(1): 2-16 (1941).

Lazarsfeld, Paul F., Bernard R. Berelson, and Hazel Gaudet, *The People's Choice: How the Voter Makes Up His Mind in a Presidential Campaign* (New York: Duel, Sloan and Pearce, 1944).

Lens, Sidney, *Poverty: America's Enduring Paradox: A History of the Richest Nation's Unwon War* (New York: Thomas Y. Crowell Company, 1969).

Lewis, David L., *W. E. B. Du Bois: Biography of a Race, 1868-1919* (New York: H. Holt, 1993).

Lindblom, Charles E., and David K. Cohen, *Usable Knowledge: Social Science and Social Problem Solving* (New Haven: Yale University Press, 1979).

Lippman, Walter, *Public Opinion* (New York: Harcourt, Brace and Company, 1922).

Lipton, Douglas, Robert Martinson and Judith Wilks, *The Effectiveness of Correctional Treatment: A Survey of Treatment Evaluation Studies* (New York: Praeger, 1975).

Logan, Charles H., "Arrest Rates and Deterrence," *Social Science Quarterly, 56*: 366-389 (1975-76).

Logan, Charles H., "General Deterrent Effects of Imprisonment," *Social Forces, 51*: 64-73 (1972).

Logan, Charles H., "Legal Sanctions and Deterrence from Crime," unpublished Ph.D. Dissertation (Indiana University, 1971).

Looney, G., "Television and the Child: What Can be Done?" paper presented at the meeting of the American Academy of Pediatrics (Chicago, October 1971).

Lott Jr., John R., and John E. Whitley, "Abortion and Crime: Unwanted Children and Out-of-Wedlock Births," Yale Law & Economics Research Paper No. 254, University of Maryland Foundation, University of Maryland and University of Adelaide School of Economics, posted May 16, 2001 to the Social Science Research Network, available at <http://papers.ssrn.com/sol3/results.cfm?RequestTimeout=50000000>.

Lott Jr., John R., and John E. Whitley, "Abortion and Crime: Unwanted Children and Out-of-Wedlock Births," *Economic Inquiry, 45*(2): 304-324 (April 2007).

Lowery, Shearon A., and Melvin L. DeFleur, *Milestones in Mass Communication Research*, 2nd ed. (New York: Longman, 1988).

Lowi, Theodore J., *The End of Liberalism* (New York: W. W. Norton & Company, 1969).

Lynd, Robert S., *Knowledge for What? The Place of Social Science in American Culture* (Princeton, NJ: Princeton University Press, 1939).

Lynn, Laurence E. (ed.), *Knowledge and Policy: The Uncertain Connection* (Washington, D.C.: National Academy of Science, 1978).

Lyotard, Jean-François, *The Postmodern Condition: A Report on Knowledge*, trans. by Geoff Bennington and Brian Massumi (Minneapolis: University of Minnesota Press, 1984; originally published in French in 1979).

Mack, Raymond W., "Four for the Seesaw: Reflections on the Reports of Four Colleagues Concerning Their Experiences as Presidential Commissioners," in Mirra Komarovsky (ed.), *Sociology and Public Policy: The Case of Presidential Commissions* (New York: Elsevier, 1975).

MacKinnon, Catharine, *Sexual Harassment of Working Women* (New Haven, CT: Yale University Press, 1979).

"Magazine Models Impact Girls' Desire to Lose Weight," American Academy of Pediatrics (1999).

Marable, Manning, *W. E. B. Du Bois, Black Radical Democrat* (Boston: Twayne, 1986).

Marcuse, Herbert, *One Dimensional Man* (Boston: Beacon, 1964).

Markert, John, *The Social Impact of Sexual Harassment: A Resource Manual for Organizations and Scholars* (Spokane, WA: Marquette Books, 2010).

Martindale, Don, *The Romance of a Profession: A Case History in the Sociology of Sociology*, 2nd ed. (New Delhi, India: Intercontinental Press, 1986).

Martinson, Robert, "New Findings, New Views: A Note of Caution Regarding Sentencing Reform," *Hofstra Law Review, 7*: 243-258 (1978).

Martinson, Robert, "What Works? Questions and Answers about Prison Reform," *The Public Interest, 35*: 22-54 (Spring 1974).

Marx, Karl, and Friedrich Engels, *The German Ideology* (London: Lawrence & Wishart, 1938; original work published in 1845).

Marx, Karl, *Capital: A Critique of Political Economy*, Vols. 1-3, trans. by Samuel Moore and Edward Aveling (New York: International Publishers, 1987).

Maynard, C., "Body Image," *Current Health, 2* (1998).

McCall, George J., "Social Science and Social Problem Solving: An Analytic Introduction," pp. 3-18 in George J. McCall and George H. Weber, *Social Science and Public Policy: The Roles of Academic Disciplines in Policy Analysis* (Port Washington, NY: Associated Faculty Press, 1984).

McCall, George J., and George H. Weber, *Social Science and Public Policy: The Roles of Academic Disciplines in Policy Analysis* (Port Washington, NY: Associated Faculty Press, 1984).

McChesney, Robert W., "The Political Economy of Global Communication," pp. 1-26 in Robert W. McChesney, E. M. Wood, and J. B. Foster (eds.), *Capitalism and the Information Age: The Political Economy of the Global Communication Revolution* (New York: Monthly Review Press, 1988).

McCroskey, James C., and Michael J. Beatty, "The Communibiological Perspective: Implications for Communication in Instruction," *Communication Education, 49*(10): 1-6 (January 2000).

McQuail, Denis, *McQuail's Mass Communication Theory* (Thousand Oaks, CA: Sage, 2003).

Mead, Lawrence M., *Beyond Entitlement: The Social Obligations of Citizenship* (New York: Free Press, 1986).

Mead, Margaret, *Coming of Age in Samoa: A Psychological Study of Primitive Youth for Western Civilization* (New York: W. Murrow and Company, 1928).

Merton, Robert K., "Bureaucratic Structure and Personality," pp. 195-206 in Robert K. Merton (ed.), *Social Theory and Social Structure* (London: The Free Press, 1957 [1949]).

Merton, Robert K., "The Unanticipated Consequences of Purposive Social Action," *American Sociological Review, 1*(6): 894-904 (December 1936).

Mestrovic, Stjepan G., "Why East Europe's Upheavals Caught Social Scientists Off Guard," *The Chronicle of Higher Education* (September 25, 1991).

Meyer, Marshall W., William Stevenson and Stephen Webster, *Limits to Bureaucratic Growth* (New York: De Gruyter, 1985).

Michels, Robert, "Oligarchy," pp. 48-67 in Frank Fischer and Carmen Sirianni, *Critical Studies in Organization and Bureaucracy* (Philadelphia: Temple University Press, 1984).

Michels, Robert, *Political Parties: A Sociological Study of the Oligarchical Tendencies of Modern Democracy,* translated by Eden Paul and Cedar Paul (New York: Free Press, 1962, originally published in 1911).

Miller, Jerome G., "The Debate on Rehabilitating Criminals: Is It True that Nothing Works?" *The Washington Post* (March 1989), retrieved October 3, 2009, from <http://www.prisonpolicy.org/scans/rehab.html>.

Mistretta v. United States, 488 U.S. 361 (1989)

Molotch, Harvey, and Marilyn Lester, "Accidental News: The Great Oil Spill as Local Occurrence and National Event," *American Journal of Sociology, 81*:235-260 (1975).

Morris, Albert, "The American Society of Criminology: A History, 1941-1974," *Criminology, 13*(2): 123-166 (1975).

Moynihan, Daniel P., *The Politics of a Guaranteed Annual Income: The Nixon Administration and the Family Assistance Plan* (New York: Random House, 1973).

Myrdal, Gunnar, *An American Dilemma: The Negro Problem and Modern Democracy* (New York: London, Harper & Brothers, 1944).

Nagel, Stuart S., "Political Science and Public Policy," pp. 180-200 in George J. McCall and George H. Weber, *Social Science and Public Policy: The Roles of Academic Disciplines in Policy Analysis* (Port Washington, NY: Associated Faculty Press, 1984).

Neftel, Klaus A., Rolf H. Adler, Louis Kappeli, Mario Rossi, Martin Dolder, Hans E. Kaser, Heinz H. Bruggesser, and Helmut Vorkauf, "Stage Fright in Musicians: A Model Illustrating the Use of Beta Blockers." *Psychosomatic Medicine, 44*(5): 461-469 (1982).

Nelson, C. E., J. Roberts, C. Maederer, B. Wertheimer, and B. Johnson, "The Utilization of Social Science Information by Policymakers," *American Behavioral Scientist, 30*: 569-577 (1987).

Nelson, Cary, "From the President: Ethics and Corporatization," American Association of University Professors website, retrieved November 2, 2010, from <www.aaup.org/AAUP/pubsres/academe/2010/JF/col/ftp.htm>

Nye Jr., Joseph S., "Scholars on the Sidelines," *The Washington Post* (April 13, 2009), p. A15.

Oh, Cheol H., *Linking Social Science Information to Policy-Making* (Greeenwich, CT: JAI Press, 1996).

Oommen, T. K., *Protest and Change: Studies in Social Movements* (New Delhi: Sage, 1990).

Paletz, David L., and Robert M. Entman, *Media Power Politics* (New York: The Free Press, 1981).

Paletz, David L., Peggy Reichert and Barbara McIntyre, "How the Media Support Local Government Authority," *Public Opinion Quarterly, 35*:80-92 (1971).

Palmer, Ted, *Correctional Intervention and Research: Current Issues and Future Prospects* (Lexington, MA: Lexington Books, 1978).

Patelis, Korinna, "The Political Economy of the Internet," pp 84-106 in James Curran, (ed.), *Media Organizations in Society* (London: Arnold, 2000).

Pearl, D., L. Bouthilet, and J. Lazar (eds.), *Television and Behavior: Ten Years of Scientific Progress and Implications for the Eighties,* Vols. I & II (Washington, D.C.: U.S. Government Printing Office, 1982).

Petersilia, Joan, "Influencing Public Policy: An Embedded Criminologist Reflects on California Prison Reform: The Academy of Experimental Criminology 2007 Joan McCord Prize Lecture," *Journal of Experimental Criminology,* 4(4):335-356 (December 2008).

Petersilia, Joan, "Policy Relevance and the Future of Criminology — The American Society of Criminology 1990 Presidential Address," *Criminology 29*(1):1-15 (1991).

Pettigrew, Thomas F., "Can Social Scientists be Effective Actors in the Policy Arena?" pp. 121-134 in R. Lance Shotland and Melvin M. Mark (eds.), *Social Science and Social Policy* (Beverly Hills, CA: Sage Publications, 1985).

Phillips, D. C., "Two Decades After: 'After The Wake: Postpositivistic Educational Thought,'" *Science & Education 13*(½): 67-84 (February 2004).

Plato, *The Republic*, translated with introduction and notes by Francis MacDonald Cornford (New York: Oxford University Press, 1945).

Pollard, W. E., "Decision Making and the Use of Evaluation Research," *American Behavioral Scientist, 30*: 661-676 (1987).

Popper, Karl, *The Logic of Scientific Discovery* (London: Routledge, 2002; originally published *Logik der Forschung* in 1934; translated by Popper himself into English in 1959).

Potter, W. James, Roger Cooper and Michel Dupagne, "The Three Paradigms of Mass Media Research in Mainstream Communication Journals," *Communication Theory, 3*: 317-335 (1993).

Powledge, Fred, *The Engineering of Restraint* (Washington, D.C.: Public Affairs Press, 1971).

Prewitt, Kenneth, "Foreword," pp. xxxvii-xli in Robert F. Rich, *Social Science Information and Public Policy Making* (New Brunswick, NJ: Transaction Publishers, 2002).

Price, Katherine, "Students March for an Alternative," *The Boar* (March 29, 2011), retrieved April 8, 2011 from <http://theboar.org/news/2011/mar/29/students-march- alternative>.

Rabe, B., *Statehouse and Greenhouse: The Emerging Politics of American Climate Change Policy* (Washington, DC: Brookings Institution, 2004).

Rae, John, *Life of Adam Smith* (London: Macmillan & Co., 1895),

Reckless, Walter C., and Simon Dinitz, *The Prevention of Juvenile Delinquency: An Experiment* (Columbus: Ohio State University Press, 1972).

Reed, Stephen K.,*Cognition: Theory and Applications* (Monterey, CA: Brooks/Cole Publishing, 1982).

Reeves, Byron, and James L. Baughman, "'Fraught with Such Great Possibilities': The Historical Relationship of Communication Research to Mass Media Regulation," pp. 529-571 in Sandra Braman (ed.), *Communication Researchers and Policy Making* (Cambridge, MA: MIT Press, 2003).

Rein, Martin, *Social Science and Public Policy* (New York: Penguin Books, 1976).

Reiss, Jr., Albert J., "Sociology and Public Policy," pp 19-50 in George J. McCall and George H. Weber, *Social Science and Public Policy: The Roles of Academic Disciplines in Policy Analysis* (Port Washington, NY: Associated Faculty Press, 1984).

Reppucci, N. Dickon, and Robert Harry Kirk, "Psychology and Public Policy," pp. 129-158 in George J. McCall and George H. Weber, *Social Science and Public Policy: The Roles of Academic Disciplines in Policy Analysis* (Port Washington, NY: Associated Faculty Press, 1984).

Rich, Paul, "Time to End Tenure: Job Protection Blocks Accountability in Academia," *Carolina Journal, 4*(3) (December 1994/January 1995), available online at <www.paulrich.net/ publications/carolina_journal_vol4_nr3.html>.

Rich, Paul, *Sacred Cow: Tenure and the Demise of Academic Accountability* (John Locke Foundation, 1994).

Rich, Robert F., and N. Caplan, "What Do We Know about Knowledge Utilization as a Field/Discipline — The State of the Art," paper presented at the Research Utilization Conference, University of Pittsburgh (September 1978)

Rich, Robert F., *Social Science Information and Public Policy Making* (San Francisco: Jossey-Bass Publishers, 1981).

Rich, Robert F., *Social Science Information and Public Policy Making* (New Brunswick: Transaction Publishers, 2001; originally published in 1981 by Jossey-Bass).

Roach, Kate, "Social Scientists Explain Many Things – But Can They Explain Themselves? David Willetts Understands Why Social Sciences Matter, But We Need to Do a Better Job of Convincing the Wider Population," *The Guardian* (February 3, 2011), retrieved February 21, 2011, from <www.guardian.co.uk/commentisfree/2011/feb/03social-sciences-david-willetts?INTCMP=SRCH>.

Merton, Robert K., *The Sociology of Science: Theoretical and Empirical Investigations* (Chicago: University of Chicago Press, 1973).

Robinson, D. L., "Head Injuries and Bicycle Helmet Laws," *Accident Analysis and Prevention, 28*(4): 463-475 (1996).

Robison, James, and Gerald Smith, "The Effectiveness of Correctional Programs," *Crime & Delinquency, 17*: 67-80 (1971).

Root, Michael, *Philosophy of Social Science: The Methods, Ideals, and Politics of Social Inquiry* (Oxford, UK: Blackwell, 1993; reprinted in 1999).

Ross, Dorothy, *The Origins of American Social Science* (Cambridge, UK: Cambridge University Press, 1991)

Ross, Edward Alsworth, *Principles of Sociology,* 3rd ed. (New York: Appleton Century Crofts, Inc., 1938)

Ross, H. Laurence, Donald T. Campbell and Gene V. Glass, "Determining the Social Effects of a Legal Reform: The British 'Breathalyser' Crackdown of 1967," *American Behavioral Scientist, 13*(4): 493-509 (March/April 1970).

Roucek, Joseph S., "A History of the Concept of Ideology," *Journal of the History of Ideas, 5*(4): 479-488 (October 1944).

Rousseau, Jean-Jacques, "A Discourse on the Moral Effects of the Arts and Sciences," in Jean Jacques Rousseau, *The Social Contract and Discourses*, translated with an Introduction by G. D. H. Cole (London and Toronto: J. M. Dent and Sons, 1923, originally published in 1750), retrieved from <http://oll.libertyfund.org/title/638/71081 on 2010-03-20.

Rousseau, Jean-Jacques, *The Social Contract*, trans. Maurice Cranston (Middlesex, England: Penguin Books, 1968).

Runes (Ed.), Dagobert D., *Dictionary of Philosophy* (Ames, IA: Littlefield, Adams & Co., 1959).

Rust, Amy, "Chicago Economist Links Abortion to Falling Crime Rates," *University of Chicago Chronicle, 18* (August 12, 1999), retrieved November 6, 2008, online at <http://chronicle.uchicago.edu/990812/abortion.shtml>.

Saint Joseph Edition of the New American Bible (New York: Catholic Book Publishing Co., 1992).

Salter Jr., Leonard A., "Global War and Peace, and Land Economics," *The Journal of Land & Public Utility Economics, 19*(4): 391-396 (November 1943).

Samuels, Warren J., "The Firing of E. A. Ross from Stanford University: Injustice Compounded by Deception?"*The Journal of Economic Education, 22*(2): 183-190 (Spring 1991).

Sapp, Jan, *Genesis: The Evolution of Biology* (New York: Oxford University Press, 2003).

Savitz, Leonard D., "A Study of Capital Punishment," *Journal of Criminal Law, Criminology and Police Science, 49*: 338-341 (December 1958).

Schmidt, Frank L., and John E. Hunter, "Meta-Analysis," pp. 51-70 in Neil Anderson, Deniz S. Ones, Handan Kepir Sinangil, Chockalingam Viswesvaran (eds.), *Handbook of Industrial, Work and Organizational Psychology: Volume 1, Personnel Psychology* (Thousand Oaks, CA: Sage, 2001).

Schneider, A. L., "The Evaluation of a Policy Orientation for Evaluation Research," *Public Administration Review, 46*: 356-363 (July/August 1986).

Schuessler, Karl F., "The Deterrent Influence of the Death Penalty," *The Annals of the American Academy of Political and Social Science, 284*: 54-63 (November 1952).

"The Scientific Conception of the World: The Vienna Circle," in Marie Neurath and Robert S. Cohen (eds.), *Otto Neurath: Empiricism and Sociology* (Dordrecht: D. Reidel Publishing Company, 1973).

Scott, Robert A., and Arnold R. Shore, *Why Sociology Does not Apply: A Study of the Use of Sociology in the Public Policy* (New York: Elsevier, 1979).

Sechrest, L., S. White, and E. Brown, E. (eds), *The Rehabilitation of Criminal Offenders: Problems and Prospects* (Washington DC: National Academy of Sciences Press, 1979).

Segall, Marshall H.,*Human Behavior and Public Policy: A Political Psychology*(New York: Pergamon, 1976).

Sellin, Thorsten, *The Death Penalty* (Philadelphia: American Law Institute, 1959).

Sharlet, Jeff, "A Philosopher's Call to End All Paradigms," *The Chronicle of Higher Education* (September 15, 2000), p. A19.

Sherden, William A., *The Fortune Sellers: The Big Business of Buying and Selling Predictions* (New York: John Wiley & Sons, 1997).

Sholle, David J., "Critical Studies: From the Theory of Ideology to Power/Knowledge," *Critical Studies in Mass Communication, 5*: 16-41 (1988).

Sigal, Leon, *Reporters and Officials* (Lexington, MA: Heath, 1973).'

Signorielli, Nancy, "Television's Mean and Dangerous World: A Continuation of the Cultural Indicators Perspective," pp. 85-106 in Nancy Signorielli and Michael Morgan (eds.), *Cultivation Analysis: New Directions in Media Effects Research* (Newbury Park, CA: Sage, 1990).

Signorielli, Nancy, George Gerbner and Michael Morgan, "Violence on Television: The Cultural Indicators Project," *Journal of Broadcasting and Electronic Media, 39*: 278-283 (1995).

Simons, Herbert W., and Michael Billig (eds.), *After Postmodernism: Reconstructing Ideology Critique* (Thousand Oaks, CA: Sage Publications, 1994).

Simons, Herbert W., and Michael Billig (eds.), *After Postmodernism: Reconstructing Ideology Critique* (Thousand Oaks, CA: Sage, 1994).

Skemer, Don, "Drifting Disciplines, Enduring Records: Political Science and the Use of Archives," *The American Archivist, 54*(3): 356-369 (Summer 1991).

Smith, Adam, *An Inquiry into the Nature and Causes of the Wealth of Nations,* Vol. X, The Harvard Classics (New York: P. F. Collier & Son, 1909–1914; originally published in 1776).

Smith, Craig, "A Review of the British Academy Report, Punching Our Weight: The Humanities and Social Sciences in Public Policy Making," *Economic Affairs* (Institute for Economic Affairs, September 2009).

Sokal, Alan D., "A Physicist Experiments with Cultural Studies," *Lingua Franca, 6*(4) (May/June 1996). Retrieved October 25, 2010, from <http://www.physics.nyu.edu/faculty/sokal/lingua_franca_v4/lingua_franca_v4.html>.

Sokal, Alan D., "Transgressing the Boundaries: Toward a Transformative Hermeneutics of Quantum Gravity," *Social Text 14* (Spring/Summer 1996), pp. 1-2.

Sokal, Alan D., and Jean Bricmont, *Fashionable Nonsense: Postmodern Intellectuals' Abuse of Science* (New York: Picador, 1998).

Stearns, Peter N., "History and Public Policy," pp. 91-128 in George J. McCall and George H. Weber, *Social Science and Public Policy: The Roles of Academic Disciplines in Policy Analysis* (Port Washington, NY: Associated Faculty Press, 1984).

Stewart, Elbert W., and James A Glynn, *Introduction to Sociology* (New York: McGraw-Hill Book Company, 1971), p.16.

Stinchcombe, Arthur L., "Merton's Theory of Social Structure," pp. 11-33 in *The Idea of Social Structure: Papers in Honor of Robert K. Merton*, Lewis Coser, ed. (New York: Harcourt Brace, 1975).

Strinati, Dominic, *An Introduction to Theories of Popular Culture* (New York: Routledge, 1995).

Surgeon General's Scientific Advisory Committee on Television and Social Behavior, Television and Social Behavior, Vols. 1-5 (Washington, D.C.: U.S. Department of Health, Education and Welfare, U.S. Government Printing Office, 1972).

Taylor, Mark C., "End of the University as We Know It," *The New York Times* (April 27, 2009), retrieved April 28, 2009, from <www.nytimes.com/2009/04/027/opinion/27taylor.html?_r=3&pagewanted=print>.

Tibbitts, Clark, "Success and Failure on Parole Can Be Predicted," *Journal of Criminal Law and Criminology, 20*: 405-413 (1923).

Tichenor, Phillip J., "The Logic of Social and Behavioral Science," pp. 10-28 in Guido H. Stempel III and Bruce H. Westley (eds.), *Research Methods in Mass Communication* (Englewood Cliffs, N.J.: Prentice-Hall, 1981).

Tichenor, Phillip J., George A. Donohue and Clarice N. Olien, *Community Conflict and the Press* (Beverly Hills, CA: Sage, 1980).

Tittle, Charles R., and Alan R. Rowe, "Certainty of Arrest and Crime Rates: A Further Test of the Deterrence Hypothesis," *Social Forces, 52*: 455-462 (June 1974).

Tittle, Charles R., and Charles H. Logan, "Sanctions and Deviance: Evidence and Remaining Questions," *Law and Society Review, 7:* 371-392 (Spring 1973).

Toby, Jackson, "Is Punishment Necessary?" *Journal of Criminal Law, Criminology, and Police Science, 55*(3): 332-337 (September 1964).

Trigg, Roger, *Understanding Social Science: A Philosophical Introduction to the Social Sciences* (Oxford, UK: Basil Blackwell, 1985).

U.S. Bureau of Justice Statistics, *Prisoners in State and Federal Institutions on December 31*, annual, and *Correctional Populations in the United States*, annual. Retrieved October 20, 2008, from <http://www.ojp.usdoj.gov/bjs/prisons.htm>.

U.S. National Science Foundation, NSF 09-300, *Federal Funds for Research and Development* (November 2008, annual).

van den Berg, Axel, "Critical Theory: Is There Still Hope?" *American Journal of Sociology, 86*(3): 449-478 (1980).

van Willigen, John, *Anthropology in Use: A Bibliographic Chronology of the Development of Applied Anthropology* (New York: Redgrave Publishing Co., 1980).

Vaughan, Ted R., Gideon Sjoberg and Larry T. Reynolds (eds.), *A Critique of Contemporary American Sociology* (New York: Rowman & Littlefield, 1993).

Vendramin, Valerija, and Renata Sribar, "Beyond Positivism or the Perspectives of the 'New' Gender Equality, *Solsko Polje, 21*(1-2): 157-169 (2010).

Viswanath, K., "The Impact of Communication Research," *Journalism Studies 2*(4): 617-620 (2001).

Voltaire, "Lettre XII: sur M. Pope et quelques autres poètes fameux,*" Lettres Philosophiques'* (1733).

Voltaire, *Candide,* 2nd ed., trans. Robert M. Adams (New York: W. W. Norton, 1991; originally published in 1759).

Wacquant, Loic, "Positivism," in Thomas B. Bottomore and William Outhwaite (eds.), *The Blackwell Dictionary of Twentieth-Century Social Thought* (New York: John Wiley & Sons, 1992).

Waldo, Gordon P., and Theodore G. Chiricos, "Perceived Penal Sanction and Self-Reported Criminality: A Neglected Approach to Deterrence Research," *Social Problems, 19*: 522-540 (Spring 1972).

Walsh, David Allen, *Selling Out America's Children: How America Puts Profits Before Values and What Parents Can Do* (Minneapolis: Deaconess Press, 1994).

Ward, Lester F., *Applied Sociology: A Treatise on the Conscious Improvement of Society by Society* (Boston: Ginn, 1906).

Ward, Spencer A., and Linda J. Reed (eds.), *Knowledge, Structure, and Use Implications for Synthesis and Interpretation* (Philadelphia: Temple University Press, 1983), retrieved December 5, 2010, from <http://www.temple.edu/tempress/titles/335_reg_print.html>.

Wartella, Ellen, "Communication Research on Children and Public Policy," pp. 359-373 in Sandra Braman (ed.), *Communication Researchers and Policy Making* (Cambridge, MA: MIT Press, 2003).

Weber, George H., "Social Science and Social Policy," pp. 215-232 in George J. McCall and George H. Weber, *Social Science and Public Policy: The Roles of Academic Disciplines in Policy Analysis* (Port Washington, NY: Associated Faculty Press, 1984).

Wedel, Janine R., Cris Shore, Gregory Feldman, and Stacy Lathrop, "Toward an Anthropology of Public Policy," *The Annals of the American Academy of Political and Social Science, 600:* 30-51 (July 2005).

Weinberg, Steven, "Sokal's Hoax," *The New York Review of Books* (August 8, 1996).

Weiss, Carol H. (ed.), *Organizations for Policy Analysis: Helping Government Think* (Newbury Park, CA: Sage Publications, 1992),

Weiss, Carol, "Introduction," pp. 1-20 in *Utilizing Social Research in Public Policy Making,* edited by Carol Weiss (Lexington, MA: D.C. Heath, 1977).

Weiss, Carol, "Knowledge Creep and Decision Accretion," *Knowledge, 1*: 384-404 (1980).

Weiss, Carol H (ed.), *Using Social Research in Public Policy Making* (Lexington, MA: Lexington Books, 1977).

Weiss, Carol H., "Congressional Committee Staffs (Do, Do Not) Use Analysis," pp. 94-112 in Martin Bulmer (ed.), Social Science Research and Government: Comparative Essays on Britain and the United States (Cambridge: Cambridge University Press, 1987).

Weiss, Carol, *Organizations for Policy Analysis* (Newbury Park, CA: Sage, 1992).

Wertham, Frederick, *Seduction of the Innocent* (New York: Rinehart, 1954) .

Whyte, William Foote, "On the Uses of Social Science Research," *American Sociological Review, 51*: 555-563 (Augustin 1986).

Wildavsky, Aaron, *The Politics of the Budgetary Process*, 4th ed. (Boston: Little, Brown, 1984).

Wilkinson, Reginald A., and Thomas J. Stickrath, "After the Storm: Anatomy of a Riot's Aftermath," *Corrections Management Review* (Winter 1997).

William C. Bailey, Louis N. Gray and David J. Martin, "On Punishment and Crime (Chiricos and Waldo, 1970): Some Methodological Commentary," *Social Problems, 19*: 284-289 (1971).

Williams, T. M. (ed.), *The Impact of Television: A Natural Experiment in Three Communities* (Orlando, FL: Academic Press, 1986).

Wilson, William Julius (ed.), *Sociology and the Public Agenda* (Newbury Park, CA: Sage, 1993).

Wire reports, "Obama Conveys Faith in Science: In lifting the Ban, He Rejects False Choice between the Two," *The* (Spokane) *Spokesman-Review* (March 10, 2009), retrieved from <http://www.spokesman.com/stories/2009/mar/10/obama-conveys-faith-in-science>.

York, Richard, and Brett Clark, "The Problem with Prediction: Contingency, Emergence, and the Reification of Projections," *The Sociological Quarterly, 48*(4): 713-743 (Fall 2007).

Zillman, Dolf, "Pornography Research and Public Policy," pp. 145-164 in Sandra Braman (ed.), *Communication Researchers and Policy Making* (Cambridge, MA: MIT Press, 2003).

Zimring, Franklin E., *The Great American Crime Decline* (New York: Oxford University Press, 2006).

AUTHOR NOTE

The idea for this book came to me shortly after I attended a plenary session at the 1997 annual convention of the Association for Education in Journalism and Mass Communication. The Rev. Jesse Jackson, a guest speaker, talked about successes that the civil rights movement has had on influencing public policy. Five leading scholars then took the stage to talk about successes in the field of mass communication, but they had trouble identifying some (see Chapter 1 for details). At that time, I had no intention of writing a book about the impact of social science research on public policy. I was too busy conducting research on the impact of corporate mass media in society. But I couldn't stop thinking about that session. It reminded me of my days as a master's student in criminology at The Ohio State University in the early 1980s. Criminologists, too, have had (and continue to have) a difficult time finding solutions to the crime problem.

In time, I might have forgotten the issue. After all, there is no great incentive for social scientists like me to question the value of what we do. In fact, raising questions about the value of a research discipline is likely to draw much criticism from colleagues, no matter how much evidence he or she amassed. No one likes to think that what they do for a living is insignificant. But questions about the relationship between social science research and public policy emerged again two years later, in May 1999, after I presented a paper at the International Communication Association meeting in San Francisco. The next presenter on the panel declared that he was going to test a theory that opposed mine. But the ax never fell. In fact, the researcher's data didn't support his model — it supported mine!

The irony of this event did not go unnoticed. During the question-and-answer session, the researcher continued to advance his theory until someone from the audience spoke up: "But your data supported Professor Demers' model." A handful of people in the meager audience of about a dozen chuckled. I suppose I should have been one of them. But I was simply dumbfounded. *How can social scientists solve social problems if they can't agree on how to interpret knowledge?*

That incident at ICA was the beginning of the end of my decade-long program of empirical research on corporate media (although I continue to do theoretical work and work with graduate students on empirical projects) and the beginning of an decade-long journey to understand and define the role and function of social science research in society. *Does, or can, social science research have a meaningful impact on public policy or solve social problems?*

I immediately began scouring the scholarly literature for evidence that might answer this question. Early results were not encouraging. A fairly large body of empirical research in policy studies had already concluded that, on the whole, social science research has relatively little impact on public policy or on solving social problems. These bothered me so much that in the summer of 1999 I suggested AEJMC use its plenary session on August 10, 2000, in Phoenix to address the impact of mass communication research.

As was the case in 1997, the panelists — three of whom were top-notch scholars in the field of mass communication and one of whom was an expert in policy studies and the law — had difficulty identifying major cases of impact. The policy studies expert pointed out that social science research is most likely to impact public policy when the research supports the ideological position of the policymaker; however, the policymaker usually ignores the research when it doesn't (see Chapter 6 for more details on the plenary).

This is disheartening to those of us who believe that truth should reign supreme whenever possible. But it does not mean social science can never have an impact when it challenges politicians' views or societal values. One of the best examples is Gunnar Myrdal's *An American Dilemma*, a 1944 study of race relations in America. A decade later, the U.S. Supreme Court cited Myrdal's study to justify in part its decision in *Brown v. the Board of Education* (1954), which was the beginning of the end of legal segregation in America (see Chapter 2 for more details). Nevertheless, social scientists would have a very tough time arguing that their research influences the policymaking process more than party ideology and campaign contributions, or that research even has more than a weak impact on public policy. As this book shows, there is just too much empirical evidence to the contrary (see Chapters 5-8). Indeed, on the political stage, social science research is almost always a minor player; rarely a lead one.

To be clear, I do not argue in this book that the social sciences are worthless. I am not a relativist, a radical skepticist, a postmodernist, a neo-Marxist, an anarchist, or a nihilist. I believe both mainstream social science research and humanist-driven research in the social sciences are capable of producing knowledge useful for making the world a better place, despite many debates over what constitutes knowledge (see Chapters 3 and 4). Nor do I criticize so-called "pure" theoretical research. Not all research or knowledge need have immediate, practical results. Knowledge for knowledge sake is as worthy a goal as are works of literature or art.

However, after studying the impact of social science for more than a decade, I do believe very strongly that the social sciences are failing to live up to their promises — promises that took form during the 17th and 18th centuries, when the United States and other Western countries were becoming more industrialized and urbanized. These two trends created a bevy of new social problems, including suicide, unemployment, divorce, crime, and drug abuse. Following the lead of the great Enlightenment philosophers, most early social scientists believed their role was to find the causes of these problems and fix them.

Many early social scientists played an active role in the public policy process. But today, many scholars working in the social sciences no longer believe they should get involved in the policymaking process. Most believe their role should be a passive one: "We social scientists do the research and the policymakers fix the problems." This attitude has insulated the social sciences from accountability and severely limited their influence in the policymaking process and in society in general. When people ask me what I do and I tell them I am a mass communication researcher, they almost always follow-up with, "What is that?"

Some scholars cherish this autonomy. They feel policymakers and the public are not competent to judge their performance. But the lower the accountability, the lower the relevance to policymaker and the public. Social scientists in the United Kingdom will back me up on this. They, too, cherished their autonomy before the government in 2010 decided to cut ALL funding to the social sciences and to the humanities at about 24 public institutions. The social sciences were easy targets for cuts because policymakers couldn't see how they contributed to a better society. In contrast, the politicians showed strong support for the natural sciences, because they were perceived as helping to build a better economy (see Chapter 1 for details).

There is, as yet, no sustained public debate about the relevance of the social sciences in America. But it's long overdue, and the funding cuts in the UK may stimulate that debate.

This book is an attempt to sound the alarm before, rather than after, policymakers try to cut funding cuts to the social sciences. It addresses a number of issues, including the history of the role and function of the social sciences, whether social sciences should fix social problems, whether social science knowledge is possible, whether research has an impact on public policy and, if so, how that impact can be enhanced. My greatest hope, though, is not that you agree with my findings and conclusions, but that you will be motivated to help jump-start a genuine dialog among social scientists, policymakers and citizens as to the role and function of the social sciences in society.

ACKNOWLEDGMENTS

I am most grateful to my wife, Theresa — who has always supported my varied writing projects and often provides opinions and comments that influence my thinking — and to my daughter, Lee Ann, who would prefer that I play with her 24/7 but understands that daddy has to work to earn money for her future college education.

I am deeply indebted to Jan Polek, a woman of extraordinary character, fortitude and intelligence, for reading and re-reading several early versions of this manuscript. Her suggestions for improving the manuscript, her moral support, and her good humor kept me motivated.

Professors Igor Klyukanov and Galina Sinekopova, my good friends and colleagues, offered so many helpful suggestions through the debates we've had over the years about the role and function of the social sciences that I no longer know where my and their thoughts start or end.

Special praise also goes to Alex Tan, who supported me in this project from the beginning and recognized that the quality of scholarship is not to be judged on the amount of grant money a faculty member brings in. Other academics who have played a direct or indirect role in this project include Phillip J. Tichenor, Paul Lindholdt, David Perlmutter, Douglas Blanks Hindman, Ryan Thomas, Tae-hyun Kim, John Schulz, John Bennitt, Joan Petersilia, Robert F. Rich, K. Viswanath, Douglas Underwood, Joanne Cantor, Theodore Glasser, Leo Jeffres, and Masahiro Yamamoto.

I also appreciate the seven librarians across the United States who took the time to read and review an early draft of this book. They provided very helpful comments, especially in terms of organization and voice. In no particular order of appearance, they are Lucy Heckman, St. John's University Library, Jamaica, New York; Ken Neubeck, Patchogue, NY; Nancy Barthelemy, Archivist, Peabody Institute Library, Peabody, Massachusetts; Andrea Tarr, Librarian, Corona Public Library, Corona, CA; Amada Scott, Librarian, Cambridge Springs Public Library, Cambridge Springs, Pennsylvania; T. G. McFadden, Director, Schaffer Library, Union College, Schenectady, NY; and Anne M. Miskewitch, Librarian, Literature and World Language Department, Harold Washington Library Center, Chicago.

AUTHOR INDEX

SUBJECT INDEX

ABOUT THE AUTHOR

David Demers is an associate professor of communication at Washington State University, where he has taught courses in media theory, research methods, news reporting, media history, media law and editing since 1996. He is author of more than 125 scholarly and professional articles and author or editor of 11 academic books, including *History and Future of Mass Media: An Integrated Perspective* (Hampton Press, 2007), *Global Media: Menace or Messiah?* (Hampton Press, 2002, revised edition), *Mass Media, Social Control and Social Change: A Macrosocial Perspective* (edited with K. Viswanath, Iowa State University Press, 1999), and *The Menace of the Corporate Newspaper: Fact or Fiction?* (Iowa State University Press, 1996).

Demers is a media sociologist. His research on corporate media structure has won five national awards. He also is an ardent advocate of the First Amendment, having brought seven lawsuits to make governments more accountable to citizens, including one that is now pending before the Ninth Circuit Court of Appeals. In February 2010, the Society for Collegiate Journalists honored him with a Louis Ingelhart Freedom of Expression Award. He previously worked as a newspaper reporter and a marketing research analyst. He earned master's degrees in journalism and sociology from The Ohio State University and a Ph.D. in mass communication from the University of Minnesota.

He currently is writing two more books: a literary journalism work that broadens the thesis in this book to include other ideals of the Enlightenment and a another book that examines the impact of the Internet on the distribution of power in society. He and his family live in Spokane, Washington.